Claiming Neighborhood

Claiming Neighborhood

New Ways of Understanding
Urban Change

JOHN J. BETANCUR AND
JANET L. SMITH

UNIVERSITY OF ILLINOIS PRESS

Urbana, Chicago, and Springfield

This book is dedicated to all those in the struggle to claim their neighborhoods, and especially to Doug Gills, our colleague and friend, who did so much for Chicago's neighborhoods.

Printed and bound in Great Britain by
Marston Book Services Ltd, Oxfordshire

Library of Congress Cataloging-in-Publication Data
Names: Betancur, John Jairo, author. | Smith, Janet L., 1962– author.
Title: Claiming neighborhood : new ways of understanding urban
    change / John Betancur, Janet Smith.
Description: Urbana : University of Illinois Press, 2016. | Includes
    bibliographical references and index.
Identifiers: LCCN 2016030961 (print) | LCCN 2016036726 (ebook) |
    ISBN 9780252040504 (hardback : alk. paper) | ISBN 9780252081972
    (paperback : alk. paper) | ISBN 9780252098949 ()
Subjects: LCSH: City planning—Illinois—Chicago. | Neighborhood
    planning—Illinois—Chicago. | Cities and towns—Growth. | Urban
    policy—Illinois—Chicago. | BISAC: POLITICAL SCIENCE / Public
    Policy / City Planning & Urban Development. | POLITICAL SCIENCE /
    Public Policy / Social Policy. | SOCIAL SCIENCE / Sociology / Urban.
Classification: LCC HT168.C5 B48 2016 (print) | LCC HT168.C5 (ebook) |
    DDC 307.1/2160977311—dc23
LC record available at https://lccn.loc.gov/2016030961

Contents

Introduction

"Real Property" (along with "construction") is no longer a secondary form of circulation, no longer the auxiliary and backward branch of industrial and financial capitalism that it once was. Instead, it has a leading role, albeit in an *uneven* way for its significance is liable to vary according to country, time or circumstance. . . . Capitalism has taken possession of the land, and *mobilized* it to the point where this sector is fast becoming *central*. Why? Because it is a new sector—and hence less beset by the obstacles, surfeits, and miscellaneous problems that slow down old industries. (Lefebvre 2004, 335)

This book examines the contradictions, contentions, and coincidences shaping urban space in the context of Chicago, the genesis of scholarly and applied studies of neighborhood change in the United States and beyond. We are particularly interested in the forces affecting neighborhoods, including what results from urban policy, elected officials, investors, speculators, planners, service providers, resident leaders, institutions, and community-based organizations. Our intent is simple: to better understand the underpinnings of neighborhood change over the past few decades and to consider what might happen in the near future. We argue that current theories—the tools used by academics and policy makers to explain how and why neighborhoods change—limit our ability to interpret what is *actually* happening while at the same time advancing in a veiled form a specific position or point of view and mandate. In particular, long-standing assumptions about what a neighborhood is and its importance in our lives rely on an image from the past that never existed and that ignores or hides the realities on the ground. Whether romantic or ideological, concealing or oppressive, this image of "the neighborhood" needs to be revisited, and its usefulness in explaining contemporary urban space and in guiding policy needs to be re-examined.

What follows has deep implications for theory, policy, and practice. Our goal is to inform the conversations people are having in communities, non-profit organizations, classrooms, local governments, foundations, and policy think tanks about addressing systemic inequalities and how best to redistribute resources and opportunities. Unemployment, crime, poor school quality, crumbling infrastructure, abandoned homes, and vacant land continue to be pressing concerns in many of our neighborhoods today. How we understand and deal with these conditions matters. In this book, we focus on the logic that underlies most of today's neighborhood-oriented policies and practices, which blame low-income people for these conditions rather than structural factors such as racism and class bias, and we focus on public policy that turns to real estate development as a primary vehicle to improve low-income neighborhoods. As a result of these policies, the conditions that deprive low-income neighborhoods of opportunities are sidestepped, residents and their communities are often criminalized, and land is cleared to induce investment. In contrast, affluent communities with higher real estate values can afford first-rate schools, new and improved infrastructure, and social services. A better understanding of the interrelationship between these disparate spaces is critical given the prominent role real estate plays in urban policy today.

This book is intended for students, researchers, and practitioners interested in neighborhoods and how and why they change. At the theoretical level, we reveal the limitations of the prevailing orthodox approaches to the study of neighborhood change while concurrently advancing a type of inquiry that is capable of generating alternative explanations. A strong theme is the role *representations* of neighborhoods play, particularly through the lens of race and class, in shaping land values and investment, causing real estate in white, middle-class communities to appreciate while disinvestment and property loss occur in predominantly nonwhite, low-income communities. The linkage, we argue, is the commodification of space that has transformed neighborhoods into sites from which to create and extract value. This includes current efforts to entice higher-income families to live in cities, replace public housing with mixed-income communities, attract tourists to ethnic neighborhoods and suburbanites to the city for entertainment, as well as many community-driven plans to redevelop disinvested commercial sites and housing. We provide rich case studies to illustrate how specific strategies aimed at improving neighborhood conditions have contributed to this transformation and will continue to do so as long as past and contemporary interpretations of neighborhood change drive policy and practice.

What Is a Neighborhood?

This is not an easy question to answer. In this book we consider "neighborhood" to be a freely used term that is often used without having a precise definition in mind. We will take into consideration the fluidness of this term as we problematize the concept of "neighborhood change." Still, there are some basic assumptions that we want to lay out before we move forward. As a starting point, most agree that a neighborhood is a place in which people live, and at a more personal level, it is the area surrounding one's home (Pebley and Sastry 2004). Neighborhoods are also assumed to have some sort of boundary to differentiate one from another, but these cannot easily be pinned down by asking residents or researchers (Taylor 2012).

Researchers treat "the neighborhood" as a unit of analysis that includes people and other things such as grocery stores, schools, and parks that are joined together in an enclosed space. Socioeconomic data and other spatial statistics are often assembled and used to analyze neighborhood characteristics. In the United States, social scientists have been doing this since the early 1900s with data delineated by the US Census as tracts, which have become proxies for neighborhoods.[1] Then and now, the average size of a census tract is about four thousand people, which, depending on the density, can be a small or large area. Urban planners in the 1920s assumed this population size was sufficient to support a local school and other amenities expected in a neighborhood (Perry 1929). More recently, transit-oriented development and walkability standards have reinforced this scale, assuming that most amenities should be within a walking distance of one's home (usually a half-mile radius), which then dictates a certain density and land use mix.

Throughout this book we will discuss how research, policy, and practice has helped to reify a particular notion of the urban neighborhood—its scale and contents—as well as the assumption that neighborhoods are relatively homogeneous. When first drawn up, census tracts were "designed to be relatively homogeneous units with respect to population characteristics, economic status, and living conditions at the time of establishment" (U.S. Census Bureau n.d.). For the most part, this continues to be the case; even as the United States becomes more racially and ethnically diverse, its census tracts are not (Holloway, Wright, and Ellis 2012). Social scientists debate how to interpret homogeneity or the relative lack of heterogeneity that has been the spatial trademark for much of the United States. In this book, we continue this debate by using aggregated data and census tracts to investigate neighborhood change to call into question how the race, ethnicity, and class of people get inscribed onto space. We argue that our understanding of these relatively segregated living patterns requires us to look at how space is produced, both in a real and conceptual sense. While recently challenged by policies and planning practices that promote "mixed" neighborhoods, we find homogeneity continues to be a significant and highly accepted measure in the study of urban dynamics.

Another assumption to unpack is the presumed colocation of a community within a neighborhood. The term "community" generally refers to a group of people that have in common an interest (e.g., business and professional associations), a condition (e.g., race and class) or an identity. Neighborhoods, for the most part, are viewed as space-based communities. We do not assume that proximity means there is community or that community is a spatially dependent relationship. Still, whether by choice or not, living as neighbors is a form of communing. At a minimum, there is the common experience of being in a place—whatever the conditions—that is shared and affects all who live there in some way. Many also assume, however, that there is some synergy between the place and the people and that what is in common is neither arbitrary nor a coincidence. In other words, some believe that one reason we are likely to find people with the same characteristics, economic status, and living conditions sharing space is because people seek out other people like them to live among and are likely to act collectively to maintain the status quo of that space over time. While we do not assume that a group of people collected in a space by an arbitrarily drawn boundary is also a community, we do recognize that this assumption has been reinforced by years of research, which subsequently has shaped how we think about the relationship between neighborhood and community (J. Smith 1998).

As this book demonstrates, language and representations of space have the ability to imagine things for us, and through repetition they can come to appear to be real, serving as lenses through which we then see and constitute reality. We assume that any representation of space generated by theory actually obfuscates social practice and operates as an ideological frame with its own power effects. This includes assuming that people in a neighborhood form a community, and if they do not they are disorganized and pathologized. In general, we see neighborhoods—however they are determined and bounded—as places of reference in which people interact with multiple other forces and hence are neither self-explaining nor self-contained. Instead, neighborhoods have to be grasped as a set of social relations and interactions historically materializing in place but at the same time surpassing space. This includes how we investigate and interpret neighborhood change.

Explaining Neighborhood Change

Scholars, through their research and writing, have generated various explanations for why and how neighborhoods change. In this book, we argue that the foundation for most theories are studies of human ecology established by researchers at the University of Chicago in the 1920s, which became the dominant paradigm both in explaining neighborhood change and in actually shaping neighborhoods through its use by policy analysts and planners (J. Smith 1998). In this framework, which is reviewed in great detail in the next chapter, neighborhoods were assumed to be *natural areas* where people of similar social, ethnic, or demographic background would live together. Change occurred when the composition of the neighborhood's population changed. Migration was a concern for these researchers, particularly given the diversity of new groups entering the city. It was assumed that the greater the difference between current residents and the immigrants "invading" their neighborhood, the greater the likelihood that newcomers would "succeed" and "push out" the incumbent residents. This process of change was often accompanied by resistance or even violence as incumbents sought to protect their space.

Early critics of human ecology theories (e.g., Alihan 1938; Firey 1945; Suttles 1972) found this view of neighborhood change deterministic and devoid of any consideration of the symbolic, cultural, and political reasons that often influence household decisions to move from or stay in a neighborhood over time. Despite the critiques and noted limitations, we contend that the ecological succession framework prevailed in some form in each new major theory of neighborhood change. This includes filtering, life-cycle, racial change, and revitalization, which in the next chapter we classify as mainstream theories of neighborhood change.

While human ecology thinking continues to influence some interpretations of neighborhood change (e.g. see Wilson and Taub 2006, Sampson 2012), the past few decades have been associated with gentrification theories. Beginning in the 1960s, a growing body of research grounded in various critical traditions (e.g., Marxism, neo-Marxism, feminism, postmodernism) raised questions about how and why cities were changing. Generally, political economists treated neighborhoods as contingent products that reflect the forces that produce them while the people living in them respond to the challenges involved in their production. According to Logan and Molotch, "within the Marxian framework, neighborhood is essentially a residual phenomenon" (1987, 100). For some, this view changed with the introduction of Henri Lefebvre's *The Production of Space*, which geographers like David Harvey employed to show neighborhood change as a flow of capital in relation to spatial production and the process of social reproduction. Still, this framing of neighborhood change is grounded in a general theory of capitalism that tends to limit agency in the process and, more generally, overdetermine the outcomes of change. In other words, gentrification was relatively unstoppable.

While these critical analyses revealed the limiting aspects of human ecology thinking, particularly the means by which theory fixes space and naturalizes homogeneity, they too limit our ability to understand neighborhood change. As with human ecology—though for very different reasons—homogenous space defined by class and race is the expected and presumed norm. By assuming that forces acting for and against community follow the same trajectory every time there is a fight over space, the ending of the story is already determined: developers will always get the land and make money by capitalizing on the rent gap, while community advocates push back, perhaps slowing the process but ultimately losing the battle.

We contend that the analysis needs to shift attention from the consumers to the production of space for consumption. Before the 2008 recession, few doubted that there must be real demand (i.e., gentrifiers) for all the condominiums built in New York, Las Vegas, Miami, Chicago, and most other cities for nearly a decade starting in the late 1990s—why else would banks invest in all this development? The nearly global burst of the housing bubble, however, revealed a disconnect between the real demand for housing, the desires of investors and elected officials, and the realities of consumers. One explanation for this disconnect is the changing nature of real estate and specifically its use in the process of accumulation and wealth creation. Land is being used more and more to create and extract value, to further advance the commodification of life and space. In simple terms, the production of value (e.g., return on investment, capital gain, profit) relies on people with the means to change the value of land, either through investment or disinvestment in space. While capital and markets make this possible—and have for many years through different mechanisms—our current period has transformed the land itself into an instrument *and* a means to extract and accumulate value (Lefebvre 1991). In broad terms, urban space is an abstract commodity and its value is independent of the actual needs of families or retailers or manufacturers. It ends up being worth what speculation can get for it because the actual consumers and producers of space are seeking to maximize its value regardless of how it is transacted or how and by whom it is used.

By the 1990s, the commodification of neighborhood space had become one of the preferred and well-supported means of producing value. What made this type of development possible was fast capital turnover via financialization and securitization, deregulation and the associated "unlocking" of fixed real estate. Equally, to assure that value accrues over time, *creative destruction*—the linked process of accumulation and annihilation (Marx and Engels 1998 [1848]; Schumpeter 1994 [1942])—made the industry of producing and reproducing space flexible, fast-moving, and free-floating. In our view, creative destruction is historically contingent, and thus forces in history determine different forms and priorities over time under different societal regimes. Made up of different formations, a societal regime does not operate equally across a society.[2]

In its current form, creative destruction is tied to a specific societal regime of investment and divestment processes shaping the built environment. While investment in some urban areas may be justified by actual population growth, the ability to quickly and strategically reinvent space for profit is really the primary driver. This includes generating all kinds of new markets. The middle class returned to the city to gentrify neighborhoods while banks and developers discovered the emerging markets of disinvested "inner-city" communities in which to invest, or, more accurately, from which to extract value created by past destruction. At the same time, empty manufacturing space became lofts for living/working/playing while public housing developments were being transformed into mixed-income communities for the middle class and a token portion of the "deserving" poor. The production of each type of space has its own narrative and set of justifications to attract middle- and upper-income homebuyers, and most of these narratives are driven by the need to find new ways to generate value from space. While some of these narratives also include social goals and aspirations such as helping get people out of poverty, they are still tied to the real estate product that is a means to the accumulation end, which is higher land value and a commodity that can be used to extract a greater return on investment. At the same time, as this book will illustrate, there are opposing forces with counternarratives that challenge the accumulation of space, which complicate and at times disrupt and even stop this process.

The past two decades have been marked by the accelerated production, destruction, and reproduction of neighborhoods throughout Chicago and other cities around the country. Regeneration or urban renewal schemes in Europe and the United States, and high-end housing production in just about every major city in the world, have also played a role. The correspondingly accelerated cycles of investment and disinvestment, evidently tied to financial speculation, have accelerated real estate turnover. In turn, real estate turnover has intensified the use of land in the production and circulation of the value of urban space and, subsequently, neighborhood change. Areas ignored or disinvested for decades by real estate agents and banks were discovered and transformed, seemingly overnight, into hip places for young singles or into family-oriented middle-class enclaves. Along the way, the priority given to stable neighborhoods has been subsumed by fluctuating real estate values, and aspirations for community are colliding with the realities of accumulation. This moment calls for us to re-examine urban dynamics and how neighborhood change is explained.

Reframing Neighborhood Change

This book re-examines the dynamics of neighborhood change after nearly a century of research, policy making, and practice, once again using Chicago as a site for investigation. We are motivated by several shortcomings in the study of neighborhoods today, which in turn affect the understanding and pursuit of change of any kind. A key concern is the way prevailing explanations "fix" how we think about neighborhoods and measure change, thereby erecting a model against which to assess reality and a paradigm for intervention that is incapable of assessing the dynamics of creative destruction and accumulation. The neighborhood constructed by mainstream researchers has become a naturalized homogeneous site even if contested and in flux.

Another concern is the way theories of neighborhood change align the space of a community within a fixed and arbitrarily bounded place on a map. We argue throughout the different case studies that a community—people sharing a common culture or belief—is in no way automatically aligned with any physical space and, more importantly, should not be assumed to actually exist in a space defined by researchers and real estate brokers. Still, as we contend, these conceptual spaces are useful in our understanding of why neighborhood change has mattered in the past and continues to be a focus of theory and policy making. This includes the role the neighborhood has played in shaping social relations, contestation, and the mutually constitutive relationships between space and class, race, gender, family, and so forth. These concerns have practical as well as theoretical implications.

A particular issue we have is with indicators that equate homogeneity with stability and then are used to measure the stability or health of a neighborhood. Not only does this naturalize contingent formations such as class- and race-differentiated neighborhoods, it also problematizes some spaces; depending on the race or income level of the occupants, not all homogeneous spaces are the same. As we discuss throughout this book, white and middle-income (or higher) neighborhoods are the standard while nonwhite and/or lower-income neighborhoods are often found to be unhealthy and unstable, a perspective that narrows our approach to policy analysis and subsequent prescriptions for fixing neighborhood problems and controlling change in the future. This includes, for example, justifying restricting the number of poor people living in mixed-income communities on the premise that "too many" will cause the neighborhood to become poor. Grounded in a framework that does not acknowledge the forces that contribute to segregation, mainstream assumptions about neighborhood stability have been used to restrict the choice and opportunity of people who typically have less of each in order to mitigate perceived fear among those who have more of both. Equally important, it has negatively branded whole groups of people, including nonwhites, the poor, and renters.

Finally, mainstream theory and conventional wisdom has also assumed that higher-income consumers moving into a neighborhood is a positive form of change when compared to lower-income families moving in, because wealth provides stability and improves the health of the neighborhood (e.g., see J. Mitchell 1974). For many planners and politicians, this is a favorable outcome, as disposable income coupled with higher home values means increased tax revenues for local government, more customers for local shops and restaurants, and families that are less reliant on social services. While research on gentrification has turned this notion on its head by revealing the destabilizing effect of higher-income families moving in and displacing lower-income people from neighborhoods, it has also revealed the negative effects of speculative investment (Betancur 2011; Curran 2004; Newman and Wyly 2006; Marcuse 1985a, 1985b; Slater 2012), one of many tension points between theory and practice. Focusing on demand and treating it as a wholly benign behavior and not on the forces contributing to the production of specific types of neighborhoods has made it relatively easy to justify policies that promote gentrification. Yet at the same time, it has become harder the past two decades even for higher-income families to live in some cities, which suggests that demand may be fictitious or at least economically ineffective relative to what is being developed.

Approach and Chapters in This Book

We believe the production of flexible space is the dominant force shaping the production of neighborhood space today. Concrete examples from Chicago illustrate how this point of view not only exposes the limits of contemporary theory, practice, social reproduction, and community-based initiatives, but also offers a more robust interpretation of contemporary urban dynamics. This approach also allows us to develop more flexible explanations for neighborhood change by combining historically necessary conditions and contingent forces shaping them on the ground. It also frees us from deterministic theoretical outcomes and allows a perspective in which neighborhoods are largely situational and open; their individual cases are driven by different actors responding to different local situations.

This book seeks to accomplish three things: (1) examine major changes in the structure and dynamics of urban space and specifically neighborhoods over the past few decades, (2) assess the role and adequacy of prevailing paradigms in explaining change and shaping neighborhoods under today's regime of flexible accumulation, and (3) offer an alternative framework in which to investigate and interpret contemporary neighborhood change. We use Chicago as our laboratory for good reason. We know the city well, having worked with many different entities grappling with change, and we have witnessed firsthand how mainstream theories and methods, which have their roots in Chicago, have framed neighborhood analyses and policy making.

We begin with our own analysis of prevailing approaches to the study of neighborhoods and neighborhood change in chapter 1. As already suggested, we demonstrate how mainstream approaches not only improperly totalize, naturalize, and homogenize space but also mirror the power relations that seek to fix a neighborhood as a place to segregate or contain people. We draw on insights from political economy and critical theory depicting neighborhoods as real estate submarkets of social reproduction to question the assumption that homogeneity is natural, and we suggest that highly contested and differentiated social processes are at work instead.

Chapter 2 illustrates and examines the effects of classifying neighborhoods through ecological indicators, both in the form of representations of space and in the policies/interventions derived from their use. We draw on two recent efforts to classify Chicago neighborhoods, which point to alternative analytical approaches and metrics that can be used to interpret the spatial impacts of creative destruction over time.

In chapter 3, we examine the racial trajectory of two neighborhoods, one predominantly black and the other predominantly Latino. We focus on the role representations play in the process of facilitating a neighborhood's shift toward gentrification. Drawing from what we have observed in both neighborhoods, we posit that racialization of the space played a central role in the ongoing shift to gentrification, with race being used against low-income families either to justify practices to drive them out or to support whites and gentrifiers moving in.

Chapter 4 examines the trajectory of change in Englewood, a South Side neighborhood that went from white to black and from middle-class to poor, to consider how its current state as a hyper-ghetto came about. We focus on the ways Englewood is defined and redefined both to demonize and imprison residents and to facilitate speculation. We discuss the ways in which these "games" of representation mask realities on the ground, including the tremendous diversity and energy that characterizes the everyday practices of residents, and we discuss how residents in Englewood respond to and relate to the current representations of this neighborhood and their efforts to offset negative change.

In chapter 5, we draw on the previous chapters to diagram how, both conceptually and empirically, neighborhoods today operate as *flexible spaces of accumulation* that range between the extremes of gentrification and ghettoization. Unlike the more stable and homogenous neighborhoods of the postwar industrial era, neighborhoods now are place-based accumulation engines simultaneously pushing toward gentrification and ghettoization, producing spaces that can contain urban poor minorities in carceral formations and provide opportunities for unfettered speculation over the spoils.

Chapter 6 builds on this framework to examine various efforts to "sell" neighborhoods and the construction and destruction of community through its commodification. Using as examples Paseo Boricua in Humboldt Park and Boystown in Lakeview, we show how particular ethnicities or lifestyles have been appropriated by cities and capital to be commodified and consumed and how some residents benefit while others confront the daily realities of continuous displacement and impoverishment created by the commodification process. We also examine how such places can become caricatures of themselves after the inhabitants whose identity is used to sell the space have moved on and even when they have not, which illustrates how community and neighborhood do not align even in a space claimed by a group.

In chapter 7, we examine the process of social engineering vis-à-vis mixed-income housing that the Chicago Housing Authority has been advancing through its Plan for Transformation. This analysis reveals how race and income help create the ghetto as a particular form of homogenous space that requires intervention, while also raising questions about how mainstream theory conceptualizes what makes a neighborhood healthy. It also documents the ways in which the representation of mixed-income developments is being used to advance gentrification, to classify the poor as either deserving or undeserving, and to further push them into super-ghettoes or destabilized neighborhoods occupied by poor nonwhites.

Chapter 8 draws on our many years of experience in the field of community development to examine how a development agenda has changed the field into something more like middlemen between neighborhoods and the outside and less like community-based organizations serving low-income people. We illustrate this point with different examples of community development that have been widely used in Chicago and elsewhere in the United States. We also consider the challenges for multiracial and multiethnic collaborative efforts to take what control they can or at least offset the process of creative destruction and accumulation through contemporary efforts to organize coalitions across neighborhoods.

Although each chapter stands on its own, when combined they aim to portray a vastly different picture from the concept of neighborhoods as ecologies and of change as a dynamic of invasion and succession. Building on this evidence, we close by outlining a grounded set of recommendations for a different approach to how we study, document, and experience the realities of neighborhood change. We posit some challenges to researchers and theorists, practitioners on the ground, and policy makers, as well as to ourselves.

Claiming Neighborhood

CHAPTER 1

Prevailing Approaches to the Study of Neighborhoods and Change

> Something that we know when no one asks us, but no longer
> when we are supposed to give an account of it, is something
> that we need to remind ourselves of. (Wittgenstein 1958, 89)

Theories of neighborhood change have been constructed since the 1920s (Keating and Smith 1996) to help make sense of the physical, social, and institutional factors altering the status quo of American neighborhoods and affecting larger urban systems. These theories aim to identify factors that cause neighborhoods to change. For example, architectural features and location can increase or decrease demand for a neighborhood, while institutional factors such as zoning, building code enforcement, rent control, lending practices, and discrimination can positively or negatively influence housing market operations. It is also common for researchers to look at changing demographics, including racial or ethnic composition, as well as change in the income level, familial status, and age of household members.

Policy makers and practitioners have long turned to these theories to guide the development of programs and strategies to either offset the negative results of change (e.g., loss in property values, decreasing quality of life) or to encourage change so as to produce positive results (e.g., increased property values, improved quality of life). And although we cannot always make direct linkages between theory and policy (e.g., see Metzger 2000), social science hegemony at particular points in time has framed both how neighborhood change is problematized and subsequent policy solutions.

Assuming that the process of developing theory is political (Foucault 1995, 1998; Flyvbjerg 1998), we focus on how theories of neighborhood change have produced a particular discursive space in which to interpret urban dynamics, a space with rules that determine what constitutes "legitimate" modes of distinguishing stable or healthy neighborhoods from unstable and unhealthy ones. Instead of viewing theory as a generalizable conceptualization of space, timeless and disconnected from context, we see it as a product of researchers that generates a particular type of space—in this case the stable neighborhood—for investigation. An early example of this is the neighborhood unit devised by Clarence Perry in 1929. In his famous diagram (Figure 1), the neighborhood

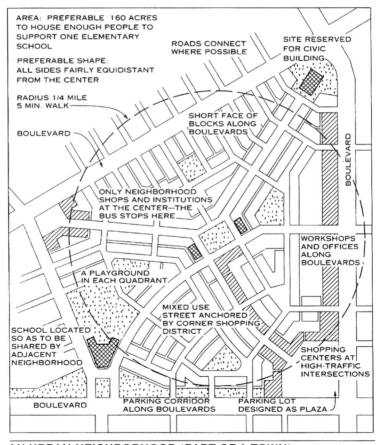

AN URBAN NEIGHBORHOOD (PART OF A TOWN)

Figure 1. Neighborhood Unit
Source: Clarence Perry, *A Plan for New York and Its Environs.* New York: 1929.

is shown as a collection of lots with single-family homes arranged around a school and community center and parks, with curvilinear streets that limit access from outside the neighborhood. Shopping and services are located along busier roads on the periphery but within walking distance of most homes. The scale is generally based on the population needed to fill an American grade school. Accompanying the diagram is a list of principles that guide the location of these different elements.

Perry's neighborhood unit is both a real and imagined space. It is *conceived*, as in being "thought of" or "brought into existence" through action, which in this case was through guidance for developing neighborhoods in a plan for the New York City region. It is also *conceptual* because Perry is projecting a particular view of what a neighborhood could or should be relative to cultural expectations at the time. Keeping this in mind, our review of neighborhood change theories considers how they not only help describe and explain but also produce urban dynamics.

Framing theory as *space producing* focuses attention on the relationship between these indicators and the place itself, which when conflated can lead to specific expectations for the site and its occupants that are only partially representative of the experiences of people actually living in the spaces studied. Theory viewed in this way is active; it is neither timeless nor disconnected from the context in which it was developed, and it draws attention to the role of researchers in the process of producing theory when examining urban space. To illustrate this we trace the trajectory of ideas that evolved from early writings of human ecologists, situating each subsequent or new theory in the context in which it was introduced.[1] A common thread we find is an image of stability that is based on neighborhoods being relatively homogeneous and occupied by a majority white, middle- or higher-income homeowners, which continues to underpin contemporary thinking about how to measure and interpret stability.

Most research on neighborhood change has been through either a human ecology or political economy lens. Human ecologists generally view neighborhoods as "natural" units, interconnected cells in the body of the city. Change was assumed to be a recurring process triggered by specific conditions essential to the growth and expansion of the city. In contrast, political economy has treated neighborhoods as historically produced spaces in the city that are contingent upon the controlling forces of power and capital. Clearly both frameworks derive from different epistemologies. Yet both have in common two fundamental features: neighborhood change always follows the same rules, and the space of the neighborhood is assumed to be relatively homogeneous in content. We explore these features next in *mainstream* (human ecology and its offshoots) and *critical* (political economy and its relatives) explanations of neighborhoods change.

Mainstream Theories of Neighborhood Change

The origin of mainstream theoretical investigations of neighborhood change in the United States is found in the work of human ecologists at the University of Chicago in the 1920s (J. Smith 1998; Temkin and Rohe 1996). Since then, academic research has posed new theories and models to describe neighborhood dynamics. What follows is a chronological review of the early work of the Chicago School and subsequent theories it generated—filtering, life cycle, racial tipping, and revitalization—and the corresponding assumptions each makes about the cause of neighborhood change.

HUMAN ECOLOGY AND INVASION-SUCCESSION

In the early part of the twentieth century, sociologists at the University of Chicago (UC) set out to explain the modern city as a product of human nature. Their premise was that the urban spatial patterns observed in American cities must somehow be essential for the progress of society. In *The City* (1925), Robert Park, Ernest Burgess, and Roderick McKenzie presented the city as a specific and orderly spatial pattern produced by economic competition and the division of labor in the industrial city. Burgess developed a schematic in which the city appeared as a set of concentric zones radiating from the central business district (Figure 2). Each surrounding zone was identified by dominant household and housing characteristics, with higher-income groups living in lower-density housing furthest from the center. Over time, the city was expected to grow, expanding out from the center. As industry in the center competed for space with surrounding residential areas, inhabitants of the inner zone would then push into the next outer ring (invasion), eventually taking over the physical space of that zone (succession).

In this framework, neighborhoods were assumed to be *natural areas* where people of similar social, ethnic, or demographic background naturally lived together. They were not alone in their thinking. Tilly (1984) suggests that a *paradigm of differentiation* evolved in social theory at the time to consider how community was maintained despite the growing diversity of urban space. In this paradigm, segregation in urban space could be explained. Not only were city dwellers expected to live away from work, they were also expected to naturally coalesce in enclaves with people of similar income and heritage to recreate a sense of community that was lost in modern city life. For the most part, these enclaves provided a separate space outside the workplace for social interaction and the production of culture (Katznelson 1981; Harvey 1989).

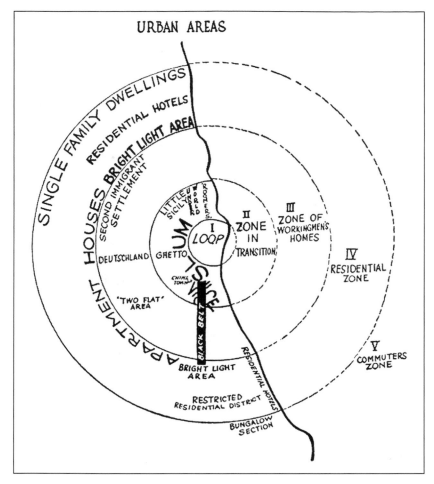

Figure 2. Concentric Zone Model
Source: Ernest Burgess, "The Growth of the City: An Introduction to a Research Project." In *The City*, edited by Robert Park, Ernest Burgess, and Roderick McKenzie. Chicago: University of Chicago Press, 1925.

The Chicago School's early research had a profound effect on the study of neighborhood change, with Chicago becoming the dominant site for investigating social life in industrial urban America. Immigration was of particular interest for these researchers. They assumed that the greater the difference between new immigrants invading a neighborhood and its incumbent residents, the greater the likelihood that succession would occur, often preceded by resistance or even violence. While some UC researchers used ethnographic techniques to produce in-depth neighborhood studies to learn more about the culture of particular groups (see for example Thomas and Znaniecki's *The Polish Peasant in Europe and America* [1918] or Zorbaugh's *The Gold Coast and the Slum* [1929]), others developed methods that could systematically track population patterns and movement (see Burgess and Bogue 1967), laying a firm foundation for qualitative and quantitative research. UC researchers also instituted the mapping of neighborhoods or *community areas* along with its demographic studies.[2] The first to employ census tracts as proxies for neighborhoods, they initiated the use of aggregate data and many of the socioeconomic indicators used today to document changes in spatial patterns, including race/ethnicity.

Developed at a time when cities were rapidly growing, human ecology theories provided a logical explanation for urban growth patterns in an industrialized economy. Given the waves of immigrants to American cities, neighborhoods were changing with the rapid infusion of people competing for space. Human ecologists' underlying assumptions about urban spatial patterns and human nature, however, limited the explanatory value of the ecological model. Assuming that the order of the city in the 1920s, segregated by race, ethnicity, and class, was necessary for social reproduction and economic progress, these theorists excluded from the explanation some factors shaping the space of the city. These factors included the active recruitment of labor to build its industrial base (e.g., Lemann 1992); the social and legal conditions that often kept residents segregated by race, ethnicity, and class (e.g., Massey and Denton 1993); and the deliberate actions of institutions opposed to integration (e.g., Abrams 1955; Aldrich 1975). The exclusion of these processes sets up a narrow interpretation of neighborhood change that privileges a view of the city that is compelled to be differentiated along social factors, particularly race, class, and ethnicity, if it is to grow and develop.

Generally, there is little accounting for exogenous factors contributing to neighborhood change in early ecological models beyond the assumption that growth varies with and is dependent on the larger economic climate. Burgess's concentric zones assume a city's growth is determined by an increasing level of commercial and industrial activity in the central business district (CBD), which then pushes out the center, causing change to occur in surrounding zones. Seemingly simplistic in thinking, the Chicago School's view of urban dynamics reproduced the dominant mind-set at the time, which assumed the CBD determined the spatial patterns of the city (e.g., see Weber 1899). While later work questioned Burgess's concentric zone model (see Hoyt 1939; Harris and Ullman 1945), it still reinforced the premise that the spatial form of the city was a natural outcome of economic activity. This was also the case with filtering.

FILTERING

Filtering refers to the process where older housing units become available to lower-income families as higher-income families move to newer units on the urban periphery. In early filtering models, the metropolitan area was presented as a single housing market, with a fixed hierarchy of housing units available to different income groups competing for the best housing value (Baer and Williamson 1988). In spatial terms, this conceptualization of the urban housing market complements the concentric zone model described above, locating newer and more expensive homes at lower densities further out from the center to meet the demands of an expanding metropolis. In contrast, though, filtering looked beyond the CBD as the sole driving economic force shaping the city and considered the effects of suburbanization.

Originally introduced in the mid-nineteenth century, filtering was first used in the 1930s by Homer Hoyt to connect physical and economic obsolescence of housing units with neighborhood change. A University of Chicago economist, Hoyt employed filtering to explain American urban spatial patterns he observed in empirical research completed for the US Federal Housing Administration (FHA). Based on a study of 142 cities, he concluded that increasing income levels encouraged residents to seek better housing being built at the periphery of urbanized space. Movement out by these residents freed up the aging housing stock, which then provided new homes for lower-income groups. Rather than invasion, these families were simply filling up homes made available to them. Considering the welfare effects of filtering, this distinction allowed filtering to appear ambiguous, a process that can produce both negative change and positive outcomes.

As a theory to explain the relationship between the aging housing stock and neighborhood change, filtering helped make sense of physical deterioration in central cities as part of a larger urban dynamic that pushed and pulled middle-class urban dwellers out to improve their living conditions. In the late 1930s, and even more so following World War II, households were leaving behind the dinge and congestion in the city and seeking out new housing opportunities in the suburbs. Filtering, however, generally assumes that this is occurring in a free market economy without barriers such as discrimination (see Squires 1994) or a spatial mismatch of supply and demand that prevents housing markets from operating "perfectly" (Baer and Williamson 1988).[3] And, as with human ecologists, filtering theories assumed that these dynamics would maintain homogeneous space over time, as did racial tipping.

RACIAL TIPPING

Often referred to as racial succession, the concept of "tipping" presumes that race is the primary cause of change in urban spatial patterns. The tipping point hypothesis states that when a certain proportion of blacks moves into a neighborhood, whites will move out, often at an accelerated rate, leading the neighborhood to eventually become all black (Grodzins 1958; Wolfe 1963). Research by Molotch (1969, 1972) and Schelling (1971) suggested that tipping was independent of white residents' decisions to move out; instead it is a threshold at which whites are no longer comfortable moving into a racially mixed neighborhood. In either case, researchers (see Clark 1991; Farley et al. 1979, 1994; Farley 1995; Galster 1990; Ottensmann 1995) concluded that resegregation was an inevitable result of racial tipping.

While previous research on invasion-succession had drawn attention to the effects of different ethnic groups' moving in, racial tipping transformed the space of the city into black and white. Derived at a time when many cities were beginning to experience population loss as whites moved out to the suburbs while increasing numbers of minority (primarily black) residents moved into the city, tipping helped to explain the rapid change of neighborhood conditions observed in many older American cities beginning in the 1950s. Tipping also linked race to declining housing values, reinforcing a negative image of the outcome of racial invasion-succession. For example, Downs (1981) attributes changes in housing values to "ghetto expansion." As blacks moved out of the ghetto into adjacent neighborhoods, housing values initially inflated when blacks moved in and then decreased as the neighborhood became predominantly nonwhite.[4] Generally, this notion supports Hoyt's (1933) observations that housing prices were linked to the racial/ethnic mix of the neighborhood. It also provides another factor to explain decisions to move that start the filtering process.

The tipping point is simply a statistical measure, yet many have interpreted it as a sign that mixed-race neighborhoods are inherently unstable (Ottensmann 1995). It has been difficult to dispute the explanatory power of tipping. Even proponents of racial integration and efforts to prevent racially mixed neighborhoods from resegregating respected the tipping-point hypothesis and assumed there was a threshold at which whites would leave or not move in. The Village of Oak Park even went so far as to propose an ordinance that would limit the number of black households on a block to 30 percent, since this was the threshold commonly found in the empirical research at which a neighborhood would rapidly become all black (Goodwin 1979). Such thresholds are also evident in pro-integrative policies and incentives (e.g., equity assurance programs) that try to persuade whites to remain in racially mixed neighborhoods or to encourage blacks to move into predominantly white neighborhoods (Keating 1994).

Beginning in the 1980s, evidence of sustained racially mixed neighborhoods (see Nyden, Lukehart, and Maly 1997; Ellen 1998, 2000; Farley and Frey 1994;

Lee and Wood 1991; Denton and Massey 1991) suggested that tipping may have been a temporary phenomenon produced by specific conditions such as the mass migration of blacks from the south to older cities and the shift from an industrial to a service economy. Others point to external forces such as blockbusting and redlining (Squires 1994). This empirical research also made it clear that interpreting the evidence is conceptually and methodologically complicated. A key problem is defining what we actually mean by integration. As Richard Smith (1998) explained, there is a significant difference between *demographic* integration and *social* integration, with the latter presenting "problems of measuring and characterizing the attitudes and interactions among community residents under anything other than the small-scale, case study approach" (3). Perhaps most important, these communities were exceptions to the rule, either anomalies or outliers worthy of study, and likely the result of deliberate programs aimed at promoting racially integrated communities.

NEIGHBORHOOD LIFE CYCLE

At the same time researchers were paying attention to racial tipping, Hoover and Vernon (1959) introduced the idea of the neighborhood life cycle to explain the differences among them. Life-cycle researchers assumed that all neighborhoods could be classified as being in some stage of development, transition, downgrading, thinning out, or renewal. Each stage was distinguished from the other by changes in the population (race/ethnicity, socioeconomic status, age) and in the physical place (land use, population density, housing conditions). While the term "life cycle" implies that neighborhoods were expected to go through all stages, the model allowed for some to remain in one stage as others fluctuated between two, or moved up or down the continuum.

The classic life-cycle model utilized a continuum of different stages to describe the general health or stability of a neighborhood. While it distinguishes each stage, it does not help to discern what conditions move a neighborhood from one stage to the next. A more complex model that focused on the roles of different actors in the change process was developed by John Mitchell (1974) for the US Department of Housing and Urban Development to help guide investment decisions (see Table 1). While useful, the model makes it appear as if all factors identified in any given stage happened concurrently. It also assumes that a stable neighborhood is homogeneous, higher income, owner-occupied, and white.

The life-cycle model and its derivations narrowed the scope of the investigation to focus specifically on the neighborhood characteristics that caused it to change. By isolating the neighborhood as an object for study itself, it was

Table 1. Indicators of a "Healthy" Stable Neighborhood (1974)

Social
- Middle to high social status
- Moderate to upper income levels
- Ethnic homogeneity
- High school graduates and above
- Family-oriented or childless adults
- White-collar and/or skilled blue-collar workers
- Pride in neighborhood and house
- Good neighborhood reputation
- Neighborhood perceived as safe
- Socially cohesive

Public Services
- Services efficient and appropriate
- Some reliance on private services

Physical
- Good property upkeep
- Sound structural condition
- Good location
- Neighborhood well maintained

Economic
- High owner investment
- Good property values
- Insurance available
- High confidence on future value

Reproduced from "The Neighborhood Change Process," J. Mitchell 1974.

no longer just a "unit of analysis" in the study of urban dynamics. Instead, the neighborhood was treated as a fairly autonomous site in which to observe different types of change occurring *within*. As in previous theories, change was considered natural, but unlike human ecology theories, which assumed that the CBD was the driver, the life-cycle theory was not necessarily determined by the relative location to the city center.

The potential to move down the continuum into a less healthy stage was a concern for some policy makers and researchers who assumed this could be prevented but also that intervention could help move a neighborhood up to a better stage. In part, this shift parallels a growing interest in targeting neighborhoods as sites in which to implement policy that could improve deteriorating cities. For example, urban renewal was introduced after World War II to clear out the bad buildings and prepare the space for new development, and then to induce private investment with public funds to replace obsolete housing and reverse deterioration. The notion that all places had a life cycle provided a common set of criteria and vocabulary to evaluate and compare the condition of city neighborhoods. Neighborhood quality and socioeconomic status of residents was always positively correlated, making it impossible for predominantly lower-income neighborhoods or mixed-income communities where the majority of residents were poor to be classified as stable or to become stable without either changing the mix of people or their economic status. Furthermore, homeowners were preferred to renters, who were expected to have higher turnover rates and limited involvement in property upkeep, as well as lower incomes. All this had implications for both local and federal policy regarding where best to invest resources to revitalize aging cities. According to Metzger (2000, 7), this explanation was used "to encourage the 'deliberate dispersal' of low-income and African-American urban neighborhoods, followed by the eventual reuse of abandoned areas," which also justified introducing different revitalization strategies.

NEIGHBORHOOD REVITALIZATION

Where previous conceptual schemes focused on the negative effects of change, the life-cycle model suggested that positive change also was possible. As research in the United States began documenting the revitalization of a small number of older urban neighborhoods in the 1970s, some social scientists shifted their attention to the conditions that facilitated positive neighborhood change. For example, Ahlbrandt and Brophy (1975) described the successful revitalization of a Pittsburgh neighborhood that utilized public resources to improve physical conditions and induce investment by the private sector. Building from the image of what makes a neighborhood healthy, it was assumed that higher levels of ownership and income were needed to improve the neighborhood.

Theories about revitalization focused on triggers for private investment. In Boston, Clay (1979) found proof of a positive market response to private urban reinvestment, distinguishing gentrification from incumbent upgrading. Most of the revitalization was the latter, with upper-income residents appearing to move "back to the city" from the suburbs to live near downtown employment. Clay also suggested that those making the improvements assumed that submitting to their social norms and behaviors, such as owning a home, would also improve the neighborhood (Clay 1979). Goetze (1979) concluded that private investment occurred in Boston because a positive perception of the neighborhoods' being revitalized had been created. He assumed that confidence in a neighborhood can be produced through positive marketing that sells the neighborhood to potential investors and incumbent residents. Goetze and Colton

(1980) developed a model to explain revitalization as a function of housing conditions and market perceptions, which are affected by a combination of factors including neighborhood location, metropolitan market dynamics, specific features of the neighborhood (topography, transportation, spatial integration), citizen expectations of government, and the culture of local government. The ideal state is a neighborhood where market perceptions are strong (but not too strong) and the housing is in good condition. Strong neighborhood confidence is indicated by the level of activity in the real estate market regardless of housing conditions. This allows a physically deteriorating neighborhood to have a strong market standing if there is confidence that it will improve, which means increasing home values and ownership rates.

In these various explanations of revitalization, the neighborhood is viewed as a submarket within the city and the larger urban space (i.e., the metropolitan area or region). The primary explanation for neighborhood upgrading, whether it be by incumbents or newcomers, is the investment potential of the neighborhood. Strategies to market the neighborhood can aid in public and private investment, particularly in the housing stock. At a time when local governments were trying to figure out how to do more with less federal support while their middle class was shrinking as higher-income families moved out to the suburbs, revitalization triggered by private market investment represented great potential.

Up to this period, Marxists and political economists had not really paid attention to neighborhoods, in part because their analysis was at a systems level. This changed as neighborhoods became sites for disinvestment and reinvestment driven by both private capital and the state (e.g., urban renewal and gentrification). In particular, David Harvey's (1973) study of the relationship between city disinvestment and suburban investment spatialized the flow of capital and put it squarely in or out of neighborhoods. Many, however, trace the expansion of critical voices back to Neil Smith's work, which reframed invasion and succession as a process driven by revanchist motivations of middle class (usually white) people to reclaim the city from the poor (usually not white) rather than individual consumers leading gentrification. From his perspective, what was happening in the 1970s was a fundamental restructuring of urban space, and the outcome depended on "how much productive capital returns to the area from the suburbs" (N. Smith 1979, 538).

Critical Approaches to the Study of Neighborhood Change

Critical analysts, including us, view urban dynamics differently than mainstream researchers. Political economists, for example, examine the change that occurs in neighborhoods primarily as a function of capital accumulation and social reproduction. In this framework, neighborhoods are sociohistorical formations originally emerging from the separation of production and social reproduction. Neighborhood change is examined in terms of the social relations of reproduction, shaped by and at the same time shaping class dynamics, and of capital accumulation and control of surplus value. Orthodox political economy focused almost exclusively on class struggle around the process of value production and appropriation. This has evolved, with new schools of thought including Regulation, neo-Marxism, and other nuanced analyses of postindustrial capitalism that have introduced space into the analysis.

SPATIALIZING THE FLOW OF CAPITAL

Like the human ecologists, political economists neglected neighborhoods in their early investigations of urban dynamics, focusing instead on production processes above and beyond neighborhoods. Much of this changed with Lefebvre's *The Production of Space*, which opened up to political economists a means to investigate neighborhood change as a form of spatial production and a process of spatialized social reproduction. But this has not necessarily led to a political economic theory of neighborhood change per se and much less to a clear means of studying particular neighborhoods. Instead, critical analyses of capitalism grounded in various frameworks—e.g., neo-Marxism, feminism, postmodernism, and more recently neoliberalism (e.g., Smith 2002; Hackworth 2007)—have led to a more concrete understanding among political economists of neighborhood change. As with human ecology theory before, this is path-breaking work that set a stage for further investigation and inspired new ideas, including this book.

At the core is David Harvey, who assumed that the production of cities, and by extension the production of neighborhoods, is driven by capital accumulation and social reproduction. Most relevant are his insights on the investment-disinvestment dynamic and differential class reproduction. The former are mechanisms of creative destruction that through devalorization and valorization processes, for instance, cause mass movement such as white flight while concurrently generating demand for suburban living and urban gentrification. Practices such as redlining and blockbusting are part and parcel of this process. As a result, through his analysis of the circuits of capital, Harvey concluded that flexible accumulation produces rounds of investment and disinvestment, which have tremendous and profound implications for social reproduction. In Harvey's (1989) words, "it is now the created spaces of capitalism, the spaces of its own social reproduction, that have to be annihilated" (192), and as a result "the social spaces of reproduction . . . lose their functional coherence" (193).

Harvey was critical of those who treated all urban residential space as a single market. Instead, he showed how investment-disinvestment dynamics segmented space into ranges to accommodate buyers' purchasing power, but not, however, in the same way human ecologists assumed that land values were determined by proximity to the CBD. Instead, it was more purposeful and interrelated with how capital accumulation worked. Differential access to capital produces residential differentiation and market segmentation. As a result, people with similar purchasing power clustered together, at times even by occupation, and formed milieus of differentiated social reproduction space "out of which distinctive value systems, aspirations, and expectations may be drawn. . . . Working-class neighborhoods, for example, typically produce individuals with values conducive to being in the working class" (Harvey 1989, 119).

Harvey also noted that "creation of distinctive housing submarkets . . . improves the efficiency with which institutions can manage the urbanization process. But at the same time it limits the ability of individuals to make choices" (1989, 121). Clearly, individuals and households are limited to the submarkets they can afford. Harvey contends that residential differentiation through housing consumption further differentiates social reproduction by market segment, so that as people cluster into their respective segments, neighborhood identity begins to trump class consciousness. Class consciousness is further fragmented as layers of social differentiation such as race, ethnicity, occupation, or age are added, resulting in place-based identities and hierarchies that emphasize such aspects over class. The result is a city that is fragmented into distinct housing submarkets that steer individuals to the particular residential formations that correspond to their class position and race, often segmenting them even further by class subgroups.

COMMUNITY VERSUS COMMODITY

Mollenkopf (1981) adds another element by examining the antagonistic aspects of community and accumulation, which he claims produces an ongoing tension that then manifests in neighborhoods. Accumulation or the *exchange value* of space is "how a society creates, expands and distributes its means of well-being," while community or the *use value* of space is found in "the bonds people build with one another which enables them to trust in and rely on each other" (Mollenkopf 1981, 320). Driven by the profits to be gained from the monetary exchange of land and property, accumulation will always seek neighborhood forms that maximize capital gains, commodify social reproduction (e.g., housing), and make it possible to accumulate capital (e.g., appreciation). In contrast, community pursues neighborhood qualities such as family, sentimentality, neighborliness, mutual reliance, concerns about stability, networks and bonds, and being independent. Both sets of values coexist, and while seemingly incompatible, they somehow adapt and coalesce, though not always with ease.

Crises redefine the relationship between exchange and use value. For example, the crisis of Fordism—the post–World War II decades where mass production and mass consumption aligned to fuel economic growth—introduced a new societal regime that rendered prior arrangements between accumulation and community inoperable. Focusing on the post-Fordist transformation of individuals and households into consumers, Mollenkopf found a highly diverse economy that needed an expanding, further segmented consumer base in order to thrive in a post-mass-production era. As a result, neighborhoods became an opportunity to promote consumption, including traditional elements like homes and schools, but also a much wider range of shopping and services as well as different lifestyles and experiences. They are now also places to be "consumed" by tourists seeking cultural experiences, diners seeking authentic ethnic food, and anyone seeking a particular lifestyle.

For Mollenkopf, regime change presented both an opportunity and a challenge for the community position as the struggle pitted use values against accumulation's push for exchange value and extraction. The two positions are not easily reconciled in this current period of restructuring, which has resulted in reductions in labor compensation globally at the same time that capital passes on the costs of social reproduction to workers and families (Tabak 1996). Globalized competition has also pushed individuals and households to produce their own jobs. We have seen entrepreneurship move to center stage just as governments are shrinking social welfare in the name of austerity. All these shifts have generated high levels of labor polarization and predation in urban areas. Combined with an intensified drive to increase the commodification of social reproduction, these changes have affected neighborhood life tremendously. Through the political economist's lens, growing polarization and poverty concentration is a historically specific form of value extraction, intensified in this case to the point of threatening the livelihoods and life chances of a growing urban mass of people at the low end, what Harvey (2006) refers to as "accumulation by dispossession." And at the high end, we have intensified commodification via symbolic capital, spectacle, and Disneyfication (e.g., Zukin 2009).

Harvey (1995) offers a vision of how these seemingly divergent paths cross and function in contemporary urban space, operating altogether as marketplaces of use values or combinations of exchange and use values. Largely fixed in place by their condition, the poor resort to and depend largely on social relations within their neighborhoods to satisfy needs and wants. In contrast, having abundant exchange value, affluent groups engage in high levels of commodified reproduction and spatial mobility. They depend far less on their neighborhoods to satisfy their needs or to provide use value, which is dictated primarily by symbolic consumption, but they are concerned about its exchange value. Mostly homeowners, they have higher stakes in the real estate exchange value of their neighborhoods, which might explain the attention given to protect against and prevent behavior that can lead to depreciation and decline.

The social and economic world experienced by much of today's urban poor is defined and contained by the neighborhoods in which they live, a space that is limited by their own scarce consumer power. Higher-income individuals and families, who have more buying power, have many more options available. The resulting economic polarization creates an urban mosaic in which some neighborhoods are excluded either because they are exclusive and therefore off-limits to most or because they have literally been excluded—shut out—from the economy. From this perspective, income and a neighborhood's use value appear to be negatively related: as one goes up, the other goes down. From the outside, however, "ghettos" (i.e., extremely poor neighborhoods) are lacking both exchange and use value.

While the path of creative destruction can be contained and value restored in some neighborhoods—at least in theory—this would not necessarily benefit the poor. The circulation of capital that started flowing back into cities in the 1970s was motivated to create and extract value, not necessarily to improve neighborhoods for poor people. The rise of gentrification was proof of that, first documented in London (Glass 1964), then New York City (N. Smith 1979; Zukin 1982), and many other spaces thereafter. People were "moving back to the city" and they did not necessarily want to live with poor people. Palen and London (1984) concluded that the salient theme in all explanations for "market driven revitalization" was intergroup conflict and competition for space. Initially, the driving force was a young, upwardly mobile professional class (yuppies) looking for a good deal on a place to fix up. As demand increased and more capital was fed into the process, however, the movement morphed into an industrial complex of real estate developers, building contractors, designers, and the many spin-off entities that were part of the loft-living scene (Zukin 1982) and gentrification in general.

We were at that point in the postindustrial second circuit of capital in which land is a major commodity. Most political economists now attribute change to gentrification, a force that is prevailing though not easily reckoned with, as evidenced by the fights to save Bryant Park, Tompkins Square Park, and so many other places (e.g., N. Smith 1996; Zukin 1996; Mele 2000; Betancur 2002; Davila 2004). As cities began to not only embrace the infusion of private capital but to incentivize it, the practice intensified and the explanation shifted to situate gentrification in neoliberalism (Brenner and Theodore 2002; N. Smith 2002). Now gentrification is a means to privatize neighborhood revitalization and to reframe how the space of cities functions in a global economy, gaining independence from the state (N. Smith 2002). As a result, the neighborhood reproduces the social relations needed to sustain it as a site for capital from anywhere in the world to invest and reinvest. In short, neighborhoods are sites of accumulation.

As historical formations tied to general and particular historical forms of accumulation and social reproduction, neighborhoods reflect capitalist relations in spatialized social forms and processes. Rather than static containers, neighborhoods constitute active spaces of capitalist-driven social reproduction. Neighborhood residents can be both passive and active, supporters and challengers, individuals and communities. From this perspective, neighborhood change is a constant, and it can assume as many forms as there are neighborhoods. Political economy theory also includes, however, elements of structuralism and reductionism similar to human ecology theory. As sites of accumulation and social reproduction, there is little or no room for resident agency. While we have evidence of resistance, ultimately all we can expect is the forces of capital to be slowed or temporarily diverted, but never stopped. In this sense, the lens of political economy finds similar themes as human ecology thinking did: change is inevitable, predictable, and expected to displace people with limited power.

Competing Paradigms, Potential Openings

Each of the theories just reviewed "produce a particular notion of what constitutes a neighborhood and neighborhood change" (J. Smith 1998). Our classification scheme—mainstream and critical—represents two paradigms, each sustained but also revised over time, differentiated by institutional and ideological factors. In broad terms, each is produced by different and competing discursive practices, one supportive of the status quo and the other critical of it. As historical products linked to the forces producing each, mainstream explanations can be viewed as hegemonic discourses and critical explanations as counterhegemonic discourses. In Table 2 we differentiate key forces and effects of these divergent explanations and the representations they produce.

Both paradigms continue to shape how we study and interpret neighborhood change. In succinct terms, the mainstream approach treats neighborhoods as self-contained *units* within a pre-existing differentiated and hierarchical urban

Table 2. Mainstream v. Critical Approaches to Neighborhood Change

Paradigm	What Is a Neighborhood?	What Makes Them Change?	Understanding of Space	Forms of Change
Mainstream	• A natural unit of homogenous space • A moral zone	• Invasion-succession • Filtering • Racial tipping • Life cycle	• Container • Passive	• Progress • Evolution • Disequilibrium-equilibrium
Critical	• A production of residential space • A process of social reproduction	• Social relations • Community (use value) versus Accumulation (exchange value) • Consumption classes • Class differentiation	• Socially produced • Structured-Structuring	• Systemic • Regime • Dialectic • Movements

system. There is a natural order for the city and a virtuous process in which different groups compete for space and get sorted. The middle class is the status quo against which the rest are measured, and each class and the space it inhabits represents a position or stage in the spatial trajectory of social progress. The neighborhoods occupied by lower classes are barely functional and not ideal; they are places families should only pass through on their way up the socioeconomic ladder. In contrast, critical approaches see neighborhoods as *contingent formations of historical processes* that reproduce particular social relations. For political economy theories, class is the product of a system of value extraction and, hence, a relationship of exploitation and domination, and it is clearly not natural. Neighborhoods result from the separation between production and social reproduction, and their differences are produced by factors of class power, value extraction, societal regime change, and uneven opportunity.

By naturalizing neighborhood differentiation, human ecologists assumed that segregation represented the essence of social life and that the existing order was the hegemonic form. In contrast, by constructing neighborhoods as contingent formations, political economists offered counterhegemonic challenges to that order and the subsequent representations it generated. Further, while mainstream theories assume a particular form of homogeneity as evidence that a neighborhood is healthy or stable, political economy explains all homogeneity as the *product* of a class system that groups people into submarkets segmented by income and occupation, and now consumption, and the corresponding processes of social reproduction. More generally, critical analyses expose sociocultural and political dimensions of urban dynamics that mainstream theories fail to problematize because it is assumed that neighborhood change is stimulated by competitive forces that naturally redistribute groups across the landscape. Critical explanations portray change as the result of instabilities associated with class and intergroup struggles that can end only by uprooting exploitation and subsequently constructing radically different social relations.

A problematic connection between mainstream theories and some critical analyses is the assumption that class struggle is always the driving force that explains neighborhood change and the spatial patterns observed. Both buy into the modernist episteme that a universally valid generalization can be offered to explain *all* neighborhood change and that a system of representation that assumes some universal laws can explain all reality. Just like human ecology theory, framing the production of space in such a way leaves little, if any, room for factors of irrationality, inconsistency, chance, or agency. It also limits our options for exploring what other socially constructed factors might contribute to neighborhood change.

Although we group political economy and other postmodernist critical theories together, we are aware of deep differences between them, especially between the tendency in political economy to reduce social alienations to class while critical theories add other sources of alienation (e.g., race, sex, gender, age, and disability) acting independently or jointly in the production of space. For example, many critical authors have showed how race has been a major historical and contingent tool of neighborhood segregation and in the construction of property values and neighborhood homogeneity in the United States (e.g. Smith 2013). Feagin suggests that political economy places "the processes and structures of racial stratification and domination . . . at the center of serious urban analysis" (1998, 8). Alluding to "the reality of enforced separate spaces," he argues that "the divide between the suburbs and the city is, in many respects, a racial divide" (1998, 12) and between ghettos it is a "practice of repression," though he does not explain whether they are expressions of the same universal order of class alienation.

Other authors that focus on the racial construction of space, such as Goldsmith and Randolph (1993) or Hirsch (1998) do so in isolation from class. In a pioneering effort, Barrera (1979) addressed the overlapping of race and class in American neighborhoods, establishing race as a segment of class with its own hierarchy of class exploitation. Meanwhile, feminist, queer, and intersectional approaches argue that gender and sexual identity can be as important as class and that they are often so intertwined that they cannot be separated (Bell and Valentine 1995; Dill and Zambrana 2009; Geltmaker 1992; Kobayashi and Peake 1994; Knopp 1992, 1998; Lees 1994; Soja 1989; G. Rose 1993). Indeed, in their mutually reinforcing combinations, they can produce forms of alienation beyond those of race, class, or gender per se (Dill and Zambrana 2009).

OPENINGS

A small but growing body of critical literature examines neighborhoods as socially contested arenas to explain the forces acting inside and outside, influencing and at the same time influenced by changes set off by restructuring and neoliberalism. While this literature ties neighborhood dynamics to systemic forces of change, it also shows how internal dynamics of resistance or accommodation can challenge the status quo. A few examples illustrate the great potential of this line of research for reframing how we study neighborhood change. Of particular interest is the inclusion of culture as a way to commodify a neighborhood as well as identify a community within it.

In *Beyond Segregation: Multiracial and Multiethnic Neighborhoods in the United States*, Maly (2005) identifies relatively stable multiracial, multiethnic neighborhoods in Chicago and New York City that he explains by factors such as availability of affordable housing and social services or exceptional qualities such as a lakefront location. He also emphasizes the role of globalization and immigration in producing this diversity, and specifically the institutions promoting and managing it as well as the existence of buffer groups such as Latinos and Asians mitigating the black-white divide.

Barrio Dreams: Puerto Ricans, Latinos and the Neoliberal City (Davila 2004), a study of gentrification in East Harlem, describes the internal and external class and racial/ethnic conflicts coupled with the larger forces of neoliberalism bent on changing the neighborhood. The book shows how promises of upward mobility and empowerment shut out many longtime residents while obfuscating representations that "Latinize" the space. Davila contrasts the roles of culture as identity and commodity to both form and challenge community while offering an innovative look at the marketing of Latino space both to "defend community" and to gentrify it in a context of class, race, and interethnic conflict. A multifaceted view of the place of Latinos in the changing urban landscape, *Barrio Dreams* is a nuanced examination of the complex social and economic forces shaping cities and neighborhoods, and the forces of resistance contesting them from within or from outside.

In *Selling the Lower East Side: Culture, Real Estate and Resistance in New York, 1880–2000*, Christopher Mele (2000) recounts local resistance to gentrification in New York's Lower East Side. The author shows how developers, media executives, and others interested in selling neighborhoods used images of urban grittiness to appeal to a cultural marketplace hungry for new fodder, co-opting negative neighborhood characteristics and turning them into positive symbols of difference. He also illustrates how political and economic forces conflate to transform neighborhoods on the ground and what happens when a neighborhood is being "consumed." The Lower East Side is an example of the forces converging in some low-income ethnic neighborhoods.

In *The New Urban Renewal: The Economic Transformation of Harlem and Bronzeville* (2008), Derek Hyra combines the ecological, political economy, and globalist paradigms to study gentrification. While political decision making is the prime driver of neighborhood change, he claims that it has to be combined with factors of location and the position of cities in the global economy to properly explain gentrification. Although "black-on-black" gentrification brings up a new dimension, the research suggests that in fact class drives the process (Hwang and Sampson 2014). While it may be taking a different form, urban renewal continues to produce the same results: in this case removing low-income blacks with heavy support from national and local governments.

In *Landscapes of Power: From Detroit to Disneyworld*, Sharon Zukin (2009) also adds a new dimension by applying the concept of "creative destruction" to the contemporary service economy to explain the critical role market culture plays in shaping the sense of place. Through case studies, she contends that abstract forces stemming from the market economy detach people from social institutions and overpower their attachment to place. The result is that different place cultures have to conform to private market values rather than to public vernacular dynamics. Architecture takes on a market-oriented franchise look as well. Along the way, places become *nonplaces*, transacted in global markets without concern for the social processes and the livelihoods involved (or destroyed).

These studies show the dramatic revalorization of central cities, especially from the 1990s to the recession, and the transformation of some but not all working-class and often minority neighborhoods into pricey clusters of exclusivity (N. Smith 1996; Atkinson and Bridge 2005), reflecting the new dynamics of flexible accumulation. They expose the tremendous conflicts and speculation involved and the displacement of residents, in short, the transformation of working- and low-class neighborhoods into highly flexible spaces and environments of spectacle, exclusivity, valorization, and privatization. They illustrate how large-scale forces impact individual lives and communities in concrete and intimate ways. They point to the ways in which space is being reconstituted and commercialized to cater to a presumed higher class of people and to the development/production of living environments suitable for them. As such, they are great examples of the shortcomings of mainstream analyses of neighborhood change, of the enormous variations within and across urban space, and of the possibilities associated with careful discussions of the forces converging to produce and reproduce neighborhoods as sites of consumption and accumulation.

The studies cited above introduce a critical dimension of contestation that complicates how we interpret the sources of neighborhood change. These studies also problematize the relationship between different representations of space and power, though they also tend to give residents little power and responsibility in the form of agency, strategies, and paths to praxis. Still, they are far more complex and provide more layers to unveil and explore. These books are also great examples of grounded analyses exposing the dialectics of neighborhood change today and the ways they affect the livelihood of residents and community. Clearly, we must incorporate social constructs such as income, class, race, ethnicity, and gender in order to produce a *historicized* analysis of the different factors that facilitate the production of uneven space and places. The analysis also should be *genealogical* to account for change over time in societal regimes (e.g., from inflexible to flexible spaces of accumulation) as well as to take into consideration particular dimensions specific to the space itself. Finally, a *dialectical* approach is needed to reveal contradictions—assuming they exist—allowing for a richer interpretation of change that occurs over time. We explore next how these approaches can combine to practically examine neighborhood change in the current regime of creative destruction and flexible accumulation.

CHAPTER 2

Understanding Change in Today's Changing Urban Mosaic

We can be sure, at any rate, than an understanding of language
and of verbal and non-verbal systems of signs will be of great
utility in any attempt to understand space. (Lefebvre 1991, 131)

The previous chapter demonstrates how each variation in neighborhood change theories reproduced social norms about what constitutes a neighborhood. Although for different reasons, both mainstream and critical frameworks conflate the relationship between the physical place and the social space that leads to specific expectations for the site and its occupants. Both also homogenize neighborhood space in terms of class and race. As critical theorists argue, we believe these spaces are problematic. But we believe the outcome of change is not fully determined or easily predicted. As we demonstrate in this chapter and the ones that follow, many forces have been at work in city neighborhoods since the 1970s, and not all are moving in the same direction.

Our starting assumption is that the existing theories of neighborhood change, dominated by mainstream assumptions, have generated a particular discursive space in which to interpret urban dynamics, including rules determining what constitutes a legitimate stable or healthy neighborhood. While we disagree with the underlying assumptions of the ecological framework, however, we are not necessarily opposed to the indicators or data used by analysts or even their methods of studying neighborhood change. What we contest is the epistemological assumptions that determine how data is interpreted that subsequently limit our interpretation of urban dynamics.[1]

Our aim in this chapter is to make the discursive space of neighborhood change visible and more political, contingent, and reflexive. The ability to see and analyze discourse in this way—as an object and as a space-producing practice—comes from joining the work of Henri Lefebvre (1991) and Ludwig Wittgenstein (1958), along with the work of other critical theorists including Bourdieu, de Certeau, and Foucault. Instead of viewing theory as a generalizable conceptualization of space, timeless and disconnected from context, we understand it to be a product of researchers and users that generates a certain type of space for investigation. Wittgenstein's (1958) notion of *language games* draws attention to the various ways researchers (including ourselves) speak about space, such as cataloging and categorizing it, and how they measure how it has changed over time. All are "games" that researchers learn how to play through formal training but also through informal means (e.g., watching others).

Wittgenstein concludes that language is "carried on in quite different ways" (Pitkin 1972) depending on the language game being played. He shifts our attention from the object to the way we speak about the object, to see the many ways language creates the "possibility" of phenomena (Wittgenstein 1958). In other words, language is both a tool used to *describe* space and a means to *generate* space. Theory viewed in this way is neither timeless nor disconnected from the context in which it was developed. To illustrate, we review the origin and evolution of the stable homogeneous neighborhood rooted in human ecology theory. We then turn to two examples that utilize data and methods similar to those of the human ecologists but that are deployed under different assumptions about what forces make neighborhoods stable and what makes them change. These examples also demonstrate how we can investigate differently and better understand neighborhoods as sites of consumption and flexible accumulation as well as social reproduction.

Constructing the Homogeneous Neighborhood

In 1931, Professors E. W. Burgess and C. Newcomb from the University of Chicago published the book *Census Data of the City of Chicago, 1930,* which divided Chicago for the first time into seventy-five communities. These "natural areas" were derived by applying the principles of human ecology to the city using existing US Census tract boundaries. Burgess had led the research team that divided the city into community areas based on several criteria: (1) the space had a history as its own community; (2) residents identified with the area (and its name); (3) it had a known trade area; (4) membership was distributed in local businesses and institutions oriented to residents; and (5) it had a defined geography including natural and artificial barriers such as the Chicago River and its branches, railroad lines, local transportation systems, and parks and boulevards. Complying with the Census Bureau's tabulation requirement that whole census tracts be used meant some compromises had to be made.

Until 1970, these seventy-five community areas and their boundaries remained fixed in space. For the 1970 census, O'Hare Airport, which had been annexed in 1956, was added as a new community area, joined to the city by a thin stretch of transit right of way, and the existing community area of Uptown was divided by carving out Edgewater to the north. Both are now part of the seventy-seven communities that make up the city (see Figure 3). The division of Uptown revealed how the community area had changed unevenly since the 1930s. The new community of Edgewater was formed by higher-income residents in the northern portion who sought to separate from the more deteriorated southern section.

Even as the city has changed over time, the so-called community areas have been retained. Many Chicagoans claim them as their home and identify with their names. While the content—people, buildings, infrastructure—has changed over the years, analysts have consistently used the same boundaries drawn by the Chicago School in 1930. The map makes the space of these community areas timeless even when the internal logic changes. For example, Englewood is still considered a single community area even though it was divided down its east side by a highway in the 1960s, separating people who at the time were neighbors but who now, decades later, do not consider themselves to be from the same community. Complicating this further are the ever-shifting ward boundaries, which currently carve up Englewood into six wards with no single ward solely in the community area. In addition, the real estate board has its own map that currently identifies approximately 170 neighborhoods, each with its own name, including several with a Chicago community area name but without the same borders. While of interest to researchers, these neighborhoods do not have the same status in the study of neighborhood change, in part because the boundaries are more fluid. For example, during the housing boom that began in the 1990s and continued to 2006, the real estate board's map was updated two times to add new markets.

The influence of the Chicago School is seen throughout the world in cities that have established geographically bounded units for analysis and comparable sets of indicators to make comparisons and monitor change over time. Of course, the benefit of having stable boundaries is the ability to track changes in population and other characteristics within and across the fixed geographies. For example, the *Chicago Community Fact Book*, which was produced with each

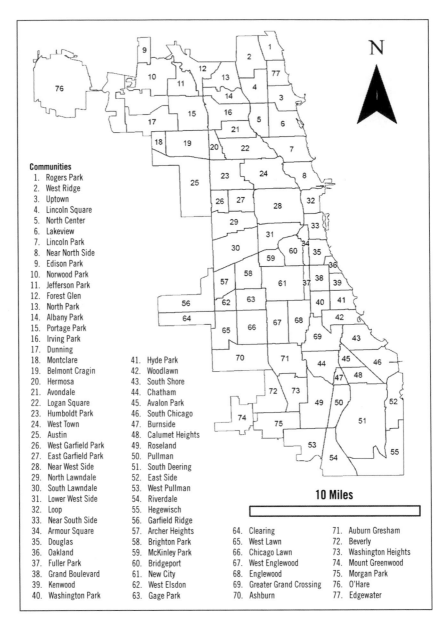

Communities
1. Rogers Park
2. West Ridge
3. Uptown
4. Lincoln Square
5. North Center
6. Lakeview
7. Lincoln Park
8. Near North Side
9. Edison Park
10. Norwood Park
11. Jefferson Park
12. Forest Glen
13. North Park
14. Albany Park
15. Portage Park
16. Irving Park
17. Dunning
18. Montclare
19. Belmont Cragin
20. Hermosa
21. Avondale
22. Logan Square
23. Humboldt Park
24. West Town
25. Austin
26. West Garfield Park
27. East Garfield Park
28. Near West Side
29. North Lawndale
30. South Lawndale
31. Lower West Side
32. Loop
33. Near South Side
34. Armour Square
35. Douglas
36. Oakland
37. Fuller Park
38. Grand Boulevard
39. Kenwood
40. Washington Park

41. Hyde Park
42. Woodlawn
43. South Shore
44. Chatham
45. Avalon Park
46. South Chicago
47. Burnside
48. Calumet Heights
49. Roseland
50. Pullman
51. South Deering
52. East Side
53. West Pullman
54. Riverdale
55. Hegewisch
56. Garfield Ridge
57. Archer Heights
58. Brighton Park
59. McKinley Park
60. Bridgeport
61. New City
62. West Elsdon
63. Gage Park

64. Clearing
65. West Lawn
66. Chicago Lawn
67. West Englewood
68. Englewood
69. Greater Grand Crossing
70. Ashburn

71. Auburn Gresham
72. Beverly
73. Washington Heights
74. Mount Greenwood
75. Morgan Park
76. O'Hare
77. Edgewater

10 Miles

Figure 3. Chicago Community Areas
Source: Scott Pouder, 2015

decennial census between 1930 and 1990, provided longitudinal data for each of the seventy-seven community areas along with a written history of how each had changed over time. These same boundaries are used by philanthropic organizations to assess and map by community area their applicants and distribution of grants, and by the city's Department of Public Health to track changes in patterns of disease and other conditions.

The Chicago School heavily influenced how researchers analyzed the economic arrangement of the city. As already described, human ecologists assumed there was a natural order to the city. From this perspective, they transformed what they observed about the real city of Chicago into a model of "The City" (1925), an urban prototype, spatially preconfigured as a series of concentric zones radiating out from the central business district. They used these principles and classification tools to then classify cities in the United States and throughout the world. From a particular moment in time and space—Chicago in the 1920s—the Chicago School became a guide to all sorts of future urban investigations and interventions, including federal policy, which affected real estate investment and neighborhood planning, and that justified and reified a hierarchical order of homogenous space based on income and race/ethnicity.

RACIAL AND ETHNIC HIERARCHY

While at the University of Chicago, Homer Hoyt (1933) developed a list of racial and national groups in order of their least (1) to most (10) detrimental effect on land use values: (1) English, Germans, Scotch, Irish, and Scandinavians; (2) north Italians, (3) Bohemians and Czechoslovakians; (4) Poles; (5) Lithuanians; (6) Greeks; (7) Russian Jews of the lower class; (8) south Italians; (9) Negroes; and (10) Mexicans. These descriptive findings were later used by Hoyt while he was principal economist at the Federal Housing Administration (FHA) to guide the agency and its employees in allocating mortgage insurance. This research was also adopted by the real estate and insurance industries throughout the United States to classify areas and as a result was often used to determine property values. Covenants, zoning, special districts, and other tools were also widely used to control the makeup of neighborhoods.

Human ecologists in the 1920s did not consider discrimination to be a factor in the production of homogeneous neighborhoods. However, they used homogeneity as the central criteria to identify neighborhoods and began generating "scientific" facts about physical neighborhoods to monitor their health. Without questioning their assumptions, the FHA and the entire real estate industry followed suit. As Hoyt's criteria for investment became the norm and was reproduced by real estate agents and researchers, urban space became racialized and hierarchical. While the Supreme Court made it illegal to enforce covenants in 1948, the FHA continued supporting differential treatment of nonwhite communities by insuring suburban housing for whites, which helped to facilitate the rapid racial transition of neighborhoods in many cities. Before passage of the Fair Housing Act in 1968, practices of redlining, racial steering, and blockbusting were used by banks and the real estate industry to control or manipulate the racial makeup of neighborhoods. Public agencies also used these methods. In Chicago, federal courts found the Chicago Housing Authority (CHA) guilty of discrimination by developing public housing only in black neighborhoods. As a result, Chicago's public housing was nearly all black.[2]

By the 1960s, more black people began moving into white neighborhoods. The practices of researchers once again helped to reaffirm race as a basis for determining neighborhood health and values. Racial tipping was widely accepted in the academy, canonizing the belief that white flight will follow when a threshold of nonwhites is surpassed. In practice, a few pro-integration communities and suburbs used the tipping point to develop strategies to produce stable racially mixed neighborhoods. The Village of Oak Park even established a threshold of no more than 30 percent black on a block in an effort to "maintain" integration and an "equity assurance" program for homebuyers to assuage fears of property value decline in a racially mixed community.[3] Similar logic is found today in the design of mixed-income communities.

INCOME AND CLASS HIERARCHY

Economic segregation was also considered natural by human ecologists, and, like racial segregation, it too was reinforced by government efforts and institutions. While some of these activities aimed to help people living in poor neighborhoods, most were intended to keep them out of middle-class neighborhoods. As Silver (1985) concludes, middle-class reformers and planners have long used their own values and prejudices to develop solutions to the social and physical problems in poor neighborhoods. Some focused on securing space further out for middle-class enclaves. Middle-class neighborhood associations began forming as early as the 1880s "as a counterpart to the settlement house movement" (Silver 1985, 164). In Richmond, Baltimore, Louisville, St. Louis, Chicago, Memphis, and Atlanta, these associations worked to influence local governments to protect their neighborhoods against class and racial change (Rice 1968; Brownwell 1980; Flint 1977; Emmart 1911; Arnold 1979). In Chicago, the Hyde Park and Kenwood communities "formed a property owners association largely to solidify resistance against racial integration," and, following the 1919 Chicago race riot, associations of white neighborhoods supported a plan "to discourage blacks from venturing out of the Black Belt" (Silver 1985, 164).[4]

Echoing similar sentiments, Clarence Perry's neighborhood unit, which promoted a self-contained middle-class development, offered a safeguard for socioeconomic homogeneity. In Silver's words, "Exclusion was a goal, not merely a byproduct, of the neighborhood unit plan" (1985, 166). Perry drew heavily on academic research, especially from the Chicago School. His neighborhood unit plan was endorsed in 1931 by a conference on home building and home ownership organized by the Hoover administration. Around the same time, the National Association of Real Estate Boards sponsored their own version of the neighborhood unit. In 1948, the American Public Health Association (APHA) published the handbook *Planning the Neighborhood*. Adopting the neighborhood unit, the APHA concluded that the safest route was "to adhere to the principle that neighborhood planning should safeguard existing urban relations" (Silver 1985, 170). Despite counternarratives beginning in the 1960s by Jane Jacobs (1961) and others, mainstream thinking and widespread development—primarily suburban—perpetuated the principle of neighborhood economic homogeneity and class separation.

The logic of mainstream theories has long been that neighborhood homogeneity is actively pursued by different groups and that heterogeneous space is suspicious and even actively rejected by most groups, especially the middle and upper classes. From this perspective, any attempt at mixing must limit the proportion of lower-income families since this is a natural threat to neighborhood quality. Meanwhile, critical theories claim that homogeneous neighborhoods are not the result of different groups seeking to keep the natural order; instead they are the result of the circulation of capital carving out submarkets segmented by class that are sustained for differentiated social reproduction and racial seclusion. While offering a different explanation, namely the power relations shaping social space, critical analysts also assume neighborhoods are relatively homogeneous in composition and function.

REINTERPRETING HOMOGENEOUS SPACE

We propose an alternative way to interpret homogeneous neighborhood space, to not only problematize its interpretation as critical approaches do, but also its construction as a site for investigation, policy intervention, and public investment. Shifting attention to the construction of neighborhoods, we believe, draws attention to how the forces of creative destruction and accumulation working across urban space sustain homogeneity. Through this lens we can see how the homogeneous space of neighborhoods—real and conceived—is maintained even when it is not. For example, reading the different volumes of the *Local Community Fact Book of Chicago* reveals tremendous changes in many community areas in the 1950s and 1960s. At those moments, the original homogeneity and natural boundaries of most were true artifacts of the past, as many of the city's census tracts were mixed-race. Rather than adjusting the boundaries, though, the assumptions were adjusted. Racial tipping provided a logical reason for the mix: the community was an interstitial space that would eventually become homogeneous again, and we could predict when by using a measurable threshold at which resegregation would take place. This allowed the homogeneous neighborhood to remain the baseline measure, and for many this provided further evidence that it was natural to segregate.

Today, the seventy-seven community areas continue to organize Chicago and, we are convinced, are used strategically even if not intentionally in the ongoing cycle of creative destruction and accumulation. This includes researchers studying neighborhood change, people searching for properties through Internet-based real estate search engines (e.g., Trulia.com or Zillow.com), and philanthropers trying to determine where to invest in order to promote redevelopment. And while this organization of space is unique to Chicago, the conceptualization and mapping of neighborhoods is not; virtually every city in the United States (at least) has some form of a neighborhood map based in census data collection boundaries that is used for research and for real estate and reinvestment planning.

The static boundaries of Chicago's community areas do not prevent the production of new space within them. In fact, the case studies in this book demonstrate how maintaining a fixed geography is not only convenient to observing change or the lack of it over time by holding the boundaries constant, but it is also part of the process of investment and disinvestment itself because it helps with branding and rebranding these spaces, which we argue is a form of strategic repositioning. Moreover, this static geography also provides a means to link people with a place in which to find real and imagined communities and to further differentiate social reproduction. Furthermore, these fixed geographies provide a means to manage, specifically to use representations of space for purposes of social control, as well as to justify interventions that perpetuate creative destruction and accumulation.

Strategically Reinterpreting Neighborhood Space: Some Considerations

From the paradigmatic perspective of creative destruction and the current regime of accumulation, we conclude that what distinguishes the neighborhood order in postindustrial society from that in industrial society was a mass relocation of people that has generated a geography of reserve and disinvestment.

These are the neighborhoods that house predominantly nonwhite, low-income people for the reproduction and containment of devalorized labor in central cities. At the same time, the suburbs became predominantly white bastions of prosperity, ownership, opportunity, and investment, specifically spaces for the reproduction of dominant social classes. Correspondingly, downtowns, large institutions, strategic locations (e.g., waterfronts), commodified cultural capital, suburban corporate campuses, and large retail concentrations became the dominant organizing practices shaping urban space, rather than public and civil life.

In this current regime, neighborhoods are reinvented selectively, some to facilitate the concentration and lifestyles of higher-income people involved in the command-and-control core functions of our economy, while others are home to a growing number of lower-income workers. This economic sorting has helped produce spaces of reserve, seclusion, and containment in the form of ghettos at one end of the spectrum while concurrently generating spaces of investment, spectacle, and high-level consumption at the other. While there are spaces in between, there is a growing distance between these extremes in the new subdivision of labor and a great potential for a highly polarized and fragmented neighborhood geography, especially when compared to the relative continuum of neighborhoods under the industrial order.[5]

We have witnessed an intensified process of neighborhood commodification pitting exchange value against use value, but also an absolute market versus an infra-economy, the space of basic activities associated with self-sufficiency and the bartering of goods and services (Braudel 1982). As Harvey (1995) did, we find a relationship between today's polarized space produced by overconsumption in affluent neighborhoods and the underconsumption of people living in low-income neighborhoods. Compounding the divide is the formation of intense and technologically advanced neighborhoods where the digital advantage means, among other things, that residents are more likely to be globally connected than people living in low-income neighborhoods. These are highly mobile and footloose environments more or less connected to the core urban economy. The result is an order in space that becomes extremely polarized, with urban geographies concurrently tending toward gentrification and ghettoization.

In Chicago, the spatial polarity line is drawn between the affluent, predominantly white North Side and lower-income, predominantly black South and West Sides. While the North Side is overinvested and highly congested, with few empty lots for development, much of the built environment and population in the South and West Sides has been shrinking. We classify these latter communities as *spaces of reserve* that can be used for future development. The management of these spaces is part and parcel of the management of people. In our current regime, segmentation can best assure a disciplined society in which everybody occupies the place that corresponds to their social condition. As in colonial times, separation was the best form of containment and control because it kept the dominated other (i.e., the colonized) confined but also within view. The spatial division of cities by race—or the spatialization of race—is "biopolitics" in Foucault's (1995) terms. The same can be said for identity by class/income as well as ethnicity and sexual preference.

As we will illustrate, neighborhoods today are *spaces of social control* in which institutions in a particular combination play a supervisory role and everybody inhabiting the space is expected to reproduce specific positions. Using Foucault's framework, these are "micro-practices that divide, isolate and objectivize" (Coleman and Agnew 2007, 321). Within these fixed boundaries, however, are fluid social relations that help us better understand the dialectics of flexible accumulation that includes the biopolitics that produce space and the tensions between the market and the infra-economy. To understand these tensions and processes, we next explore ways to examine neighborhoods as fixed sites of continuously produced space and an interpretation of change that it is more political and reflective.

Reinterpreting Neighborhood Change

Studying any type of change requires something that is held constant over time. In the case of neighborhood change, we see why the Chicago School and others held constant the boundaries of the space (i.e., the neighborhood) to observe the change of social and physical characteristics within. Of course there are dangers and tremendous limitations with any analysis that relies on fixing geography in order to trace changes in variables over time. The first is the potential to *fetishize the geography* as some kind of absolute subject that can be measured and classified based on who comes and goes and who stays. Studying neighborhood change in this way also tends to focus on the "transients," attributing change to the residents entering or leaving rather than to the forces acting to push and pull people around in urban space, which, as we have noted, includes the mechanisms of creative destruction that manipulate spatial factors to produce profit. Another potential limitation of holding constant boundaries is that the trends observed are merely the result of making *time* the variable without accounting for how the production of the space itself has changed. This includes representations of space that rebrand or alter the image of a neighborhood, such as how investors and developers talk up a neighborhood to promote gentrification or city officials classify neighborhoods for purposes of deploying police into areas targeted for gang activities.

Taking these various concerns about boundaries and classification into consideration, we propose an alternative view for interpreting neighborhood change: treat the bounded area identified as a symbolic, socially produced space with contents that are in constant flow and whose circulation produces and extracts value via investment and disinvestment and that clusters populations for different purposes. In Lefebvre's typology of space, symbolic or *representational space* is usually passively experienced; it's a real space but its cultural meaning is derived through the imagination, which transforms symbols and images into a meaningful place. From this point of view, a census tract, which is an arbitrary vessel to contain data, becomes a neighborhood through its repeated use as a *representation of space* to study neighborhood change, something that has been done for a hundred years (J. Smith 2013). The same can be said of Chicago's seventy-seven community areas, which since their origin in 1930 have been fetishized and transformed into real places through repeated use to show change or the lack of it over time. The corresponding representations including maps and classifications not only reinforce them as actual bounded sites, but have become the default ways in which we look at reality and the baseline for our judgment and understanding of it. By holding space constant, such analyses can easily reduce it to a neutral container rather than make explicit the production of neighborhood through forces such as creative destruction, racism, and segregation.

Along these lines, we view census tracts as tools that *produce sites for investigation and manipulation*, not sites of lived experiences. In research, these tools are quite useful if decoupled from the human ecologists' assumptions about naturally homogeneous space and the deterministic assumptions about the outcomes of change. As described above, the data chosen to document the contents of these spaces also represents specific ideas about what makes neighborhoods change. But if we look at these data as evidence of change, as descriptive of conditions at different points in time, and not as causal variables that explain why change happens, then we are at least outside the human ecologists' framework when interpreting these data. We need to go further, however, and pay attention to the factors and forces contributing to change or the lack of it in relation to creative destruction and accumulation including the actual processes involved. In this current regime, this includes the combined forces shifting us from a Fordist to a post-Fordist economy, resulting in specific investment and disinvestment strategies, factors that racialize space and conflate it with class, and also changing the dynamics of social reproduction and control. Countering these forces and factors is individual and social resistance to change, adaptations, coping, and appropriations (de Certeau 1988) as well as the search for stability. All are what Lefevbre would call *spatial practices*. Figure 4 below illustrates how these three modes of production work together to produce the discursive space of neighborhood change. It also provides an analytical framework for investigating neighborhood change in relation to a particular context, which can produce symptoms of something that needs to be explained.

Following Lefebvre's trilogy, we consider all neighborhood classifications to be representations of space. Classification schemes can be powerful. By definition, a classification system fixes particular characteristics to what is being classified so it then can be sorted and comparisons can be made across classes. These classifications often reduce complex information such as racial identity, educational attainment, or income to a simple data point or scaled distribution, which then can be used to map trends and compare geographies. In this way, neighborhoods have been simplified, becoming a "central tendency" measure such as median income or a single composite score based on a set of

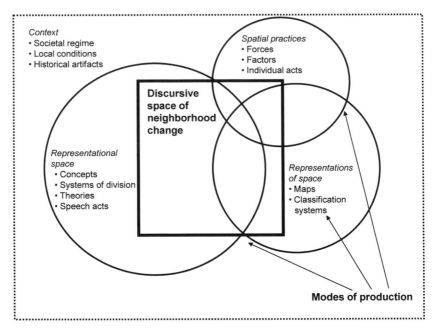

Figure 4. Producing the Discursive Space of Neighborhood Change
Source: Janet Smith 2015

characteristics. While such rankings and comparisons can be useful, they also reinforce and essentialize the significance of what they measure.[6] For example, some researchers have classified neighborhoods with more than 40 percent of the people below the poverty level as "high poverty" (Jargowsky 1997). While this means that as much as 60 percent of the people are not poor, the label "high poverty" can brand every individual living there. Such measures also can lead some to generate ecological fallacies (i.e., using a statistic about a group of people to describe individuals in that space). All these data shortcuts can homogenize neighborhoods in ways that can and do shape public perceptions, especially as they are sustained through repetition in research and in public discourse, which is often the case with crime statistics; even if the statistics change, the community identity is likely to remain intact or it may even become a self-fulfilling prophecy.

Aware of the effects such data shortcuts have, we believe that classification systems still can be used to find out what different spaces have in common, and then we can consider what forces and spatial practices are producing these commonalities in and across space. Two exercises of neighborhood classification help to illustrate this approach.[7] The first is a typology of rental housing communities in Chicago developed to examine where rental housing was being lost and gained and potential challenges and opportunities for affordable housing advocates. The second is a gentrification index derived from the theories reviewed in the previous chapter to assess where investment and disinvestment was occurring in Chicago. Both are composite measures constructed with US Census data commonly used in the study of neighborhood change, and both examples demonstrate how these quantitative data can be used to find evidence of the commodification of space through bounded processes of creative destruction and accumulation. Composite measures also help us capture some of the complexity in the production of space by offering different angles simultaneously, which may either complement or contradict interpretations of conditions.

Both measures were developed in response to changes being observed by community-based organizations in Chicago and are intended to help mobilize people and to strategize. We acknowledge that this is clearly a biased starting point, but so are mainstream and critical frameworks. Where we think we differ is our starting assumptions. We assume any type of space observed in these classification schemes is the result of both *exogenous* factors and forces limiting access to parts of the city for some while opening up access for others, and *indigenous* drivers of capital including institutional and personal action. We also consider different spatial practices including biopolitics and the infra-economy.

As a result, any changes observed are neither fully determined nor completely explained solely by value-seeking behavior or by prejudice.

RENTAL HOUSING COMMUNITIES

Between 1990 and 2000, Chicago lost an estimated sixty thousand rental units. Advocates concerned about the loss of affordable apartments and the out-of-reach for-sale market in the late 1990s, as well as shifts in where lower-income populations were living in Chicago, wanted to document how conditions had changed by community area. Using data from the 1990 and 2000 censuses, the seventy-seven communities of Chicago were classified based on their dominant tenure (for sale or rental), and rental communities were then further sorted by change (increase or decrease) in vacancy rates, the overall number of rental units, overcrowding, and new construction. Seven distinct types were identified: homeowning, thinning, tightening, converting, filling, booming, and bursting areas (see Figure 5). The study concluded that "though each neighborhood is unique, cluster communities are linked by similar housing market characteristics. When viewed in the map showing cluster groupings, one can see how Chicago's communities face common challenges and policy solutions that require us to work across geography, political and cultural boundaries" (Chicago Rehab Network 2003, 1).

The classifications produced were not assumed to be a collection of naturally occurring geographies—as in the zones for different classes found by the Chicago School—but rather the result of capital shaping development patterns in the city in individual areas and in groups of community areas. While demographic homogeneity was identified in some community areas, the study by design focused on the evidence of common market features and/or processes at work across the city, highlighting trends in public and private investment and disinvestment that was homogenized by factors such as race and income.[8] Using much of the same data that human ecologists use, the researchers found that the common features across community areas suggested that investment had turned parts of the city around in a short span of time while disinvestment drained wealth and capital from other parts.

Unlike mainstream investigations of neighborhood change, which privilege owning over renting on the assumption that renting leads to an unstable community, the research assumed that the loss of rental housing between 1990 and 2000 was a negative outcome and was more importantly the result of specific public policy decisions intended to induce ownership and destabilize renters. This included public housing demolition, which helped to *tighten* and *fill* some community areas as families moved with vouchers to other parts of the city to rent

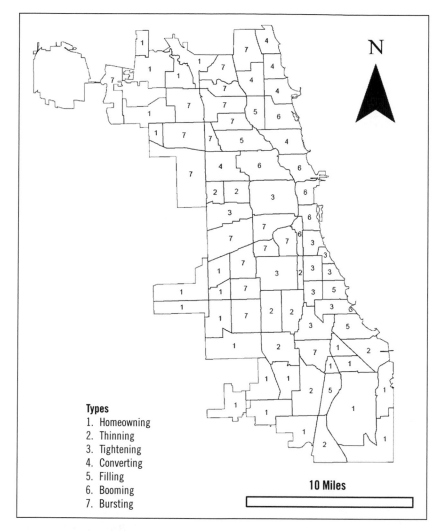

Figure 5. Rental Community Typology, 2003
Source: Redrawn from "Rental Community Typology, 2003," Nathalie P. Voorhees Center and Chicago Rehab Network, 2003.

in the private sector. These community areas also saw a change in their demographics as new higher-end housing began filling up the now available space that had been public housing. The most dramatic case was that of Bronzeville, a neighborhood south of downtown that had several thousand public housing units demolished. In ten years, the community went from being extremely low-income (using HUD's definition) to showing some signs of improvement and even gentrification in parts based on rising housing prices and income levels. As discussed in chapter 3, however, this was not a natural outcome but the result of intentional interventions on the part of the city of Chicago.

In contrast, *converting* communities along the lakefront north of downtown included neighborhoods that most would agree had been gentrifying since the 1970s. Converting meant that the percentage of rental property had declined but also that home ownership rates had increased significantly, accompanied by the steepest decreases in vacancies, in poverty rates, and in the numbers of publicly subsidized rental units. Communities in this category were also the second most overcrowded, most likely as a means for families to afford rising rents. Often nearby were the *booming* community areas, which were in advanced stages of gentrification based on continued decreases in poverty and rental vacancies and increasing home ownership rates and values, rapidly rising rents, and a lot of construction of high-end condominiums.

The *bursting* communities pointed to another force changing Chicago: immigration and migration. This included many traditional second-settlement white communities to the northwest and southwest that were rapidly changing to majority Latino. Rather than interpret this change as invasion-succession, however, the analysis focused on how suburbanization opened up these communities to new immigrants as whites moved out, and the analysis raised questions about why they quickly became the most overcrowded in the city and why population increases did not trigger new construction. Along similar lines, *thinning* community areas that were overwhelmingly low-income and majority black— often close to 100 percent—also were tied to whites leaving the city beginning in the 1960s. While many of these community areas had changed quickly from white to black, over time they had lost a significant number of families. Data on demolition, the lack of private investment by the banks, and later subprime and predatory lending suggested that public investment strategies such as urban renewal and community revitalization strategies had contributed to the continuous loss in home ownership and abandonment of nearly 20 percent of the housing stock.

The *homeowning* category, which had a majority owner-occupied housing units (60 percent or more, which was above the city's average of 45 percent), included several community areas on the edges of the city, many in the zone human ecologists identified in the 1920s as where middle-class families lived in single-family homes and bungalows. In 2000, these communities were far from homogeneous, with both young families with children and older adults without kids, each with distinct needs. And while the label recognized the tenure of the majority, the analysis included renters and differentiated their needs from owners. What united both from a housing advocate's perspective was that many more renters and owners were burdened by excessive housing costs than had been in the previous decade, suggesting that many families were struggling to keep their homes.

The evidence from this analysis suggests that in this current regime we have entered a period of more erratic, fast, and extreme forms of investment and disinvestment. While strikingly different depending on the rental housing community type, the change observed across the city makes sense in a regime based in capital accumulation and an ever-growing need for new space and ways to generate value. As the cases discussed in the following chapters will illustrate, there are highly speculative and larger development schemes producing gentrification in some neighborhoods while simultaneously generating a growing reserve of abandoned homes and vacant land in many others. These new subregional trends, however, are also not necessarily orderly or following a natural progression that mainstream descriptions would predict, especially when looking at where some of the community areas are located in space, but also relative to other factors established through specific on-the-ground analyses. In comparison, the patterns found when looking for evidence of gentrification suggested a long arc of disinvestment in large parts of the city even as intensive investment took place in relatively few community areas.

GENTRIFICATION AND DECLINE

As with the study of rental housing communities, the development of a gentrification index evolved from a request by a community-based affordable housing developer challenged by changes in the neighborhoods it served.[9] Rapidly rising land values and what were labeled as "gentrification pressures" from upscaling neighborhoods next door was making it hard to buy land (Voorhees Center 2003). The research aimed to help the organization better anticipate what was likely to happen in the near future should trends continue and to identify opportunities to intervene in order to stave off the loss of its primarily Latino population base due to a shrinking supply of private rental housing and rising home prices. Building on that project, the research was expanded to include the whole city, and researchers expected to find evidence of wide-scale gentrification given the rising housing values everywhere and the tight rental market evidenced by a low vacancy rate. Instead, the study concluded that "the vast majority of Chicago's neighborhoods have not experienced gentrification or massive new development at any time during the past 30 years" (Hudspeth 2003, 1). Furthermore, the majority of community areas had declined between

1970 and 2000 based on an assessment of variables typically associated with gentrification that were used to score each area relative to the city and to construct a neighborhood typology (see Table 3 and Figure 6).[10]

Dividing Chicago's seventy-seven community areas first into *stable* and *changing* revealed that thirty-seven of them had not really changed much since 1970. The *stable* category included four types of communities that had been consistently either below or above the city's average between 1970 and 2000:

- *Stable Upper* (Type 1) included nine community areas located on the far northwest and southwest edges of the city, six of which have been consistently 80 percent or more non-Latino white and three of which had recently become more evenly Latino and white mixed. These areas have remained near the top with respect to income, and as real estate markets these areas have retained high property values even as some transitioned to be more Latino.
- *Stable Middle* (Type 2) included thirteen community areas, most with homeownership rates of 70 to 80 percent, and while most were majority "white ethnic" in 1970, several were between 40 and 60 percent Latino in 2000. As with Type 1 community areas, racial and ethnic change was not accompanied by economic decline as middle-class Latino and African American homeowners replaced middle-class white homeowners.

Table 3. Gentrification Index Variables and Association Score (Voorhees Center 2003, 2014)

Variables	Type of Association
% White (Non-Hispanic)	Above City Average, Positive (+1)
% Black	Above City Average, Negative (−1)
% Latino	Above City Average, Negative (−1)
% Elderly (Age 65+)	Above City Average, Negative (−1)
% Children (Age 5–19)	Above City Average, Negative (−1)
% College Education (Bachelor's degree or higher)	Above City Average, Positive (+1)
Median Family Income (Adjusted for inflation)	Above City Average, Positive (+1)
% Owner Occupied	Above City Average, Positive (+1)
Median House Value (Adjusted for inflation)	Above City Average, Positive (+1)
% Families Below Poverty	Above City Average, Negative (−1)
% Manager Occupations	Above City Average, Positive (+1)
% Female Households with Children	Above City Average, Negative (−1)
% Private School Attendance (Pre-K through 12)	Above City Average, Positive (+1)

- *Stable Low-Income* (Type 3) included *Poverty* (Type 3A), and *Extreme Poverty* (Type 3B). Several of these community areas, located on the West and South Sides, had concentrated public housing projects. All but one of the Extreme Poverty areas (West Englewood) had been 95 percent or more African American since 1970 and all were near that in 2000. Some of them had recently lost population when large public housing projects such as

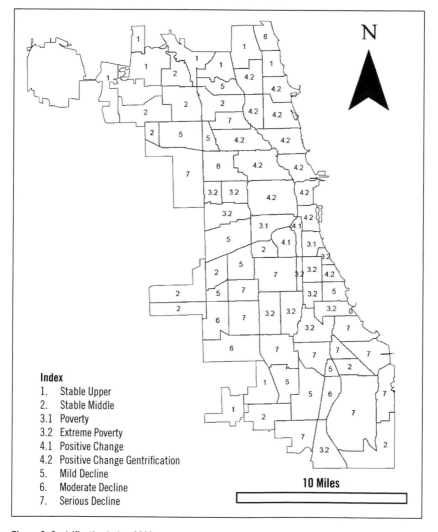

Index
1. Stable Upper
2. Stable Middle
3.1 Poverty
3.2 Extreme Poverty
4.1 Positive Change
4.2 Positive Change Gentrification
5. Mild Decline
6. Moderate Decline
7. Serious Decline

Figure 6. Gentrification Index, 2003
Source: Redrawn from "Gentrification Index, 2003," Nathalie P. Voorhees Center, 2003.

Robert Taylor Homes and Stateway Gardens had been demolished, while others had been steadily losing population over the decades.

Changing communities were divided into gentrification and no gentrification/decline (referring to the change in score value, not the condition of the community).

- *Gentrification* (Type 4): Twelve communities with significant changes driven by gentrification were identified, including the Loop and surrounding community areas, as well as communities on the North Side along the lakefront and northwest of the Loop and two on the south lakefront. Many of these scored high on the gentrification index, exhibiting housing values well above average, declining rates of older adults and children, and rising home ownership.
- *Mild Decline* (Type 5), *Moderate Decline* (Type 6), and *Serious Decline* (Type 7) included twenty-eight communities, with thirteen in serious decline. All experienced an overall decline in their score regardless of their starting condition. Most of the decline occurred between 1990 and 2000 in areas that prior to 1990 would have been considered Type 1 or Type 2 stable upper or middle areas.

We include this index to illustrate how these data and measures can be combined to identify change that is both independent of but also in relation to factors of class, race, or some combination of both.[11] Still, using traditional ecological indicators to identify change as either positive or negative can raise a red flag for some, as does the use of central tendencies. In this case, positive and negative are simple directions away from an average city value at a point in time, measured to track change over time. Similarly, "stable" means unchanging, while "decline" describes change based on data that is trending below the city average. Still, we use this measure with caution. As we emphasized with the rental housing community study, this investigation of gentrification illustrates how we can use these variables to identify trends without attributing change to the indicators themselves. So the claim here is not that whites cause gentrification or that blacks cause decline, only that there is a spatial association between race and gentrification. From our critical perspective, we instead investigate in the following chapters how racism and racist systems facilitate the uneven and racially correlated accumulation of wealth and real estate.

The data describes an intensified process at work to extract surplus value and ghettoize space, a process that is likely tied to race/ethnicity, though not exclusively. Where race did matter was in communities classified as either gentrified or stable low-income. The index design assumes that white in-movers signal gentrification, and there was clear evidence of this in gentrifying communities. The opposite was found in stable low-income communities (i.e., little change since 1970), which were predominantly African American and Latino. To better understand why these correlations exist in the first place and for so long, we turn to the forces acting on these spaces.

While these data cannot confirm displacement of lower-income nonwhites from gentrifying areas since the 1970s, they do show a pattern that suggests certain factors and forces are likely to be shaping where, depending on their race, people can and cannot live in the city. One thing that is striking about the gentrified community areas is that the increase in higher-income whites also occurs with a decrease in families with children and older adults. In contrast, higher and increasing rates of children and seniors are found in communities with consistently above average rates of poverty that are also majority nonwhite. The concurrent existence of these two types of communities—high-poverty with families and an aging population, and younger, high-income households with few children—especially when compared over time, reveals a city that is becoming more polarized, diverging further into gentrified and ghettoized neighborhoods with few places in between. We believe there is a relationship between the intensification and geographical spread of poverty and the gentrification of the center and North Side. While there are some spaces in between, the data suggest that these community areas, including those that are "stable" upper- and middle-income, will be pushed toward one end of the spectrum or the other over time if trends, as determined by the forces that produce residential space, continue.[12]

The two studies reveal a highly differentiated geography resembling more a changing mosaic than a permanently defined and stable set of natural areas and groupings. Families and older adults and people of color are moving out of gentrifying neighborhoods, or at least not moving in at the same rates as in the past. We assume it is not necessarily by choice to relocate to and live in, generally speaking, worse neighborhoods. While there still is a correspondence between race and position in the urban spatial hierarchy, the geography has changed even in these aspects. Rather than finding self-contained homogeneous areas, we find tremendous fluidness, instability, and diversity and we find evidence of the interaction of forces from outside and from within that warrant investigation.

Looking Ahead

Neighborhood classification schemes such as those presented in this chapter have their utility in making macro-level comparisons and rankings as long as they are used with care (i.e., they must be qualified and their limitations acknowledged). But the extent to which we can classify, represent, and interpret segmented urban space in any form really depends on how capable such measures are at clueing us in to the processes that produce differentiated space in the first place. While this may sound like simply a specification problem, it is really more a matter of getting the starting assumptions right. In the current regime of accumulation, we believe and therefore assume that market formations change continuously, with the strategies of real estate actors concurrently producing investment and disinvestment. The value of real estate or rent rates charged, however, can only partially capture what is happening on the ground and cannot determine the outcomes of struggles for power, space, or control.

We think classification systems such as the gentrification index, when used as a tool to open up a site for further investigation, can help in understanding better what is happening across time and space. The knowledge such measures produce is only a snapshot of an ever-changing process, which then requires us as researchers to adjust and reposition ourselves in space so we can assemble many images from different angles and perspectives. The resulting composite snapshot should be more complex and at the same time still open to interpretation and interrogation.

Keeping all this in mind, the following chapters examine how a selection of different Chicago community areas (neighborhoods) have changed over time through processes tied to accumulation and creative destruction. We begin by comparing and contrasting the presumed gentrification of two neighborhoods, Pilsen and Bronzeville, followed by a historical account of how Englewood became a ghetto. These cases were chosen because they are good examples of how representations of space, spatial practices, and representational space weave together to produce neighborhoods as sites of flexible accumulation and consumption as well as spaces to be consumed through different forms of creative destruction. They also provide the basis for our argument that in this current regime neighborhood space is becoming increasingly polarized, which raises questions about the future of communities at both ends of the spectrum. We also include two cases, "Boystown" in Lakeview and "Paseo Boricua," which includes large sections of West Town and Humboldt Park, to illustrate how cities and capital appropriate particular ethnicities or lifestyles, but also how communities of identity appropriate space to ground themselves. The challenge in both neighborhoods is the threat this commodification poses for some residents who face potential displacement, particularly if they are lower-income and/or renters. We then look at how the transformation of public housing changes neighborhoods, focusing on Cabrini Green on the Near North Side and Lakefront Properties in Bronzeville. These sites demonstrate how representations of homogeneous space are used to justify policies that sort the poor into deserving and undeserving and use public funds to advance gentrification.

These cases were selected because each presented interesting changes taking place, all in the public eye and presented through a narrative of change we suspected was much more complex and nuanced than was being captured in the media and research. For example, Bronzeville and Pilsen have been framed as neighborhoods that contain a community of a specific homogeneous ethnic identity that has then been used to personify and pursue a gentrification project. As we spoke with people and dug deeper into the narrative, however, we found contradictions. Gentrification was far more advanced conceptually than in reality, and the cultural identity in each community was much more complex and contested. In all cases, to understand the complex and compound nature of the neighborhood, we consulted secondary resources including published and unpublished reports, scholarly research, newspapers, blogs, and websites, and we then conducted dozens of interviews as well as spent time in each community observing the conditions over several years.[13] As we recommended in the previous chapter, we aimed to make the analysis historical, genealogical, and dialectical.

CHAPTER 3

Recasting Race/Ethnicity

The Gentrification of Bronzeville and Pilsen

> We are under the sway of a surgical compulsion that seeks
> to excise negative characteristics and remodel things
> synthetically into ideal forms. (Baudrillard 1993, 44)

A *New York Times* travel article in 2008 referred to Pilsen as Chicago's Latino Quarter.[1] Speaking to potential tourists, the article noted how the area drew in people from the suburbs and other parts of the city every second Friday of the month for an art walk, but "like much of Chicago these days, the affair draws its real energy from the city's surging Latino population" (Baily 2008). This image of a vibrant Pilsen (Lower West Side) does not reveal that most of Pilsen is populated by working-class immigrant families. At the same time, Bronzeville, an African American concentration located further southeast, close to Lake Michigan, has been portrayed as the future black Mecca of Chicago.[2] The *Chicago Tribune* stated, "Today, amid the renovated graystones and brownstones, Bronzeville is witnessing revitalization efforts. . . . [H]eritage is a living thing, says Harold Lucas, president of the Black Metropolis Convention and Tourism Council. It's the story of a city within a city—that still exists today" (Williams-Harris 2008).

Despite this hoopla, Bronzeville and Pilsen are still quite poor. Bronzeville has many vacant lots and boarded-up buildings as well as large, vacant strips of land along its eastern edge where a decade ago several thousand public housing units stood. The snapshots above are not inaccurate; they are just incomplete and misleading. Neither story reveals what has triggered these changes and neither talks about the many lower-income families that have felt the pressures of gentrification, of having to choose between moving away or enduring huge rent increases, while others have lost their homes to the demolition of public housing. In both neighborhoods, change has been the result of intensive efforts by real estate agents and public officials as well as other institutions, including community-based organizations (CBOs) that work with lower-income families and individuals and advocate for affordable housing preservation and development. With a few strokes of a pen, the above representations reduce and simplify a contested reality but also tell us a lot about *neighborhoods for sale*.

Representations of space indeed are techniques of power. They operate in such a way that the representation often does not reveal a trace of the powers that produced and reproduced them. Recall the famous concentric zone diagram created by Park and Burgess in *The City* (see chapter 1). This simple image shows an abstracted set of spatial relationships arranged in a particular way and centered on the business district. The pattern was assumed to be found in most cities, and through selective empirical evidence was found to be present in many. While the diagram embodied the power relations that produced those specific patterns, including the rules and behaviors that sustained racial segregation, there was no direct evidence of those power relations, which allowed this diagram to become widely accepted as an objective characterization of modern cities in the United States.

As Foucault states, "The exercise of power generates objects of knowledge, makes them emerge, accumulates information, utilizes them. . . . The exercise of power perpetually produces knowledge and inversely knowledge produces effects of power" (1992, 99). Or, as Flyvbjerg adds, "Power determines what counts as knowledge, what kind of interpretation attains authority as the dominant interpretation. Power procures the knowledge which supports its purposes while it ignores or suppresses that knowledge which does not serve it" (1998, 226). In other words, knowledge and power are closely interwoven, both with each other and with the interests and desires each stands for. A key to this argument is the relationship between the dominant and the dominated. The dominant, while in a seemingly superior position, is not in total control, and neither controls the relations of power in "a simple, absolute way" (Foucault quoted by Flyvbjerg 1998, 121). Instead, control is produced through the actions of those in the power relationship, both the dominated and the dominant. The results are neither linear nor completely predictable, which is why we must focus on the struggle itself if we are to understand how knowledge works to shape neighborhood change and the perceptions of it.

Representations are not just explicitly fabricated by individuals or forces seeking to dominate, deceive, or defend (as in a conspiracy). Rather they emerge in the practices and relations of those individuals and forces.[3] In the cases examined here, mainstream theories characterize racial and class struggles as natural (ecological) marketplace processes. As a result a lower-income nonwhite family being replaced by a higher-income white one is not problematic, because those involved—the families moving in and the families moving out—have been cast respectively as deserving and undeserving. It is confusing, however, when change results in a noticeable number of new and higher-income households of the same race/ethnicity moving into the neighborhood. The tension appears to arise, we think, because the higher-income households tend to identify by class rather than race or ethnicity, while the lower-income households do the opposite.

In this chapter, we argue that both reactions to neighborhood change are opposite sides of the same coin and intricately linked to the widespread acceptance of higher-income, usually white people displacing lower-income, usually nonwhite people. Each trajectory provides evidence of the power relations shaping neighborhoods and specifically how race and ethnicity get attached to neighborhood change, which is further complicated by creative for-profit destruction. Representations such as market opportunity and revitalization justify or entice deal making while ascribing value to disinvested real estate in areas like Pilsen and Bronzeville. Unlike traditional versions where the gentrifiers moving in are of a different race, these cases illustrate how members of the "minority middle class" function as middlemen that help to facilitate the penetration of their neighborhoods by buying into representations of progress that actually profit from racism.

Producing Ghettos and Barrios: The Cases of Bronzeville and Pilsen

Bronzeville and Pilsen illustrate the dialectics of race and class in the commodification of space. Initially, Bronzeville housed white middle- to upper-class as well as working-class German Jews, Irish, and Italians.[4] Starting with the relocation of wealthy elites from south of downtown to the Near North Side Gold Coast and the suburbs at the turn of the nineteenth century, the area underwent disinvestment along a north–south corridor around State Street.[5] Coming en masse from the South during the Great Migration (1910–1930), blacks were segregated in this corridor that widened progressively to cover the area bounded north–south by Twenty-Sixth and Sixty-Third Streets (except Greater Hyde Park to the east) and west–east by what is now the Dan Ryan Expressway and Cottage Grove Street. Named Bronzeville by residents to counter the white-coined Black Belt

(Drake and Cayton 1993), the area also has been known as the Black Metropolis. In this overcrowded neighborhood, black families were at the mercy of mostly white property owners who engaged in blatant forms of discrimination such as high rents, illegal subdivisions, and code violations. These continued into the 1950s and 1960s, when the second wave of black immigrants moved in.

The Black Metropolis prospered during the so-called Golden Age (1920–1960) as blacks of all classes were packed into one community, forming a space that many described as "a city within a city, . . . [with] its own commercial center . . . churches, social clubs, illegal gambling . . . beauty salons, nightclubs and theaters . . . even its own taxi firm called Your Cab Co." (Reardon 2000, 3–4). Indeed, Bronzeville competed with Harlem for the title of major northern center of black commerce and culture. *Time* magazine (1938) reported that total sales of commercial goods in Bronzeville were $4,826,897 in 1938 compared to Harlem's $3,322,274. After the Supreme Court struck down restrictive covenants in 1948,[6] racial tension reached a boiling point as whites resisted black expansion, provoking riots, burning buildings, and blocking the entry of black students to their schools. The real estate industry exploited the situation to generate the largest and most profitable (racial) turnover in the city's history, gaining from both black expansion and white flight. Blacks also started leaving as the class compact dispersed.[7]

The city played a leading role in this process by displacing thousands of households to build the Dan Ryan Expressway and to accommodate a three-mile-long development of public housing. The State Street corridor was transformed and the Black Belt became the country's largest concentration of poverty. Only a few middle-class pockets remained, and most businesses closed or left as local demand for their services and products dwindled. Bronzeville then declined precipitously as property owners cashed in their real estate.[8] While many churches, tenants, parents, youth, and community-based organizations joined hands to address the challenges of poverty and disinvestment, the eventual result was a ghetto, with many abandoned, delinquent, burned-out, overcrowded, and devalued properties along with tear-downs and empty lots. Around 1990, however, Bronzeville became a major target for redevelopment.

In contrast, Pilsen always had been a low-income working-class port of entry. At its peak in 1920, there were eighty-five thousand inhabitants, declining to around thirty-five thousand by 2010. Starting with German and Irish immigrants, it was home next to Poles and Czechoslovakians, followed by Italians, Lithuanians, and Yugoslavians. In the 1960s, with white flight and Latino displacement from nearby urban renewal and expressway construction, coupled with a wave of new Latino migration to the city (from 1942 on) and the 1966

Family Reunification Act, Pilsen became the first Latino (primarily Mexican) majority neighborhood in the city. Trained previously in the struggle against urban renewal and inspired by the Chicano movement, many Latino leaders engaged immediately in community building and taking over local institutions that were still in the hands of previous immigrants (e.g., churches) and leading a community-based movement grounded in civil rights. Pilsen quickly became one of the most distinct and organized community areas in Chicago and a home for many Latino struggles in the city and beyond. Culture was a centerpiece of resistance and identity in Pilsen, as reflected in murals on viaducts and buildings depicting scenes from the Mexican revolution, in the "Mexicanization" of churches, in the organization of festivals such as Fiesta del Sol, which is the largest neighborhood-based ethnic festival in the city today, and in the establishment of Latino businesses catering to residents. Classified as an ethnic neighborhood, Pilsen and its residents joined the ranks of stigmatized and neglected low-income minority neighborhoods. Deindustrialization abruptly curtailed mobility and their ability to pursue their American Dream.

Pilsen did not have the historic theater and music venues, businesses, or architectural jewels associated with the higher-income households in Bronzeville, nor did it experience the massive urban renewal, public housing development, and subsequent destructive disinvestment. Arson, public neglect, and disinvestment, however, did follow Latino settlement. As with Bronzeville, pent-up demand made rental housing an extremely profitable business for absentee slumlords. Pilsen became one of the most overcrowded areas in the city as landlords carried out illegal subdivisions, while Latino families doubled up or sublet rooms in their already small apartments. New Mexican-centered retail filled many of the vacancies that white ethnic retailers left behind. Most, however, rented rather than owned the real estate, which meant they had little control over the permanence of their businesses. Meanwhile, development pressure from the north brought gentrification pressure to the east side of Pilsen starting in the late 1980s and accelerating in the 1990s, when a seemingly citywide wave of gentrification hit.

Although different, these two areas have much in common. First, they were the initial sites of consolidation and struggle of two large "minority" groups in the city: Mexicans in Pilsen and African Americans in Bronzeville. Second, both have experienced the convulsions of racism, disinvestment, and gentrification. Together they epitomize the apparently perpetual state of neighborhood transition of capitalist cities (Lefebvre 1996), while mediating spatial racism resulted in increasing hardship for racial minorities, who often had to move where the dance of investment and disinvestment took them. Finally, as more people believed gentrification was inevitable, their rich cultures were appropriated by gentrifying forces to rebrand them for gentrification.

The Production of Racialized Spaces of Accumulation

Pilsen and Bronzeville are symbols of Latino and African American struggles, pride, territorialization, culture, identity, and memory in Chicago. They speak to segregation, displacement, racial manipulation by the real estate industry, and the construction and destruction of neighborhood-based ethnic/racial movements. Their trajectory brings out pasts that are real and imagined, oppressive and liberating, inspirational and frustrating, united and fragmented. As *blighted* neighborhoods, these sites have provided homes for people even after they had been discarded by white ethnics. But when the marketplace came back to reclaim these neighborhoods, resistance within transformed them into spaces of struggle against displacement and the right to stay put. In the process, their very cultures were appropriated and then used to displace them.

As noted in chapter 1, similar processes have been documented for New York City's Lower East Side (Mele 2000) and East Harlem (Davila 2004). Similarly, but at a more specific level, Zukin (2010) offers a compelling study of authenticity and gentrification. Building on such works, we present a reflexive story of the mutually supporting dynamics of representation and actually existing gentrification as mediated by race. Representations that branded each in terms of heritage and racial/ethnic pride had two primary power effects: the gentrification of prices that resulted in a housing boom and a generalized but overwhelming sense that each neighborhood had already gentrified even when it was still majority low-income. Furthermore, the term gentrification operates as an overlaid rebranding of these communities, making the outcome appear as a fait accompli. In reality, the process has been episodic, erratic, and definitely overrated. This suggests that there is a new form of fragmented or episodic gentrification that we need to better understand, what we are calling *gentrification before gentrification*.

A precondition for gentrification is managing the perceptions of a space, usually represented in the public realm as slum and blight, in order to entice investors and dispel the fears among gentrifiers. Racial (or racist) perceptions of a neighborhood are also a major obstacle to gentrification, requiring strategies that can erase fears of outsiders but also avoid stirring up opposition from within the neighborhood. In Bronzeville, a sanitized version of black cultural heritage helped temper white fears but more precisely was used to attract higher-income blacks. In Pilsen, representations of Mexican culture were transformed to appeal to outsiders but also to existing residents. While subtle, such representations sought to appropriate the current identity of residents and colonize their space by attracting minority middle-class families. Such representations and the forces behind them actually had a fragmenting effect on residents and community leaders.

BRONZEVILLE

Bronzeville is perhaps the best case of publicly produced disinvestment and investment mediated by racism in Chicago beginning with urban renewal in the late 1950s. After property values in the neighborhood hit bottom and citywide restructuring was in full swing, Mayor Richard M. Daley (1989–2011) became involved and was unconditionally supported by three institutions—Illinois Institute of Technology (IIT), Michael Reese Hospital, and the University of Chicago—ready to transform what was then called the Mid-South. Joining the effort were local aldermen, black business owners, and middle-class investors. The rationale and specifics of this transformation are spelled out in documents such as the *Mid-South Strategic Development Plan: Restoring Bronzeville* (Mid-South Planning Group 1993), *Bronzeville Redevelopment Plan and Project* (1999); *47th Street and King Drive Redevelopment Plan and Project*, the Chicago Housing Authority's (CHA) *Plan for Transformation* (2000), and various pronouncements and city ordinances (e.g., TIF districts).

Leading the charge was the South Side Partnership (SP), which had been established in 1989 and included major institutions (University of Chicago, IIT, Michael Reese Hospital, Mercy Health Systems of Chicago, Provident Hospital, Bank One, the MacArthur Foundation, the Chicago Urban League, and Bethel New Life) and local nonprofits (Center for New Horizons, Ahkenaton Community Development Corp., Elliott Donnelley Youth Center, Grand Boulevard Federation, STRIVE / Partners in Community Development, Gap Community Organization, and Lugenia Burns Hope Center). The SP presided over the production of *Restoring Bronzeville* (RB) and spawned the Mid-South Planning and Development Commission to oversee implementation. RB was a land-use plan preaching development without displacement around heritage tourism and historic preservation that envisioned a "vibrant, mixed-income African American community with plentiful jobs, affordable housing, top quality schools, accessible health and human services, well-maintained parks and public spaces, and safe streets. Economic development and public welfare and housing policies are combining forces to produce rapid changes in Bronzeville" (South Side Partnership 1999).

Using this plan and the commission as an entry point, the mayor appointed his own people to a blue-ribbon commission in 1997 to drive the process, snatching it from the Mid-South Commission and its black promoters. The mayor mandated his commission to work on a development strategy that would link the area to conventions and tourism. At the time, the city's convention center, on the northern edge of Bronzeville, had just been expanded. Unlike Mid-South's vision of a mixed-income community, Mayor Daley's plan imagined a Bronzeville of splendor and activity (Reardon 2000). A goal was to increase the city's tax base by helping to position it in the global corporate circuits of capital, both as a high-services economy and a cultural tourist destination. To this end, the mayor started investing in major infrastructure improvements, turning city-owned land over to private developers and working to develop a Blues District on Forty-Seventh Street. A plan advanced in 2004 by Housing Bronzeville, a coalition of local organizations, to set aside 26 percent of the 1,156 city-owned empty lots for affordable housing development was dismissed even after 86 percent of voters in the four wards that made up Bronzeville supported it in a nonbinding referendum (J. Briggs 2006). In the words of a former department of planning head, "There is a lot of decision-making going on, but we are not being involved in these decisions" (J. Hill 1997). Plans for Forty-Seventh Street attracted harsher reactions as business owners and community leaders felt the city had rammed what they considered an inappropriately located and likely unfeasible Blues District down their throats (Huebner 2000).

But the main driving force came in 1999 as the CHA began demolishing thousands of public housing units throughout Bronzeville. The plan was to turn the land over to private developers to produce mixed-income communities, once again using federals funds, this time the Housing Opportunities for People Everywhere (HOPE VI) program. Added to this were empowerment zone (EZ) funds and designation of tax increment financing (TIF) districts to subsidize private commercial investment, landmark designation of eight historical buildings, and, equally important, boosterism. The intent of City Hall was best summarized by Christopher Hill, commissioner of the Department of Planning and Development at the time: "Bronzeville will be a thriving middle class *neighborhood* for the city. . . . This is a community that because of its incredible proximity to downtown will be one of the places that people will want to live in. It is really the South [Side] equivalent of Lincoln Park" (Reardon 2000, 10).

The *Bronzeville Redevelopment Plan and Project* classified the area as "blighted," applying the same indicators used in urban renewal, such as building age, dilapidation, depreciation, vacant lots, lack of maintenance, or percentage of land vacant, most of which was actually a result of the disinvestment the city itself had generated decades earlier with the mass concentration of public housing in the area. Meeting such criteria was needed to justify the removal of blight in order to "protect, attract and support residential and commercial investment within the Area" (Manley n.d., 15). This was the first step of a new cycle of investment. Along with it, the plan incorporated an imagined space of black history, heritage, culture, and entertainment, a city within a city for and by blacks. The Mid-South became Bronzeville, an icon and the basis of identity and pride for the black community articulated in *Restoring Bronzeville*. Michelle Boyd describes in *Jim Crow Nostalgia* (2008) how this theming acted to subvert the past forces that segregated blacks while at the same time presenting a unified and strong black history of a Bronzeville that never existed.

The *Bronzeville Redevelopment Project Area Tax Increment Financing Program Plan* (approved in 1998 and amended in 2003) was created to defray the land costs of private investors. *The 47th and King Drive Eligibility Study* (2000) identified this part of the city as a "Conservation Area in need of revitalization" and included one of the main pieces of heritage tourism: to "promote the Chicago Blues Entertainment District on 47th Street as a tourist attraction and excellent location for cultural and entertainment venues." Both plans placed Bronzeville in the context of the city's agenda. Whereas the *Eligibility Study* described conservation as a "contribut[ion] to the long-term enhancement of the City," the *Bronzeville Redevelopment Plan* stated as one of its goals "to establish a link from Bronzeville to the City's tourist and convention industries." In other words, black culture and heritage were for sale.

These plans list the major assets of Bronzeville as proximity to the CBD and the McCormick Place convention center complex and the lakefront, accessibility to the rest of the city and metropolitan area via expressways and public transportation, and proximity to the Museum of Science and Industry and the University of Chicago on the south and Lake Michigan to the east. But what appears as most valuable about the area is its location vis-à-vis downtown and the possibility of effectively making it part of Chicago's corporate core and economy. Echoing this, James Hill (1997) referred to the area as "one of the last frontiers for development left in the city and a logical extension of the new McCormick Place South and the ongoing development in the South Loop area, which largely has been driven by Daley's vision." In this context, black heritage designation is a convenient representation tied into the city's tourist agenda that also appealed to blacks in and outside of Bronzeville and, whether willingly or co-opted, facilitated middle-class blacks' role in the displacement of lower-income blacks.

POWER STRUGGLE: PLAYING THE MIDDLE CLASS Historical heritage presented a powerful tourism magnet, but statements and elements in the plans expose a different intent: using middle-class blacks to colonize Bronzeville on behalf of the growth coalition. In Patillo's words, "middle class blacks act as brokers—as 'middlemen' and 'middlewomen'—spanning the space between established centers of white economic and political power and the needs of a down but not out black neighborhood" (2007, 2). It's a clever game of representations that worked out so well because it effectively appropriated the interests of the different stakeholders, that is, low-income residents, City Hall, middle- to upper-class blacks, potential gentrifiers and businessmen, and the gentrification industry. Residents long had been advocating for investment and the designation of the Douglas community as a conservation area, but they had in mind a resident-controlled process of redevelopment without displacement (articulated in *Restoring Bronzeville*). The administration represented a corporate agenda seeking to absorb the downtown's surroundings while expanding the CBD—the city's economic engine—a vision first articulated in the 1958 *Plan for the Central Communities* and then reiterated by the *Chicago 21 Plan* of 1973. By appropriating the community's repeated call for development and the aspirations of black leaders, Mayor Daley gained control of the process and the agenda by appointing his own Community Conservation Committee for the area:

> We always wanted development; but the thing about development is that it runs over, under, around and above you. It's a beast. . . . KOCO [Kenwood Oakland Community Organization] advocated for the conservation area but it has been a thorn in our back and a feather in our hat. . . . This gentrification thing really ran up on us. It's like Plymouth Rock: it landed on us type of thing. (Interview with Bronzeville grassroots organizer)

Many residents jumped at the chance to reap the benefits of gentrification. They also assumed that City Hall would deliver on its commitment to making Bronzeville a new Lincoln Park: "Buyers . . . feel safe knowing that the City of Chicago plans to build its new central police headquarters at 35th and State Street, bringing a strong police presence to the neighborhood" (Adler 1997).[9] But unlike white Lincoln Park, this was still the Black Belt. While few whites moved in, black middle-class families did, which suggests that unlike their white counterparts, middle-class blacks could cope with living with low-income blacks. In the words of one new resident:

> There is a huge gap between poor blacks and whites. The average white person isn't used to people blasting their music. It doesn't bother me because I grew up with it. For the most part, blacks can't tell that I am affluent, especially if I'm walking around in my T-shirt and shorts. As a black person, you fit in. (Reed 2005)

From another angle, the director of a grassroots organization in Bronzeville explained to us,

> It was easier to market to black folks; the process required people who were not a stranger to crime and the conditions of black communities. Gentrification would have never come in the way it did without blacks moving in first as a buffer. The trick was bringing in people with the same color and playing to people's aspirations. This façade of a growing middle class that has moved in, truth be told, a lot of them are fighting tooth and nail to make payments on predatory loans; the middle [class] group is also struggling. The first wave of people moving in were not even middle class, they maybe had middle-class aspirations; they've got what some would call "short money"; they don't have that "long money." (Interview)

Aware of the displacement of lower-income blacks, some newcomers processed it using class representations and their own aspirations. As this black economist residing in the area described, "what is happening in this neighborhood is the natural result of the most basic economic principle, supply and demand . . . setting aside lakefront property for public housing conflicts with natural economic demand" (Reed 2005). Furthermore,

> People who are on government subsidies, in general, don't have a right to any particular land because taxpayers are the ones paying for it anyway. If I am supporting the whole thing, should they get a better view of the lake and I get a view of a south suburban neighborhood and an hour-and-a-half commute? (Reed 2005)

Ultimately, white and powerful institutions appropriated the aspirations of both classes in order to advance a real estate agenda. Rather than using power outright to take land, they made their interests appear as mutually beneficial for everyone. The president of the Illinois Institute of Technology, John L. Anderson, said at a 2007 Bronzeville Summit convened by black politicians representing the area: "IIT is pleased to be a collaborative partner in the continued revitalization of the Bronzeville community and the proposed Black Metropolis National Heritage Area. . . . We invite others to be a part of this bold historic and innovative initiative" (South Town 2007, 14). Not surprisingly, Mayor Daley presented what was happening in Bronzeville as public investment to benefit the entire city:

> We've invested more than $6 billion into our neighborhoods to achieve those goals. They are essential to maintaining quality of life for all Chicagoans. And, here in the 3rd Ward those investments are proving invaluable to old and new residents alike. They are very much a part of the rebirth of Bronzeville, an opportunity to return this historic part of Chicago back to the prominence it enjoyed

for so many years. You just have to look around: the new Police headquarters, the Bronzeville Academy, the Chicago Bee Library, new, affordable homes through-out the area created through the City's New Homes for Chicago and City Lots for City Living programs. (Mayor Richard M. Daley speech in the Third Ward, August 1, 2000).

In reality, different groups produced representations that reflected their interests and aspirations. Some corporate interests condemned the area while the city saw it as a liability to remove, and to the engineers of the imagined Bronzeville it was a dream to build. In contrast, some residents and advocate organizations viewed these representations as threats, while others, self-identifying as "old timers," were in opposition to any new people moving in. From the perspective of newcomers, longtime residents could be looked down upon because they were cast as drug dealers, gang bangers, riffraff, people on government subsidies, or generally people who belonged elsewhere (Patillo 2007). The director of a grassroots organization in Bronzeville put it this way:

> We live in a capitalist society; if you can afford it, it's your right; if not, they believe that there's something wrong with you and you should go elsewhere. Poor folks are seen as criminal. . . . The thing is, for some of the middle-class blacks mov-ing in, a lot of them tried moving to Beverly and people made them feel like shit. They tried to move to downtown and people made them feel the same. "Well, maybe I can go here and not have to deal with that." But they don't realize that they are coming into other people's neighborhood and doing the same to them. . . . And in truth it hurts even more to see people of the same skin who got all this hurt and confusion, who know they will never be good enough for their own standards, but who push their own people aside to try to get there. (Interview)

Paraphrasing Harvey (1989), discursive construction of the community is as important for the success of the symbolic order it represents as it is for the actual development of the land. Representations were critical in attracting the first wave of middle-class black households to Bronzeville, while the prospects of buying cheap and selling high assured that gentrification was around the corner (Boyd 2000). These representations played into the myth of an imag-ined past where all blacks lived together, had everything at hand, and were part of a community of blues and gospel musicians, writers, and businessmen that made history. One developer even used the phrase "coming home" to sell his newly built subdivision (Smith and Stovall 2008).

Reading what happened in Bronzeville through the lens of a growth machine framework, the plans to redevelop the neighborhood tied Bronzeville to the health and prosperity of downtown businesses and black middlemen and ruling-class elites. In this way, we could say residents were forced into the schemes of the local growth coalition to transfer land from the working poor to propertied elites. But they also were active participants in the process. Bronzeville was the name some residents chose to erase the Black Belt label. It was a self-empowering act. Also, by countering mainstream and often racist descriptions of the area and replacing them with their own version of history that highlighted the place they helped build, members of the black community removed from sight the suffering and exploitation they endured.

Mythical Bronzeville has become a universal representation of renaissance that different groups view differently. For many old-timers, it represents the aspiration to be a black community that everybody is proud of and where everyone fits in (e.g., Adler 1997). The new people see renaissance in class terms: "This really is a prime area, and in its heyday, Bronzeville and this neighborhood [North-Kenwood Oakland] were really for upper-middle-class blacks. It's kind of going back to that day" (Reed 2005). Many old-timers feel ambiguous about the realization of their dream, fearing displacement and the possibility that their sought-after black heritage community will become Lincoln Park South. Most importantly, they feel that things got out of control. Historian and lifetime leader Timuel Black assessed the situation in these terms:

> As the changes take place . . . the image (of what Bronzeville once looked like) will be very difficult to evoke, simply because so much of it has been wiped out. And so, when you want to learn about the history of Bronzeville, you're going to have to go to books and read about it. . . . Bronzeville will probably wind up in the next 10 to 15 years becoming a well-organized, sanitized middle class, predominantly black but racially mixed . . . [with] Starbucks scattered through. . . . The use of the name Bronzeville for the soon-to-be reinvented community is misleading. . . . It gives a thin veneer of historical cachet to a neighborhood that, unless current trends change, will have little connection with its past. . . . It's a mockery. . . . It's a caricature! (Reardon 2000)

In contrast, a middle-class black newcomer expressed ecstatically, "I want people to know: you've got the Gold Coast. You've got the South Loop. Now, you've got Bronzeville too" (Reardon 2000, 10).

GENTRIFICATION BEFORE GENTRIFICATION? Although Bronzeville was "gentrified" in many representations and in the perceptions of many, on the ground the reality is (1) a tremendous gap between the income and housing prices, which is keeping lower-income residents on the edge (as reflected in the proportion of rent- and mortgage-burdened households)[10] and (2) clusters of development along the lakefront next to vacant lots, unfinished projects, boarded buildings, foreclosed properties, and a predominantly blighted environment to the west of Bronzeville. While the rhythm of development in some parts gave some validity to the perception that Bronzeville was gentrifying, the process brought further hardship to the majority of residents. In the words of a local affordable housing advocate, "I don't think it's fair that poor and middle class people are getting pushed out" (J. Briggs 2006). Others still believe in the ideal of a mixed-income community, as a homeowner and a businessman echoed: "We need all of us to be here; I don't want it to become an exclusive neighborhood where the children feel they are an elite of society; the apartment buildings keep the neighborhood grounded, preventing it from growing too swank" (Reed 2005) and "In building these communities, they should be friendly to all economic spectrums; it's a community, low housing, mid-level housing . . . we have to make it a melting pot of our culture . . . the haves and the have-nots functioning as one" (Interview with longtime Bronzeville business owner).

When the Great Recession brought development to a screeching halt in 2008, most expected the pace would resume once the market picked up—which it has—but the process has not followed the pace and trajectory of white gentrification on the city's North Side, as these locals describe:

> There was excitement, interest rates were good, projects were going up, giving people more confidence; [but] in 2007, 2008, 2009, developers couldn't finish projects, people couldn't afford their houses, and the project people, lots of them didn't leave . . . even if people were interested in investing, they drive around the area and see the blight; business and people have come and gone . . . more have gone than come; most businesses are struggling. . . . The problem is that a lot of cultures won't come here due to the black history and that alone will not attract non-blacks. They won't come here based on what they hear in the news . . . their perception is not of black history; it's of violence, crime and corruption. It's part perception and it's part reality. . . . People didn't come here for that [a rich culture]; they came because of the closeness to the city's downtown and got a good deal on the home or condo, no traffic, parking on the street, surrounded by museums, the Green and Red Line and the baseball field. (Interview with business owner)

> The concept of Bronzeville as a Black Metropolis and a black tourist destination is worth advancing and investing in . . . this area is the hub of the black community but . . . where did the money slated for businesses from the empowerment zone go and who benefited from that money? . . . I don't think Bronzeville will ever be a collective community, which is where the interest was. It will be a high-end

community; it will take a while but that will be the direction . . . poor people are being used in this process: the institutions going after grant monies, they use the stats of the underserved, they say this community is blighted; they get the dollars and funnel them into infrastructures of what is to come. (Interview with longtime Bronzeville business owner)

We are in a depression in the black community and there are resources coming out of the Obama administration but because of the ineptness of our own political leadership, we haven't been able to access or utilize them to build capital in the black community . . . the only real estate being built right now in this area is mixed income housing . . . but do you really think the upper-class white people are going to come in and move in when they see babysitting on the porch over there . . . so upscale units are not selling well . . . those people [currently moving into the housing] are marginal in terms of their liquid income beyond their mortgage obligations, in terms of being the person who has enough capital to go out and start entrepreneurial businesses and hire one or two people in the community, that's how you build the community (Interview with Bronzeville leader)

When the Bronzeville rush began, it was for the hope of we are gonna make this into the Black Belt, all the culture, arts. What happened is, the economy was booming for a minute, developers and speculators were coming, all these different interests were coming. . . . This was a city collaboration with federal funds bringing in homeowners that filled in these empty spots . . . the alderman had a very strong interest in bringing homeowners, that was the focus. . . . People were sold a dream, those [the low-income] would be gone. . . . But there really isn't a lot of culture . . . after 10:00 p.m. there is nothing open . . . the reality is, if you do open a business, you might have to deal with that vacant lot, you might have to deal with those young brothers on the corner who need a job. . . . The up-and-coming people that are moving in . . . they see it as a means to an end. . . . That's why we've given up on the idea because it was never real to begin with, meaning it was never understood the work that it was going to take to do it. . . . It can't be done by just the cultural piece. . . . It's bigger than that; it's about power, politics, that's what Chicago is. (Interview with Bronzeville community organizer)

The effects of the depression have been really devastating: values have declined in excess of 50 percent, short sales and foreclosures have increased dramatically . . . the mixed income housing developments . . . have been a disaster . . . people are now giving up and saying why should I stay? I can go to the South Loop. . . . The idea for the black metropolis or black culture destination should be part of an overall strategy to bring Bronzeville back but that alone won't bring Bronzeville back. . . . Time will help . . . the major investors . . . need to perform

principal write-downs of mortgages, particularly in hard hit, economically devastated areas like Bronzeville and that will keep people from walking away . . .
the upwardly mobile young professionals of 2006–2007 are leaving . . . many
first time homebuyers who can afford less . . . teachers, firemen . . . [are replacing them]. (Interview with Bronzeville real estate agent)

We were promised there would be a total shopping metropolis, but in my three
years, I never saw anything done. We couldn't get inspired by anything down
there [explained the owner of a trendy store that left]. (Cromidas 2010b)

It's a great area for buying a condo, buying a home, understanding that you will
be pioneering and there will be challenges coming . . . from four or five decades
of poor dominating the area . . . and of course the overall perception of a black
area, especially in the United States where a black area is perceived, you know,
as not safe or not well-kept. (Interview with Bronzeville businessman)

These testimonies speak volumes about the racialization of places like
Bronzeville and the challenges of undoing society's representations of blacks
and their neighborhoods. Underlying many of the comments from residents
was a sense that only "whitening" the area could redeem it: "You know this
neighborhood is starting to do well because we are getting a lot of white people.
I don't think the neighborhood should be viewed as a black neighborhood, but
just a regular neighborhood" (Reed 2005), or "I think the neighborhood will
continue to grow, considering there's different people, different races and age
groups moving in" (Cromidas 2010a). While it is possible to have a stable all-
black mixed-income or even high-income neighborhood, many still believe
that being all-black prevents this from happening—particularly because of
the association people make between blackness and crime—but also because
traditionally in Chicago, whitening is the forerunner of revalorization. As much
as people blame the lack of progress on the recent recession, they also see race
as the reason why private capital did not respond and why predatory lending
has been a far larger factor in Bronzeville than in areas of white gentrification.
Furthermore, efforts to gentrify the South Side only occurred when opportunities starting drying up on the North Side and near downtown, and only when
City Hall stepped in and offered incentives. Even then, developers and investors
were extremely cautious.

Bronzeville seems to be between a rock and a hard place: black-only gentrification has wavered and seems less feasible today, while some see the need for
whites to join in if it's going to really gentrify. It may be that middle- to upper-
class blacks provided the entry to gentrification but that only white power and
capital can consolidate it. Asked about the imaginary Black Mecca in which

blacks buy from blacks and circulate black dollars, a white real estate agent living and selling in the area considered this a racist motto, arguing that:

> This community should be embracing diversity more than it does. Everyone thinks of Bronzeville as an African American community and it is predominantly African American but what makes Bronzeville interesting is its history and its history isn't just African American. I mean, it didn't start out that way; it got a whole story that is forgotten before the migration from the South; it's a very narrow focus. If you embrace the entire history of Bronzeville from the very beginning and really develop the historic focus from a broader angle . . . you can make it a more interesting community and attract more businesses here, more restaurants, things like that. (Interview with Bronzeville real estate agent)

As of this writing, the Great Recession appeared to be coming to an end and the real estate market was in a slow upward trend. Most of the property circulating, however, consists of foreclosures and short sales. In this environment, speculative cash buyers have the upper hand as banks holding the properties prefer it to financed buying. It's hard to know with any certainty how this will change—if at all—in the near future, though there is a sense that the availability and number of these kinds of properties is dwindling.

PILSEN

Immigrating in large numbers to Chicago after World War II, Mexicans displaced from several neighborhoods consolidated in Pilsen in the 1960s. Soon after, the city and Podmajersky, a well-known developer in the area, put them on notice. The developer began acquiring blocks of contiguous properties in the neighborhoods' east end, or East Pilsen as many call it, in order to build an artist colony or enclave. In 1980, community leaders opposed to this plan organized against his proposal to redevelop an old brewery, occupied at the time by three manufacturing businesses, into a residential and performing arts complex. They were able to convince the city to reject the conversion. In response, the developer said, "gentrification is just a dirty word for 'changing' . . . If I wasn't doing what I'm doing, there wouldn't be a neighborhood here" (Cunningham 1988, 62). Meanwhile, City Hall was promoting and subsidizing wholesale redevelopment immediately north of Pilsen in partnership with the University of Illinois at Chicago (UIC). This included building University Village, a middle- to upper-income community, relocating the South Water Market activities and converting the buildings into condominiums, and demolishing the ABLA public housing site to make way for a mixed-income development named Roosevelt Square.

The city did not intervene in Pilsen as massively and directly as in Bronzeville. But as the representation of Pilsen became more racialized to outsiders in the 1960s with the entry of Mexicans, it was transformed conceptually and concretely from an orderly and well-maintained working-class white ethnic enclave supportive of family life to one of social disorder, decay, and rowdiness with increasing predatory landlord behavior, disinvestment, redlining, and public neglect. As a seemingly self-fulfilling prophecy, Pilsen then qualified for slum and blight intervention; Mexican occupation was dysfunctional, and as a result the neighborhood needed to be rescued.

In 1996, Mayor Daley appointed a Latino, Danny Solis, as alderman for the Thirty-First Ward, which included most of Pilsen.[11] Solis was one of a growing number of councilmen appointed to put different neighborhoods in the hands of the growth coalition. While many residents believe Solis triggered a wave of gentrification, he framed the situation differently:

"My vision is to make Pilsen the preeminent Mexican-American community as Chinatown is to Chinese-Americans—not only for the families who live here but for people who visit," says the alderman. "We have a good mix of working-class and professional people who are fixing up the older buildings, getting involved in the community and putting down roots. We've always been a port of entry, but now we are more than that." (Alderman Solis, quoted by Mann 2009)

Because of the wave of speculative development coming from the north, many long-term residents felt that a state of siege had been declared on Pilsen and its disposable Mexicans.

Unlike Bronzeville, Pilsen's gentrification process followed from the beginning the path of white middle-class pioneers displacing and replacing low-income Latino residents. As development absorbed the east end of Pilsen, a growing collection of deal hunters and politically connected developers, along with Latino professionals who added legitimacy to the process, threatened to swallow much of the remaining land. Trendy retail followed and progressively ventured deeper into Pilsen, moving west along Eighteenth Street, the main commercial strip. Also unlike Bronzeville, gentrification ran into formidable opposition from organized residents and activists, who advanced an ordinance seeking more resident control of zoning and who blanketed the community with "Pilsen is not for sale" signs and murals publicly stating that "*Aqui estamos y aqui nos quedamos*" (We are here and will stay here). Meanwhile, many long-term residents were trying to stay put by taking on extra work to pay rising rents.

As in Bronzeville, these struggles also were waged at the representational level. A key difference, however, was opposition and disagreement around the solution being offered to the so-called problem. Wilson, Wouter, and Grammenos (2004) studied this in detail and identified three contending growth discourses representing three mutually exclusive coalitions:

- "Affluent restructuring" consisted of for-profit developers, the UIC, and some homeowners; they saw the need to clean up Pilsen physically, restructure the social fabric, and control escalating crime.
- "Protect Pilsen" consisted of a nonprofit organizing group, a nonprofit housing development organization, and long-term residents (mostly renters); they stood for the need to keep Pilsen for current residents, provide more affordable housing, and preserve the area's cultural heritage.
- "Commodify ethnicity" included a nonprofit economic development corporation, the city's cultural affairs office, and the alderman; they coalesced around the need to upscale Pilsen physically, cultivate an entrepreneurial spirit, strengthen the area's retail base, and embellish and display Mexican ethnicity.

These discourses provide a point of departure to study the dynamics of representation and its role in the process of gentrification in Pilsen. Rather than a static process, we find a quite fluid one with a limited correlation between the actual positions taken and these researchers' categories. We challenge their assumption that each coalition and its discourse were mutually exclusive and synchronous, and we identify key actors missing from their list while pointing to others that strategically changed positions. We also question how these different representations operated in the power struggle.

POWER STRUGGLE: CLASSIFYING COMPETING DISCOURSES AND CHANGE AGENTS. The discourses identified by Wilson, Wouter, and Grammenos make representational constructs a critical component of the gentrification struggle. Examining their contending discourses and coalitions, however, we concluded that what many of the different actors they grouped together actually stood for and did was not that easily classified or classifiable. By definition, representations reduce reality to generalities that then appear fixed and monosemantic. Our goal is not to discredit the classification scheme but rather to draw attention to how the struggle over gentrification is fluid, as are the positions of those involved and how they were grouped. In this way, the classifications above have to be used as tentative and ever-evolving categories.

Affluent restructuring: Rather than a single common discourse among developers, City Hall, and homeowners, we found at least four different directions within this discourse and coalition. In some cases, the viewpoints diverged across and within each subgroup, while at other times they borrowed from or even completely overlapped positions outside it. This was especially evident among developers and homeowners. For example, the developer creating artist space projected a patriarchal image of his role and a romanticized version of the community he was creating, which was appealing to his actual and potential tenants. He also presented himself as the savior of East Pilsen. In his words, "I have a commitment to bringing it back. It's been my life" (Cunningham 1988, 62). This self-representation cast his work as an act of love rather than a money-making enterprise: "If I had just wanted to make money, I could have done things in Lincoln Park" (Cunningham 1988, 62).[12] While denying any role in gentrification, he did exhibit a negative opinion of the forces opposing his work. From his perspective, he was working independently of gentrifying developers, and he did not need help from the city to improve Pilsen.[13]

Many developers of large condominium buildings and new retail business owners also listed in this coalition did not see their work as displacing anyone or extracting rent from the neighborhood. Rather, they claimed they were adding value to it. In the words of a restaurant owner, "I don't think we are actively displacing anyone, we hope to place people by employing them" (Behrens 2009). Similarly, an investor saw his intervention in these terms: "The hope is that the economic momentum around the UIC campus expansion will continue into the South Side, but it doesn't change the character of Pilsen" (Roeder and Spielman 2005). Furthermore, he claimed they were helping existing families by including so-called "affordable" units (which also would give him access to public subsidies and zoning concessions). While technically affordable as per federal income standards, the selling prices were still out of reach for most Pilsen families.

A nonprofit CBO doing development in Pilsen listed in the "Protect Pilsen" coalition actually took a position that overlapped those in the Affluent Regeneration category: gentrification was an inevitable market process *and* it was an opportunity to develop affordable housing for residents. Referring to a set-aside requiring 20 percent of the units in buildings with more than ten units be affordable to lower-income families, a spokesperson for this organization stated, "That's the highest set-aside in Chicago and a good example of using the private market to create [affordable] housing" (Behrens 2009). Similarly, the alderman and many other local actors (placed in a different coalition) saw development per se as a blessing because it allowed them to advocate for a mixed-income community.

We assume most developers would not admit publicly and perhaps not even to themselves that they were trying to make money at the expense of the poor and instead would say that the development they were doing was good by defi-nition. Many developers said they believed they were giving people options they did not have elsewhere. Yet from inside Pilsen, the representations were clearly aimed at potential renters from outside and at middle-income buyers. One advertisement reflected this well: "Tired of High Wicker Park rents? Move to sunny Pilsen. Close to the Loop, expressway & public transportation. Pets welcome" (Lutton 1998, 28). Or the flashy poster that read, "Yesterday's Heri-tage. Tomorrow's Treasure," advertising homes for sale in University Village next door.

Developers used alternative representations depending on the audience (e.g., the alderman, the city, or banks). Only rarely did developers interact directly with activists or take sides publicly. Instead their positions were often represented through the alderman but also through police and City Hall. For example, the alderman once stated that "every development in Pilsen has been questioned. . . . If you took just about any community and you talked about the expansion of a university into a vacated area nearby, that community would be fighting to bring that development in" (Lutton 1998, 22). Similarly, a journal-ist who made a name for himself by branding neighborhood groups resisting gentrification as "anti-development rabble rousers" argued that some of the people of Pilsen were holding developers hostage rather than welcoming badly needed development to their deteriorated neighborhoods (J. McCarron 1988). Responses to his newspaper series, which were buried in an inside corner of the paper, represented different positions and perspectives but still fell into the Protect Pilsen camp: "Some perceive the poor as obstacles to the redevelop-ment and improvement of our city. It goes to show that it is easier to get rid of the poor instead of dealing with poverty" (Martinez 1997), and "Unfortunately for my community, we were hoodwinked by a developer and a good-ole-boy alderman. We could have used an articulate and effective spokesperson . . . to defend our community from this inappropriate and unwanted development which was rammed down our community's throat" (Marshall 1988).

Homeowners in Pilsen demonstrate why we need to be careful using repre-sentations that suggest that all members of a category take the same position or act collectively. While we were unable to identify who the actual homeowners were in the affluent restructuring group, we did learn from a focus group with Latino homeowners that not all shared the same viewpoint about what was happening. Although enticed by the prices offered for their properties, several knew the amount could not buy them a comparable home elsewhere. Yet they also felt the pressure to move as gentrification was increasing the costs of home-ownership through higher taxes, maintenance costs, and inspections for code violations. One owner, explaining the "stick and carrot" approach real estate firms use to acquire properties, suggested that the "opportunity" presented was more of a threat:

> They say, are you a homeowner? . . . because I tell them yes, they start in. "Oh, don't you want to sell your property?" "We'll offer you such and such amount. . . . This is a good opportunity to sell" and "You're going to have to leave anyway down the line and if you wait you won't get anything." (Lutton 1998, 20)

Similarly, we know that gentrifiers themselves are not a monolithic group. Belonging to different income subgroups, some become a casualty of the process they perhaps inadvertently facilitated (e.g. see Lloyd 2006). Many artists renting from the pioneer developer apparently were displaced from East Pilsen, as this posting in the Chicago Arts District (aka East Pilsen) suggests:

> Unfortunately, it seems as if the Podmajerskys have really priced out all of the working artists in Pilsen. About 10 years ago almost all of the buildings between 18th street and Cermak along Halsted were filled with high quality fine artists. From photographers to large scale installation artists. I personally knew the tenant who rented the building smack dab on the corner of Halsted and 18th and . . . he was priced out of the space. Moved to LA where the rent is just as high but the exposure and acceptance of artists is much more viable." (P., Laura 2010)

Missing from the "affluent restructuring" coalition were gentrification forces who by just sitting on the fence ended up supporting gentrification. This included various local nonprofit community development groups associated with (and some say co-opted by) City Hall that were considered part of the Protect Pilsen coalition.

Protect Pilsen: Characterizing this group as reactive in the struggle loses important nuance by masking what was really being advocated, namely democracy, accountability, self-determination, the end of race-based anything, and support for community-led and community-oriented development.[14] Here is how a few people lumped in this category described their positions:

> It's not that we don't want development. But the problem is that . . . they think that the only development that is possible for our neighborhood and for the city in general are [*sic*] the models that they propose. And they are models that are very authoritarian and very anti-poor. They are models to attract the middle class and to get rid of the poor." (Resident quoted in Lutton 1998, 22)

> [I]f there is progress in this community, it has to be a progress that's going to benefit everyone. . . . The only thing that that type of development [gentrifica-

tion] has done is displace people." (Nonprofit CEO quoted in Lutton 1998, 22 and 24)

The key is will the residents have a chance to map out their own future? (CEO of a local nonprofit quoted in Puente 1997)

Characterizations of opposition as antidevelopment and of community organizers as rabble rousers are common. What is often overlooked is that the "protectors" are usually advancing an alternative appropriate form of development that is done with their participation and without displacement and without taking money from schools by using tax increment financing (TIF). As the president of a community organization declared, "There is development that can be done without a TIF. It's been done before. Why not here?" (quoted in Puente 1997). And instead of private developers, many in this group were pushing for nonprofit CBOs engaged in affordable housing development as well as other initiatives to take the lead in improving Pilsen. The assumption was that these organizations aimed to benefit lower-income families through things beyond housing, such as job training and placement, providing services and advocating for better schools, and an improved built environment.

Unlike Bronzeville, where black middle-class gentrifiers—both willingly and unwillingly—became the face of corporate (white) Chicago, community organizations filled this role in Pilsen, though not always willingly. Often leaning on their ethnic identity to oppose gentrification, some community organizations demonstrated a contrary position through their actions and inaction. These included self-exclusion, a "wait-and-see" paralysis, and representations masking the class or position of the organization and its staff. Some even provided qualified support for gentrification-oriented development, as this person articulated:

We have to be where people are and that implies addressing the issues that are affecting them daily. Gentrification is a case in point. They deal with it every day as their rents and taxes go up to levels they cannot afford and as people around them have to move. This is real to them and [our agency's] approach is to let people lead and work on matters that affect their daily life. It's about self-empowerment and bringing residents into the conversations and the decisions. . . . People seem to have accepted that gentrification was a fact and all we could do was to work around it. . . . [They] seem to be more interested in their institutions and in providing services and make their choices on behalf of the community without bringing in the base. (Interview with representative of a group opposing gentrification in Pilsen)

The position of some members of the Protect Pilsen group was a moving target as well. As development moved forward, they made adjustments and adapted their strategies, some digging in their heels further while others acquiesced:

> Pilsen is one of the best neighborhoods in the City. It has *character*. It has all the ingredients that developers want, that yuppies want, that downtown folks want. But you know what? They are not gonna get it. (Old-timer quoted in Cunningham 1998, 18)

> As far as the housing issue I think that at first there was a big struggle in understanding affordable housing with the neighborhood developing as it was. It was hard to obtain the percentage of affordable housing that developers needed to include and we were able to win some battles securing a percentage for affordable housing. That was hard and we had to adjust our strategies. (Interview with staff person from local organization)

> My role is to give the community and its leaders the best possible information so they can make a decision. (CEO of a local CBO)

After being displaced from the current site of UIC in the 1960s, many Pilsen residents opposed the *Chicago 21 Plan* in 1973 and then the proposal for the 1992 World's Fair in 1979. Since then, new organizations have formed and leadership turnover has brought in staff members without ties to the old guard, many with other loyalties and visions. Also, some groups became more institutionalized, often competing with each other for the same funding or city support or to be the middleman of choice for the neighborhood.[15]

Looking back, the Pilsen Triangle proposal (1988) seems to mark the official breakup of a neighborhood-wide compact against displacing development. The proposal sought to improve the business strips through the establishment of a "Mexican festival district patterned after a zocalo and centered on the Pilsen Triangle site" (formed by Eighteenth and Laflin Streets and Blue Island at the heart of Pilsen) (Betancur and Wright 1988, 1). The Triangle was to operate as a place of convergence for residents and a tourist destination, a Mexi-town. Unsatisfied with disinvestment and neglect, many leaders looking for alternatives embraced the Triangle proposal "as a way that change could come" (Betancur and Wright 1988, appendix). Tremendous infighting followed as local leaders[16] and business owners took sides, with some expressing that nobody had been included in the discussions and others referring to it as gentrification. At least one of the groups in the middle, viewing itself as a defender of the community, supported the proposed Pilsen Triangle.[17] Although the project disintegrated, it brought to the surface the differences that had been emerging; loyalties to the outside (e.g., City Hall) and reliance on city funding and foundations tied the hands of many nonprofit agencies. According to the CEO of a key CBO, "As organizations increased their dependency and mutual ties to politicians and funders, they lost their ability to be independent voices for their communities" (quoted in Betancur and Wright 1988). All these changes had effectively undermined the compact. Rather than be a staunch "defend community" group, each in its own way took positions that fit their organization's interests and needs first and foremost.

A common direction taken by some was to support mixed-income development, which, as one person described, was "gentrification in the sense that it is an improvement in the neighborhood." (Behrens 2009). Still, a small nucleus of activists and residents continues to steadily confront gentrification head-on while promoting what some call helpful development. They have gone as far as to give up the funding that compromised their position and have challenged other community-based organizations for settling so fast and for so little. Addressing affordable housing, a member of this group said to us:

> They [other community groups] say they support affordable housing but, affordable to whom? Not for residents of the community. The majority cannot afford even their housing [referring to the affordable housing built by a nonprofit]. They support development that does not serve the base of the community. (Interview with community member)

Commodify Ethnicity: Wilson, Wouters, and Grammenos's vision of a commoditized Mexican community, as with the other two coalitions, does not represent all parties that could be included and includes some we think it should not.[18] While several businesses supported efforts of the Chicago Office of Tourism to sell the brand of the ethnic business strip/district destinations, many businesses did not, and others were indifferent. More importantly, we found, as Wacquant (1998) did, that many firms offering specialty ethnic goods feared losing customers or even their business in a gentrified neighborhood. At least seventy businesses left the community between 2000 and 2006, and only a comparatively small group of those remaining actually had the customer base that would allow them to stay in business or expand in a gentrified community (Tamalechica 2008). Meanwhile, the alderman insisted that Pilsen become a Mecca of Mexican culture consumption while artists in East Pilsen promoted their own cultural center and organized separate art festivals.

The business of marketing ethnicity sidesteps the issue of gentrification and does not necessarily put anyone supporting it in contradiction with other visions for the community as long as they do not oppose gentrification outright.[19] A good way to avoid taking a position on gentrification is to work around it. This can be done by promoting affordable housing, assisting local businesses, and making sure that Pilsen retains a Mexican footprint:

> We want to continue to see and remain a community that is representative of the Mexican cultural heritage but I think that we have to be also at the same time welcoming of diversification . . . we want to be able to sustain a mixed-income community that provides affordable housing for the families as much as possible. But I think that we have to be mindful also of certain dynamics: communities change, it's something that history has proven . . . over and over again. . . . It may be unfortunate in some way but that's how things happen. What is important for us is that fifty years from now or one hundred years from now that Pilsen, though it may no longer be a predominantly Mexican community, that we leave behind that we were here. We also understand as far as that goes that we have to support affordable housing but be mindful that of course these are market forces at play and these organizations and institutions have to make a living selling and buying houses. We have to be realistic in our demands. (Interview with staff person at a local CBO)

Even the alderman's position cannot be contained exclusively in this one coalition. His rhetoric also adjusted with the moment, avoiding some questions and resorting to ambiguous and slippery language, as these statements suggest:

> It's difficult for me to define [gentrification]. I think there was improvement. I think there was development; I think we had a lot of construction going on." (Behrens 2009)

> Addressing a controversial proposal mentioned earlier, the alderman said that the Hispanic ownership and hiring commitment included in the proposal "are good indicators of something that I could support," [adding that] "They have filed for a zoning change, but that doesn't mean this is a done deal."[20] (Roeder and Spielman 2005)

> More people have left this community, not because of gentrification. They left because of gangs, because they did not get educational opportunities. I want to change that. (Puente 1997)

> People make a decision whether to stay or leave once it [the neighborhood] improves but it's not a conspiracy to ethnically clean a neighborhood. I believe that a lot of these people decide, "Hey, I'm being offered ten times what I paid for my house—I'm gonna sell." (Lutton 1998, 30)

Missing from these three discourses, as in most discussions on Pilsen, are ordinary residents. Many of Pilsen's residents have showed tremendous resilience, itself a form of resistance. While rarely invited to participate, many have come forward and, as a local leader observed, have often offered the best solutions and ideas. While we cannot map out all their positions, hearing residents speak in public meetings, joining them in actions, or having conversations with them, it is clear that each has his or her own vision for Pilsen and not all agree. This is evident in the ways people talk of gentrification, a word that does not have an equivalent in Spanish. Instead, Spanish-speaking residents talk about those factors directly affecting their lives: being pushed out, condominium construction, whites (*güeros*) and students moving in. "Where were you when we cried for help?" asked a resident to a developer seeking community support at a public meeting for a project requiring the support of an alderman. And as Latino professionals started moving in, low-income residents differentiated between us and them (some called them "muppies" or white proxies). All of these comments suggest nuances and struggles that go much deeper, are more fluid, and cover a wider range of contradictions as both the representations and actors changed over time or as needed.

GENTRIFICATION BEFORE GENTRIFICATION? In the early part of 2000, there was evidence of gentrification before gentrification in Pilsen (Betancur, Deuben, and Edwards 2006). Today, although still majority low-income Latino, Pilsen bears the marks of gentrification, especially on the east side, where population has declined and there are fewer families and lower school enrollment. There also is a noticeable change in racial composition: Latinos have declined by 25 percent at the same time that whites grew by 24 percent, though they were still only about 12 percent of the population in 2010 (A. Williams 2011). New retail accommodates yuppy/muppy /millennial lifestyles. Housing values and rents are near the city's median, and postrecession increases in housing prices are higher than those in the city.

Language condenses perceptions into generalities, and words, especially when written in the popular press, have helped shape outside perceptions of the neighborhood. Declaring Pilsen blighted with gangs and poor schools had set it up for intervention in the 1970s. Attaching the label gentrification before the community actually started to gentrify invited investors and developers while telling residents that gentrification was a fait accompli. The ascription of these different labels has transformed Pilsen's image and how people react to it over time. Initially, many residents and local groups responded with self-affirmation, but as resistance weakened and external forces penetrated the community, the struggle fragmented.

Once the image of blighted Pilsen started to disappear, an exciting and cultured Pilsen replaced it. The dominance of an imagined future Pilsen helped push opposition and actual conditions out of sight. It is largely this rebranding that has driven up housing prices; people believed the discourse even if it was for the most part fiction. Culture also played a major role in the representation dynamics, especially in making the transition from perceptions of slum and blight to that of excitement and valorization. The Mexican appropriation and cultural branding of the community via murals and festivals, the National Museum of Mexican Art, and omnipresent Mexican signs and colors and symbols was then appropriated to attract and sell Pilsen to others. And as the image of an exotic Mexican village that included street art, ethnic food, art galleries, and studios—the spectacle—took over, the Pilsen of struggling low-income Mexicans has for the most part been removed from view. After all, "the credibility of a discourse is what first makes believers act in accord with it. It produces practitioners. To make people believe is to make them act" (de Certeau 1988, 148).

Learning from Pilsen and Bronzeville

Neighborhood change results from the ongoing power exchanges of forces acting within and outside a neighborhood, operating at different scales and in ways that are neither linear nor determined. Analyzing Pilsen and Bronzeville unveiled some of the ways in which representations emerge, evolve, and interact with those forces, and thus *represent* power and produce power effects. Indeed, these representations tend to fix reality to serve their interests. Of interest to us was how people, as individuals but more importantly as representing the neighborhood, could embrace representations of space that did not align with the people they claimed to represent. In some cases, loyalty to—and too often dependency on—resources controlled by the forces advancing gentrification was a contributing factor. Some organizations, however, ended up legitimizing gentrification in the name of an imagined future of mixed-income communities based in a common culture, whether Latino or African American, in which class differences are reconcilable.

This is not simply a story of class struggle, however. Neighborhood change cannot be reduced to class struggle, given the ambiguities and mediations that transform class itself. Class is not such a straightforward concept; it gets defined or suppressed in our daily lives, and in the case of Pilsen and Bronzeville it is clearly mediated by racial and ethnic identity. Similarly, relationships of power are not always relationships of domination, and power is not necessarily only a possession of the state and the dominant classes. As Foucault believed, we find in these cases that power is far more dispersed, assumes many forms, is ever-evolving, and has many other effects. Thus we do not read representations here as positive or negative, right or wrong, but as *producing particular effects* on behalf of particular parties or positions under given circumstances. Representations are contingent and multifaceted and can be fixed or appropriated and resignified. They also can assume lives of their own. In both neighborhoods, we saw how discourse was used to guide people in one direction or the other, often veiled and under unqualified hegemonic messages about culture, development, heritage, progress, etc. And while images can bring people together, they can also divide.

Representations substitute the actually existing conditions for a snapshot that removes from view the complex and often fragmented and contradictory realities on the ground. In any case, the power of representations lies with the forces that advance them. Just as the writing of history can make history, representations can make a neighborhood change. They definitely sold Bronzeville and Pilsen to some investors, but this fact does not prescribe the same outcome every time. In Bronzeville, on paper, the black middle and upper classes were at the helm, but they actually relied on resources (including government) under white control. While their visions of a mixed-income community were well-intentioned, they ran against the forces of capital and a real estate marketplace they did not control. In the case of Pilsen, the marketing of Mexican culture relied on Mexican elites, outsiders, and the city's effort to sell diversity to the world. But white artists, gentrifiers, students, and developers changed that image.

In both cases, culture clearly helped to promote gentrification. A common feature that may have further facilitated it was another representation of the future: the mixed-income "community" sustained through the inclusion of affordable housing to help lower-income residents stay in the neighborhood. As we discuss in chapter 7, however, this position was not based on a belief that income mixing could mitigate poverty. It was more a means to appease higher-income people, especially those who needed assurances the poor would be contained (by location, number), and make them feel confident about buying into a changing neighborhood. This view also reassured others who were conflicted about the addition of higher-income development. Income not only cushioned the effects of racism, it gave the middle-class minorities power akin to the majority. As the Brazilian saying goes, "money whitens."

Adding our insights to Wilson, Wouters, and Grammenos (2004) and Mele (2000) demonstrates the complicating role representations play in struggles around neighborhood change. It also exposes some of the dynamics that gentrification processes unleash and specifically the challenges it poses for making generalizations and classifying neighborhoods. As Baudrillard (2005) reminds us:

> Speculation, like poker or roulette, has its own logic of enthusiasm, chain reactions, escalation (*Steigerung*) where many people find the excitement of the game, outbidding. (This is why it is impossible to oppose it with economic logic. This is also what makes these phenomena exciting: overrunning economies with an aleatory and vertiginous form). (158)

Gentrification has been described in many ways, including a pioneering act that speaks to the inner desires of consumers, an act that opens the land to developers, and the cleansing and then redemption of a place. From these two cases, it appears that gentrification forces needed to first condemn and then rebrand the neighborhood. In Chicago, urban renewal not only cleared the space, it set the stage, created the market, and even mobilized early representations of these spaces as ripe for investment. When the program officially ended in 1973, the stage had been set for gentrification led by growth-machine politics and public-private partnerships. The process also triggered resistance in the form of representation wars between the well-off and low-income residents, with many others in between. The twist in Bronzeville and Pilsen was that race and ethnicity complicated resident claims and how to interpret the struggles. The next chapter looks at similar challenges, but in a declining African American community.

CHAPTER 4

Constructing Carceral Space

How Englewood Became the Ghetto

Very few people who have better options would choose to live in
Englewood. There are basically three types of residents who live
there: The 70% who simply don't have a better option within
their means, the 10% who could leave if they wanted to but are
attached to or don't want to give up on the neighborhood where they
grew up, and the 20% who are running the place into the ground
and making life miserable for the other 80%. (Nina64 2009)

At one time Englewood was considered a normal, healthy, and prosperous neighborhood in Chicago. Today it is considered a ghetto—deviant and abnormal—and the keepers of the status quo have slammed the gavel down and found it guilty of going against the norm, justifying specific and often drastic forms of intervention. This includes the surgical demolition of vacant buildings presumed to be home to drug dealers, zero tolerance policies, and the establishment of what many residents call "a police state." The negative image is also reflected in the views of both insiders and outsiders:

> The thing about Englewood is that if the crime happened outside of my door they would call it Englewood when it is not Englewood. It could be 87th and State and they are calling it Englewood when it's negative, they're calling the name of another neighborhood when is positive. (An alderman whose ward partially includes Englewood)

> Compared to a "baseline" Chicago neighborhood like, say, Belmont-Cragin or Hermosa, it's bad. Compared to an upper-middle-class to upper-class neighborhood like Sauganash, it *really* sucks. Compared to what Englewood was like

in the early 1990s, the Englewood of 2009 is Paradise. But it's still one of the worst neighborhoods in the city in terms of crime, blight, urban decay, disinvestment, engrained generational poverty and welfare dependency, etc. (A resident of Englewood)

We view Englewood as a historically produced ghetto of exclusion and seclusion in which African Americans living there have long struggled to gain control of their lives. In this chapter, we trace the material and representational construction of this neighborhood, exploring two major moments that helped produce the current space of Englewood: the production of "normal" and prosperous white Englewood followed by the production of abnormal and poor black Englewood.

Englewood's story, like that of any other neighborhood, can be told only in fragments of the ongoing convergence and divergence of processes shaping and reshaping it over time. Here we present it as open-ended, both constituted and in the process of being constituted, space that is dominated and contested by multidirectional forces and actions framing the everyday practices of people. This case exposes a dynamic and nuanced picture in which factors such as class, race, and gender within groups find expression, and in which outside and inside forces clash, diverge, and converge as people carve out their spaces for survival and resistance "within the dominant culture" (de Certeau 1888, xiv). From this vantage point, Englewood is a product of a set of deeply uneven social relations that shape local conditions but also blame the weak and vulnerable for them. This is evident in reflections by a resident and an outsider:

> Once I read a book called *Dysfunction by Design*. Some of it [conditions in Englewood] I think is by design. (Director of local nonprofit)

> Where did it all begin? I think that yes it does deal with the political part of it. But it also deals with the family. . . . So again, you say, "what's going on, why did this happen?" I think it begins with the deterioration of the family . . . you have to be pretty strong to survive in this community. (Head of local social service agency)

We find evidence of residents pushing back against this representation but also coping with it. But these are not stories of passive underdogs; rather they are descriptions of nuanced relationships between people and the factors that shape where they can and do live. What follows creates an opening to expose the complementary and contradictory power struggles shaping Englewood, including the tactics residents use to gain control and avoid oppression and to resist forces seeking to suppress their agency.

Neighborhood Change in Englewood

Urban ecologists would likely say Englewood has traversed almost the entire life cycle, going from a successful neighborhood to one of decline. Starting around the mid-1800s as a settlement of railroad workers at the junction (hence the initial name of Junction Grove) of Sixty-Third and LaSalle Streets, seven miles south of downtown, it became a neighborhood of both first and second settlement. By 1880, Germans, Irish, and Scots were the largest group of residents, followed by Poles and eastern Europeans at the turn of the twentieth century. But then, a process of racial turnover and associated disinvestment transformed the neighborhood after World War II, as African Americans entered and whites moved out. In the 1990s, concerted efforts by local institutions and the city of Chicago to jump-start the economy failed to bring back the commercial business district, and the community suffered further population and real estate losses.

Englewood's trajectory of steady growth between the 1880s and 1940s is attributed to its being a major transportation hub. By 1887 horse-drawn trolley lines took residents to downtown; electric trolleys were inaugurated in 1886, and the elevated line connected it to the metro area in 1907. By 1922, street railways, elevated trains, and suburban trains serviced Englewood, attracting businesses and people. Growing steadily, the population peaked at ninety-seven thousand in 1960, despite the exodus of fifty thousand whites in the 1950s that set off a trajectory of decline. In seventy years the community went from 99 percent white in 1930 to 98 percent black by 2000. By 2010, Englewood had declined to fewer than thirty-one thousand inhabitants.

Few communities in Chicago have lost as many people, businesses, institutions, and housing stock as Englewood. Mass clearance of a stretch of black-inhabited tracts displaced thousands to the east to make room for the Dan Ryan Expressway and large public housing projects in the 1950s. Families seeking accommodation in next-door Englewood set off a process of disinvestment and property deterioration that devastated the neighborhood. Attempts by the city in the 1960s to restore its shopping district with urban renewal funds were unsuccessful, but they did result in the clearance of more housing. In the 1970s, Sears and Wieboldt's department stores closed, and Chicago State University moved south to the Roseland community.

By the end of the twentieth century only about a hundred small shops were still operational, with more than 75 percent managed and owned by Korean and Pakistani merchants (Stockwell 2005). Teamwork Englewood's web page explains that "There is an annual leakage of $69 million as the 80,000 residents of the greater Englewood community [Englewood and West Englewood] have little option other than to shop for groceries and visit restaurants in other communities." Despite new housing units built by the Antioch Baptist Church and others (e.g., Saint Bernard's Place, Rebirth of Englewood, New Birth, conversion of the Strand Hotel and Columbia Pointe), there has been no gain in population. Englewood is characterized today as the epitome of the black ghetto or a super-ghetto, and its name evokes crime, destitution, and social disorder.

Data typically used to assess neighborhood conditions depict an Englewood of deficits in almost all fronts when compared to the city of Chicago: higher rates of female-headed families, poverty, unemployment, etc. The situation is not likely to improve as Englewood lost 9,500 people between 2000 and 2010, the second-highest number lost in the city after West Englewood, which lost 10,000 people. It ranked third in the number of new foreclosures in 2007 (Jackson 2008) and remains among the top three today (Woodstock Institute 2012). In describing these conditions, these data also define the neighborhood and determine its future. Few people know that the majority of families (56 percent) are actually not below poverty and some are actually working and middle-class. But the entire neighborhood is condemned by a ranking and by being characterized as high-poverty, a label that is then applied to all residents in that space, reducing each and every one to the same generic persona. In research terms, it is the classic problem of the ecological fallacy: making assumptions about the individual based on the average for the totality. While researchers should know not to do this, there really is nothing to prevent policy makers, reporters, or anyone living outside or inside the neighborhood from doing it. But why should it matter? Clearly, being poor is a real experience for many residents and should be of concern. Still, what is the effect of the label itself? In current terms, Englewood is classified as "high-poverty" because it exceeds the established 40 percent threshold (see Jargowsky 1997). Based on fifty years of research on the "culture" that is presumed to be associated with poverty, there is a whole collection of characteristics this label evokes. For example, we would expect to find—and usually do—more single females becoming parents at an early age. The same is true for higher rates of crime. And because poverty has been high for a couple of decades, it is presumed to be generational; that is, poverty begets poverty.

The label "high-poverty" generates a narrative that creates a space that is in part real but largely imagined. The imagined space conjured up by a string of statistics provides no information about *why* change has happened over time or which forces have produced it. It also doesn't help us understand *how* change is distributed throughout the neighborhood, or how such a characterization affects, for instance, property values. As a result, the conditions of the neighborhood are both cause *and* effect, repeating the same dynamics over time. Looking back through the timeless lens of human ecology, the trajectory of Englewood suggests a natural ecology of mutually enforcing deficits attributed to the change in race of the population. In such a case, the culprit is race rather than class in this natural succession.

The 1980 *Chicago Fact Book* describes Englewood's change in these terms:

> The *migration* [our emphasis] of African- and poor Americans into Englewood during and after World War II coincided with a series of events that eventually led to the decline in Englewood's prosperity. New residential construction . . . ceased . . . and many black residents could not conserve older deteriorating buildings and streets. Racial changes in the neighborhood led to an exodus of white residents . . . considerable demolition in homes . . . took place during the 1950s in the community for various city projects. (Chicago Fact Book Consortium 1983, 175–76)

From this perspective, racial change turned Englewood into a neighborhood of last resort where crime prospers and hope disappears, or, as a former resident describes, it has "a mentality of defeat." No explanation, meanwhile, is provided about the "series of events that eventually led to the decline of Englewood's prosperity." The *Fact Book* associates the area's deteriorated condition with black migrants and their inability to keep the neighborhood up after the departure of working- and middle-class whites. The aging real estate and various city projects are presented as a natural outcome of this movement of people in and out and of the ecology of disorder and destitution, a neighborhood presumed to be at the end of its natural life cycle. But does this mean that blacks ended the neighborhood's life cycle? These data transform Englewood into a *subject* that sustains a culture of poverty and capital deficits associated with blackness. As a form of failure (e.g., Beaty 2012; Terry 2012; Sweeney 2006; Polk and Dumke 1999), these deficits have triggered several possible policy remedies including:

- *Do nothing.* Applying the Chicago School's doctrine, it could be said that this outcome is, after all, natural, a self-contained community for the derelict. People and places are in a natural flow in which those that succeed move up and out and those that do not stay behind; like-types seek other like-types and each ends up where she or he belongs and gets what she or he deserves. If the neighborhood "dies" it is a natural process of attrition, a natural end of life.
- *Social control.* Although natural and self-contained, this neighborhood is perceived as a threat to the moral order, which calls for the reinforcement of standards to contain and neutralize the problem. Measures include

increased policing and zero tolerance from the top but also community-development strategies from the bottom aimed at youth to keep them from getting involved in gangs and drugs.

- *Dispersal.* Assuming poverty concentrations are generational, a logical step is to disperse residents into "normal" middle-class environments so as to expose them to people with a culture of work that can show them how to lift themselves up by their own bootstraps. Here poverty is a matter of wrong choices and behaviors. This philosophy underlies the mixed-income concept employed in the redevelopment of public housing and inspiring programs such as Moving to Opportunity.
- *Urban renewal.* This approach replaces the "abnormal" slum with a normal ecology that includes the right residents and physical environment. This correction aims to counter the natural tendency to decline and provides a means to return to a better state similar to where the neighborhood was before it started to decline. This philosophy spurred controversial federal projects such as urban renewal but also, in reaction to it, the grassroots community development movement that continues today in the United States.

All these one-size-fits-all interpretations of space are both authoritarian and hegemonic, tainted by ecological determinism and racism. Cause and effect are merged into a self-reinforcing cycle while the area and its residents are classified by racialized moral rankings, all under the code of objective measurements of community conditions. As a homogenizing discourse it pre-empts alternative interpretations by excluding residents who exercise self-determination. In Foucault's terms, "From all that happens, you won't understand, you won't perceive but what has been made intelligible because it has been carefully extracted from the past; and speaking properly, has been selected to make the rest unintelligible" (1992, 33).

This hegemony still dominates current thinking about neighborhoods. And while it has currency in research and practice, it is perhaps more striking how many residents use the same framework to explain their conditions and their neighborhood. Newspaper article titles reveal this thinking all too well: "Englewood violence limits summer for children: For one family, kids spend time in safe havens or under watchful eyes of parents" (Bowean 2009); "High School with Culture of Failure to Be Shut" (Ihejirika, 2005); "Durbin Hears Englewood Frustrations: Meets Gang Members to Explore their Side: 'A Lot of Broken Lives'" (Sweeney 2006); and "Englewood needs help repairing its human infrastructure" (The Chicago Reporter 1999). We also see it in documentaries such as "Englewood: The Growing Pains in Chicago" (Cochran 2011) and hear it in residents' own words: "There's no escape. . . . Living in Englewood, I feel like I'm robbing my children of their childhood" (Terry 2012). Commenters on web-posted articles, bloggers, and interviewees join the fray, blaming conditions on behavioral or cultural factors such as poor parenting, resident neglect, culture of poverty, defeat, crime, local disorder, and so forth.

These representations are not unique to Englewood or Chicago. Many US neighborhoods have experienced this trajectory of racial change accompanied by decline and rising crime and unemployment, and they have been portrayed in the same reductionist, moralizing, and victim-blaming ways. Residents are described as hopelessly trapped in the spaces where they belong. Although we find this common narrative at work in Englewood, we also find evidence that creative destruction via race and class—rather than people's *free* choices, character, or a natural cycle of decline—produced and continues to produce such conditions.

Creative Destruction and Spatial Racism

We turn to the insights of authors like Bourdieu (1988), Foucault (1995), and Lefebvre (2004) to see how creative destruction and spatial racism worked to transform Englewood into a ghetto. From this vantage point, Englewood is a socially produced and continuously re-enacted process in which dominant forces—policy makers, researchers, investors—have the upper hand but have to deal with local actions and reactions, contexts, and structures that complete the process. Using a genealogical approach, we can trace these struggles back and follow their trajectory forward to illustrate accumulated effects that frame the production of Englewood today. We include insights from Harvey (1989), who adds the perspective of a differentiated class reproduction by which neighborhoods become housing submarkets. From this perspective, the production of black and poor Englewood cannot be separated from the earlier production of white and middle- to working-class Englewood. Although each is distinct as defined by race, income, housing values, etc., both are in the same space, separated not just by time but also by shifting residential patterns that have sustained racial segregation in cities like Chicago. To see how this works, we first review in more detail the production of prosperous white Englewood and the subsequent disinvestment and destruction that produced black Englewood and transformed it into a ghetto.

PRODUCING A WHITE MIDDLE-CLASS NEIGHBORHOOD OF SUCCESS

Starting as a small settlement of railroad workers surrounded by farms in the 1850s, Englewood quickly urbanized through the establishment of subdivisions with well-developed infrastructures and the opening of institutions such as the Cook County Normal School in 1860 (later Chicago State University) that attracted middle-class professionals. Soon it became the home of Swedish, German, and Scottish immigrants with their Catholic, Baptist, Methodist Episcopalian, Swedish Lutheran, and German Evangelical churches and their respective institutions. Immediately following the Chicago Fire of 1871, waves of middle- and working-class whites made it their home due to its excellent location near their workplaces and its railroad connections to downtown and the rest of the metropolis.

In 1889, the city of Chicago annexed an area that included Englewood. Then the decision in 1891 to hold the Columbian Exposition in Jackson Park to the east of Englewood spurred a real estate boom. Development was further advanced by the completion of the Jackson Park elevated train line (1893) and its Englewood branch (1907), and the establishment of electrified surface lines on Halsted, Sixty-Third and Fifty-Ninth Streets (1896). Many other major developments, such as St. Bernard Hospital (1905) and Wilson Junior College (established in 1935 and renamed Kennedy-King in 1969), followed. Englewood's boom peaked with the success of the Sixty-Third and Halsted shopping district, anchored in the mid-1930s by a Sears Roebuck store located in a block-long building that included a major theater, a Wieboldt's, Becker-Ryan, and other department stores, various banks, and many small and midsize retail businesses and shops. At this point, the shopping district became the largest in Chicago outside the Loop, serving the entire South Side of the city. The neighborhood was also home to a large and successful working class employed in nearby manufacturing plants and the Union Stock Yards to the north.

Although the Great Depression was a major blow for smaller businesses, banks, and households, the population of Englewood kept growing, reaching ninety-three thousand people in 1940. In short, this was a period of settlement, growth, and consolidation led by the right population, attracting the right institutions and businesses, and receiving tremendous City Hall support, all amounting to a healthy and booming real estate and economy. As the regional industrial economy expanded, more European immigrants came seeking employment and housing opportunities. This match between economic opportunities and a working- to middle-class white neighborhood lasted until the 1950s, when racial turnover and ensuing deindustrialization turned the tables for Englewood.

PRODUCING A "FAILED" BLACK NEIGHBORHOOD

Around the 1860s, Englewood had a small black population. Two small clusters of low-wage railroad and domestic black workers lived south of Garfield

Boulevard near Stewart Avenue and near Loomis Boulevard and Sixty-Third Street and Ogden Park at Sixty-Seventh Street and Racine Avenue. For decades, they remained less than 1 percent of the population and related well to the rest of the community. This picture, though, started changing after World War II, when various factors combined to bring out some of the worst expressions of racism. The most critical were a new mass wave of black immigration to the city from the South, the bitter reaction of whites to the expansion of the Black Belt into their neighborhoods, the civil rights movement, Chicago's urban renewal program, racial steering and redlining, and the associated massive white flight from neighborhoods principally in the South and West Sides of Chicago in the 1960s and 1970s.

Restricted to the Black Belt, new black immigrants overflowed it, and their push into Englewood caused much anxiety among whites. Small incidents could trigger a violent reaction, as was the case in 1949 when blacks attended a union gathering at the home of a Jewish family near Fifty-Sixth and Peoria. The rumor that the home was being sold to a black family led to the mobilization of thousands of whites against blacks, "Jews, Communists, and University of Chicago meddlers" (Hirsch 1998). Feelings ran high, and whites reacted to black households moving to Englewood with bombings, arson, physical attacks, and pickets seeking to prevent black kids from attending their all-white schools. Despite the resistance, blacks had become 11 percent of the local population by 1950. In response, whites started "fleeing" west and southwest to all-white areas.

Underlying and accelerating these moves was rampant race-based speculation by the real estate industry and owners, which further stirred up the waters. Banks, landlords, and real estate concerns joined forces to profit from white flight and black immigrations. Panic peddling and blockbusting pushed panicky white households to sell in a rush. Banks and landlords helped blacks move in, charging them higher rates and rents because, as one banker stated, "When a lender makes a loan on a house, he looks at the total financial position of the borrower. The rate is determined by risk. The Negro has to pay a *higher rate* because he is not as secure in his job" (Stockwell 2005). Real estate agents "doctored" applications to qualify black households on paper for FHA-secured mortgages to acquire the properties from real estate agents at inflated prices. Owners of rental property engaged in illegal subdivision to rent to black households. Many owners used arson to recover some value of their homes through insurance. Along the way, banks redlined Englewood, making home purchase and maintenance difficult and contributing to high foreclosure rates. In response, the Metropolitan Housing Alliance requested in 1975 an investigation of ten savings and loans and mortgage companies, asking for government intervention to extend the time for Englewood homeowners to settle debts (Polk and Dumke 1999).

In the end, blacks had gained little from moving to Englewood. Not only had they helped push up home values, giving a second lease on life to the real estate there, they also had financed white flight and then *paid* dearly for it.[1] Working within the Chicago School framework, this change could be interpreted as a natural process of invasion-succession or a natural life cycle of decline. In truth, it was produced by a racist real estate industry (banks, real estate agents, landlords, and associates) and public policies (both on the part of the city of Chicago and the Federal Housing Administration), with white residents actively or passively playing into the hands of racism. An example was the gathering of young whites in Marquette Park in 1974–1976 under the Nazi leadership of Frank Collin that carried out violent marches into black Englewood. This provoked a defensive action by blacks and their supporters, who responded by marching into white areas.

Englewood became one of the first go-to communities for blacks (after the Black Belt), while the white population erected a Maginot Line on its western (Marquette Park), northern (New City), and southern (Auburn Gresham) white neighborhood borders. An Englewood resident moving in 1958 described the experience in these terms:

> As soon as the blacks moved in, and the whites saw they weren't moving out, the [for sale] signs went up like a disease. One house in her neighborhood that was owned by a black family was bombed. Threats of burning and bombing were regular occurrences. She and her siblings regularly were insulted and treated badly by those living in their own block. At some point, police protection was made available to families in the area. For nearly a year, officers were stationed around the clock on both the family's front and back porches. (Edman 2006)

To add fuel to the racial fire, in the early 1960s the city of Chicago constructed the Dan Ryan Expressway along the western edge of the Black Belt (allegedly to separate it from white east) and sliced off the east edge of Englewood. The city also erected a five-mile-long wall of public housing high-rises along the expressway, on the western edge of the former Black Belt (northeast of Englewood), further concentrating and segregating the black population.

Meanwhile, large retail malls such as Ford City and Evergreen Plaza opened in the 1960s, providing substitutes for the retail district in the heart of black Englewood. Although the city tried to save the district by converting it into a pedestrian mall (1964–69) and developing a new eighteen-acre campus for Kennedy-King (inaugurated in 1971), the intervention proved to be not only too little too late, but also inappropriate. Both Sears and Wieboldt's department stores closed shop soon thereafter (mid-1970s) as did the Englewood Theater, various banks, and the remaining department stores. Other major institutions such as the Englewood Hospital followed (1988).

Racial turnover in the 1950s brought the black population to 69 percent by 1960. High levels of rental housing (70 percent in 1950) helped the transition. Englewood became 96 percent black in 1970 while the Irish, the Swedes, and the Germans moved southwest to Morgan Park and Beverly on their progression to the suburbs. By 1980, Englewood and West Englewood had become all-black, forming a continuum with the expanding Black Belt to its east.

Englewood also became poorer. Local economic changes and race-based practices further condemned many black households to poverty. Deindustrialization, William Wilson (1987) claims, undermined the ability of blacks to advance by removing the ladder of mobility that had helped European immigrants succeed. Also, as jobs suburbanized, blacks saw their opportunities for employment and mobility shrink further. Shaped early on into a low-end labor pool, chronically deprived of opportunity and crowded into a secondary labor market, blacks had migrated to Chicago at a time when the opportunity for mobility through industrial jobs was closing. The combined forces of deindustrialization, disinvestment, racism, and segregation reinforced the "residual forces of class structuration" (Harvey 1989, 113).

Through the lens of creative destruction, spatial racism is more complex than simply segregating low-income blacks in neighborhoods such as Englewood. The exploitation of property and development of high-rise public housing helped to contain black demand to certain areas of the city while at the same time expanding white demand for suburban living. In the 1960s, housing options for blacks were limited even though neighborhoods were supposed to open up to them with the 1968 Fair Housing Act. For whites, the options were relatively limitless in space. For blacks, access to the for-sale market meant paying inflated prices, then having redlining and disinvestment limit their returns on investment. Over time, blacks were deprived of the benefits of property that European immigrants before them had had in the same spaces. As a real estate submarket, black Englewood stripped the assets of black home buyers while race-based lower property values and disinvestment minimized any profit they might have gained from selling their homes. In this sense, Englewood is more than a container of poverty; it's a space in which real estate also produces and sustains it. This is true for renters too, who usually have limited resources to purchase property but also have limited access to credit and jobs because they live in a poor neighborhood. And as gangs, drugs, and other practices found fertile grounds in the spaces created by disinvestment and racism, the state moved in to criminalize and police black Englewood in ways that worsened the situation for residents.

Constructing the Carceral Neighborhood

Harvey reminds us that "[t]he power to shape space appears as one of the crucial powers of control over social reproduction" (1989, 187). Naming has such power that it can be a major factor in engineering the fate of a neighborhood (Mele 2000). Even though racial turnover stigmatized all black neighborhoods in Chicago, Englewood became the leading site for one of the triggers of white flight: crime. In Chicago, Englewood and crime are synonymous. Mayor Rahm Emanuel "has used the word 'Englewood' as almost shorthand for gangs, guns and the dangers facing the city's children" (USA Today 2012). But Englewood already had a reputation on this front well before blacks moved in, although far less publicized and stereotyped. Probably most famous is the serial killer, Dr. H. H. Holmes, whose World's Fair Hotel in Englewood was used to lure and then kill women in the 1890s. The World's Fair Hotel was built with a gas chamber, secret passages, and a crematorium to dispose of the bodies, and Holmes was responsible for the death and disappearance of many women, as well as other illegal activities, before fleeing the city (Larson 2004). By 1957, the neighborhood was so plagued by crime that the Tridden League of Englewood, a local crime prevention group, formed an armed police force of its own to patrol it, alleging that the Chicago police allowed vice and crime to prosper and actually profited from it. After a rough encounter with the police commissioner, they disarmed, but the longstanding issues of corruption and vice continued well past racial change. And so did the crime associated with it.

Today, no other neighborhood in Chicago has the criminal brand-name recognition of Englewood. The media often locates crime incidents there even when they have taken place elsewhere. But crime did not cause the neighborhood's plight or at least it didn't when the community was white; rather it is part and parcel of a series of factors that feed on each other. Between 1950 and 1980 housing units went from 28,000 to 19,000 and the vacancy rate from 1.7 to 8.1 percent (Chicago Fact Book Consortium 1983). By 2000, Englewood had 15,210 housing units, 17 percent of them uninhabitable or vacant (Northeastern Illinois Planning Commission 2002). At this time, vacant and other houses were being used as a real estate tool that allowed investors (often white and from the suburbs) to purchase homes and then extract value by selling them to an accomplice. Taking advantage of rapidly rising property values in the city, they inflated prices often through bogus appraisals. As a result, Englewood's median home value shot up above the city median but then went back down in less than two years. As the *Chicago Tribune* explained, "The scams sent land values seesawing, scaring off families who might have bought other homes nearby. The vacant buildings deterred renters and beckoned criminals" (Jackson and McCormick 2005). This was not a small phenomenon. The *Tribune* found that sixteen of the thirty-four census tracts in Englewood and West Englewood were high-intensity fraud areas, which meant they had at least two frauds per tract and ten frauds per 1,000 owner-occupied housing units. One woman used a single address to generate mortgages for ninety homes.[2] In 2010, inhabited housing units had declined to 11,750.

Institutional life was another major factor in the production of black Englewood. According to a former white resident, "Much more important than the racial change was the instability and breakdown of community institutions. This was a tragedy. . . . Had there been less panic about the racial change, there would have been much less change" (Adams and Cohen 1959, quoted by Haines 2000, 32–33). White Englewood had a dense and well-synchronized set of institutions and associations. Branded as "the suburb of churches" (Haines 2000), white Englewood contained many churches operating for the most part as local branches of large institutions downtown. It also had many civic organizations and a large association for businessmen, which were well-connected both in and outside the neighborhood. Various clubs and ethnic groups also held the neighborhood together. Unfortunately, this did not encompass black newcomers, who had to start from scratch with fewer resources and no political standing or ties. The Southtown YMCA closed and the Kiwanis and the Rotary Club left, and several churches closed. The Southtown Planning Association, which coordinated real estate and commercial interests, folded, while Englewood's Business Men's Association went from 450 members in its heyday to 14 in 2000.

Many organizations left and took their assets with them. Valuable real estate formerly housing these organizations and other anchor institutions sat idle (e.g., the South Side Masonic Temple), was lost (e.g., most of the buildings in the business district and the housing surrounding it), or got recycled in denigrating ways (e.g. the Southtown Theater, which many considered a landmark, became a discount store). Most retail eventually left or closed, leaving behind empty stores and underserved residents. Race turnover meanwhile caused a massive loss in purchasing capacity. Such events sent the neighborhood into a downward spiral of abandonment and disinvestment, opening the doors to landlord abuse, code violations, demolitions, and tax delinquencies while also depleting its support systems. Mayor Richard M. Daley began a tear-down program in the 1990s that accelerated demolitions and set off an added burst of clearance and further depletion of property values. By 2010, approximately 7,500 lots were vacant in the neighborhood (Joravsky 2010).

Another major blow came from political changes. Prior to racial turnover, Englewood had a unified political representation with strong national and local ties. But following racial turnover, it fragmented in many ways. People we interviewed identified politics and political representation as one of the main culprits. The number of wards increased in proportion to population loss, as electoral politics and machine priorities gerrymandered Englewood every ten years. In the 1940s, the neighborhood had only two aldermen. This grew to three wards in 1947, then to four in 1961, five in 1992, and six since 2001 (see Haines 2000). Only two other communities in Chicago included five wards, the Near West Side and Humboldt Park (Haines 2000). Moreover, Englewood was included in three congressional districts. Although residents identify strongly with Englewood, political representation fragments their identity as each ward includes pieces of other neighborhoods. Aldermen, however, ignored grassroots calls to correct this. In 2011, RAGE (Residents Association of Greater Englewood) led a series of resident forums and asked the city to break Englewood into a maximum of two wards with clear majorities in the community area, but to no avail (Lydersen 2011). One alderman retorted, "all six of us are putting a little bit into Englewood and West Englewood, so they are getting more than what one alderman would get for the area."

Authors have characterized the incorporation of blacks into Chicago's Democratic machine as "plantation politics" (Grimshaw 1992). The machine slates the candidates and uses its wide net of patronage and resources to get them elected, and then controls them tightly. It also goes after independent candidates and makes sure that if they are elected they cannot deliver jobs or services to their constituents. Under the circumstances, residents have to default to the machine to get some attention and perks. Machine aldermen "put loyalty to the Machine over loyalty to their constituents" (Preston, Henderson, and Puryear 1982, 164) and independents could not deliver much to their wards. Our interviewees spoke of unresponsive, absentee elected officials with no accountability to the neighborhood or any collective vision (see also Levin, McKean, and Shapiro 2004).[3] In the candidate forums RAGE organized for the 2011 aldermanic election, residents criticized aldermen for privileging downtown and the central neighborhoods of the city at the expense of neighborhood like Englewood (see Cardona 2011). The fact that none of the six aldermen lives in Englewood speaks volumes. The combination of gerrymandering and plantation politics not only separates residents and politics but is also a major factor in the production of an underrepresented Englewood.

REINTERPRETING CHANGE

Human ecologists could argue that neighborhoods like Englewood are natural in a society where poverty and unemployment are expected in general and where both are higher for blacks than for whites. In contrast, political economists would reject this explanation and instead claim that these spaces are the means to reproduce low-wage workers (as mediated by race). We add that while structural and institutional racism has helped segregate our cities through uneven development and investment (e.g., see Squires 1994), creative destruction like what we are describing in Englewood has produced our ghettos and provided space for urban problems to be reproduced. Assuming as Harvey does that "hierarchical structures of authority or privilege can be communicated directly through forms of spatial organization and symbolism" (1989, 187), a neighborhood like Englewood is needed—perhaps even required—in the space of contemporary urban America. But they are not needed as places simply to house poor people of color to exploit in the labor market, but as places to literally and symbolically contain—"incarcerate"—a permanent class of people.

In turn, if the "neighborhood [is the] primary source of socialization" (Harvey 1989, 119), then we can expect black Englewood to produce individuals with habits and conditions conducive to being in the so-called underclass. The transformation of space tattooed on the bodies and minds of residents conveys the notion that racial inequality is natural and that blacks should accept not only the blame for decline but also the responsibility to fix it. This is evident when talking to staff members of community-based organizations about the problems of poor parenting, teenage pregnancy or kids raising kids, single-mother households, fatherless kids, and gangs. In the words of a nonprofit staff person who lives in the neighborhood, "A lot of it stems out of the home . . . many parents need to be trained in parenting, life skills, conflict resolution because most of our crime is caused by conflict, people who do not know how to solve problems at all." Taking this further, another said, "I know there is nothing I can do about that generation. They're gone. That's why I devote all my time to the younger children. They have no fear in their life, these kids, no fear at all, no fear of being shot, no fear of dying when they go home." (Staff member of community organization)

We see a neighborhood like black Englewood more as a "fragmented terrain held together under all manner of forces of class, racial and sexual domination" (Harvey 1989, 178). Thus, it can be argued that many residents had to fend for themselves by inventing ways to survive and that even if they tried to advance, they lacked the resources and opportunities needed to do so in the ways the market and society dictate. This includes the development of alternative tactics to avail themselves of what they needed—or wanted—and to construct their own identity. Using de Certeau's words, their "inferior access to information, financial means, and compensations of all kinds elicits an increased devious-ness, fantasy, or laughter," and their tactics "must constantly manipulate events in order to turn them into 'opportunities'" (1988, xvii). In contrast, academics and authorities brand such practices as ecologies of social disorder. Actually, this behavior is not unique to any one group of people or place. We *all* compose our own practices of appropriation and self-determination (and our own diver-sions) in the context of a hegemonic order. But when you are black and poor and discriminated against, that order and its representations are used to watch your behavior closely and, further, to criminalize your tactics, which then, in a potentially endless circle, spirals into yet other illegalized activities. The com-mon official response is to intensify discipline and punishment in a context of zero tolerance. In Englewood, the dominant official strategy has been race-mediated law and order. Both vigilance and encroachment have transformed it into a carceral space that excludes many from the opportunities that affluent (mainly white) neighborhoods are afforded: mobility, choice, and the ability to seclude themselves from public (and police) view.

At the end of the day, those without the means have to appropriate space by other means. Whereas gangs protect their turf and generate income and jobs as they can, homeowners seek appreciation through tactics of exclusion and social control (Harvey 1989), such as block club vigilantism. Yet in neighbor-hoods like Englewood, immobility and isolation increase with the removal of opportunity. As Harvey argues, "The power to shape space appears as one of the crucial powers of control over social reproduction" (1989, 187). In Englewood, this power lies with government and more precisely with the police.

DISCIPLINE AND PUNISH

Englewood has been a preferred site for police experimentation and training using ever more force and different schemes of discipline and punishment. For example, facing a wave of rapes in 1985, the police tried foot patrols, knocking on doors to make checks on people. The patrols were stopped soon after they started. While the police department claimed this was due to staff shortages, residents pointed to local resistance related to police intrusiveness and lack of respect for residents (Polk and Dumke 1999). Again in 1993, Englewood was selected as one of five districts for one pilot project, Chicago Alternative Policing

Strategy (CAPS). Hailed by many, CAPS has not made much of a dent in crime levels (e.g., Eigs 2002), but it has created a sense of mistrust and suspicion in many residents and others who see the CAPS meetings as opportunities for neighbors to tell on each other with no assurance that anything will be done.[4]

Residents have staged initiatives of their own and have tried to collaborate with the police. But many residents feel the neighborhood has been converted into a police state in which racism, zero tolerance, and disrespect is ingrained, leading to a generalized mistrust and even resentment (Barnes 2012a, Barnes 2012b). Examples abound of excessive use of force, with males subjected to asphyxiation and unwarranted searches and outright harassment, and suspicious shootings and encounters between the police and the policed. This environment has increased the number of conflicts and detainees to the point that a large proportion of the male population in Englewood ends up with a criminal record of some sort, which in turn justifies further police intervention and abuse.

As highly publicized crimes continue to bring attention to Englewood, policing has tightened. Responding to a flurry of killings—most of them gang-related—Mayor Emanuel and Police Superintendent Garry McCarthy announced yet another new major crackdown on gangs and drug marketers. This included targeting selected blocks where suspected drug dealers are operating, coming in with a small army of police in a highly publicized manner, making arrests, and then "cleaning up" the area. Taking it a step further, the mayor announced that the city was going to demolish up to five hundred homes in several high-crime areas including Englewood to clear out drug dealers. In reaction, neighborhood leaders have been ambivalent (Beaty 2012), warning about the lack of resources to address the rampant issues of poverty, governmental neglect, mental illness, malnutrition, lead poisoning, drug abuse, and joblessness that make Englewood an attractive environment for drugs and violence. While agreeing on the need for police in their neighborhood, leaders also see them as part of the problem, wondering whether the "overwhelmingly black neighborhood was about to be rescued by the cavalry or trampled in its charge" (Beaty 2012).

Not only has Englewood been a war zone among gangs and drug dealers, but it has also to an extent been one between police and residents. This "state of siege," residents report, has had serious effects on local safety and the integrity of households and families, while it has produced tremendous stress among residents. If not causing conflicts, it has reinforced them and promoted retaliation. Choosing policing as the main and often only strategy to address these problems punishes and criminalizes everybody; unless the factors incubating crime and stress are addressed, heavy-handed and extensive policing may only postpone or stifle a crisis that has deep social roots. Extreme lack of opportunity is a major factor: "the lesser the need for youth in the labor market is, the higher is the police" (Foucault 1992, 82). At the end of the day, for the unemployed and underemployed poor, the alternative often is between going to jail and joining the army (Foucault 1992, 64).

High levels of incarceration have deprived many families and households of their fathers and brothers and have deprived kids of positive male figures, which weakens families or causes them to disintegrate. As a result, Englewood shows a lower rate of married couples than Chicago (19 percent versus 31 percent) and nearly one-third single-mother households (32 percent compared to 13 percent for Chicago). Incarceration means a lower rate of "marriageable men" in the neighborhood. Add to that the practical near impossibility that those formerly incarcerated will be able get a job, and a different picture of Englewood appears, one in which blaming conditions on a culture of poverty or actual resident choices needs to be re-examined. What can we expect of fatherless youths growing up under such circumstances and undergoing so much scrutiny, in households with few resources to satisfy their needs and with so few prospects for tomorrow? These youths have the same aspirations as the rest of society but lack their opportunities; in these circumstances, when they join the drug trade or engage in criminal activities, they are pursuing the same career as their counterparts. They do not see much of an alternative.

Robert Hill (1988) argues that fragmented, unbalanced, deficit-oriented, static, and ahistorical approaches to these challenges have produced the wrong explanation and perception. Discourses of normalization and discipline explain Englewood's conditions as self-inflicted and thus that the community deserves strict actions to eradicate deficits. For them, the deviant and criminal black Englewood "merits" a "state of siege" that represses resident agency and creates alternatives that range between "falling-into-line or illegal drifting away" (de Certeau 1988, 130). But if, as we conclude, local violence is actually a manifestation of larger (mainly external) forces producing a carceral environment, then the "dissident" behaviors of residents need to be interpreted differently. While no violence should be condoned, we can see how it is a means for some residents to cope with conditions, to appropriate and take advantage of whatever is available in order to create their own opportunities, and to develop an autonomous sense of themselves within the suffocating constraints they confront in their everyday lives.

Focusing on the dialectics of spatial production and social reproduction reveals how a construct such as "the ghetto" reflects the powers that produce and maintain it. From this perspective, explanations for why a neighborhood like Englewood is the way it is rationalize specific social-management strategies and a "unique brand of power" to pre-empt or repress spatial contestations. Despite the constraints and repression this power discourse and associated actions impose on residents, "people are not fools" (de Certeau 1988, 176) or passive consumers; they create their own paths of self-determination (even if they make things worse in the eyes of the dominant power). In Englewood, we find, as de Certeau does, that "users make innumerable and infinitesimal transformations of and within the dominant cultural economy in order to adapt it to their own interests and their own rules" (1988, xiii–xiv). Hence, the more residents are forced into repressive discipline, the more they need to engage in diversionary practices to go around it and create their own identity.

Local Voices, Local Agency? The Struggle for Self-Determination

People become "subjects" through their engagement in social relationships. For many in Englewood, this seems to happen mainly through resistance, divergence, and coping. Interviewees and data suggest that most residents actually do not fit the neighborhood stereotype (i.e., they are not in gangs, drug pushers or users, rapists, welfare queens, criminals, or prostitutes) and that their daily life is infinitely diverse, intimate, productive, and nuanced. Clearly, most manage to live "normal" lives despite the stress and contradictory to characterizations of social disorder and chaos. Rather than watching things "crumble" around them, as urban ecologists would expect, they actually make things happen as they struggle through daily practices and join others to resolve problems in the neighborhood, on their block, or at home. In other words, instead of being helpless victims, even those branded as derelict also construct their subjectivity, power, and place, forming the basis for their circumstances and access to resources.

Resident actions are engagements in power relations and thus forms of resistance and self-determination pushing back the dominant power (Foucault 1995). Community building initiatives further illustrate local agency and the struggle to expand it. But it's not a homogeneous or single response, as in "the community" did this or that. What we found were many efforts, including wholesale participation in the national and local civil rights movement. As more blacks moved into the neighborhood, they valiantly endured the racial hostility of incumbent residents and neighboring community areas. Some chose to pursue interracial cooperation through the establishment in 1971 of United Block Clubs of Englewood, a multiracial organization seeking to bring everybody together in the construction of a new place in which both blacks and whites could prosper.[5] But when attacked by mobs from Marquette Park at different times between 1974 and 1976, some black residents formed their own block club to defend themselves and their properties. Some also worked to rebuild from scratch the institutional life of the neighborhood, to establish networks to address the deterioration however they could.

Unfortunately, defense against a racist outside frustrated some, making community network building particularly challenging. Many organizations have formed to address this and many other pressing issues and crises such as rampant disinvestment and displacing development, public neglect, unaccountable authorities and public representatives, and low-quality schools. Although limited in resources and confronting monumental challenges, different leaders and community-based organizations have kept the struggle alive over the years despite being cynical at times and angry at others.

Residents have pursued locally controlled political representation and have been able at times to elect some of their own grassroots candidates. For example, in 1971, the Sixteenth Ward elected as their alderman civil rights activist Anna R. Langford. Although she lost to the machine in 1975, her campaign continued until voters elected her again in 1983. Neighborhood churches and nonprofits have never stopped advancing community-based approaches to security and safety. Most recently, RAGE, Imagine Englewood If, Englewood African American Male Initiative, PEACE (People Educating Against Crime in Englewood), Englewood Safety Networks, and Black Youth in Action have led the effort and have strategized with residents. They have held protests, violence dialogues, youth summits, teach-ins, and candlelight vigils, they have provided counseling, support, and safe passage for students walking to school, and they have met with police and politicians (see Barnes 2012a; Beaty 2012; Moore 2012; Terry 2012; King 2008). Over time, the list of community-based organizations and actions has been long, as has resident resilience.

Research sponsored by the Woods Foundation concluded that "Englewood is rich with individuals that have the potential to build and strengthen the community" (Levin, McKean, and Shapiro 2004, 12). In contrast, some residents and researchers consider Englewood to be a fragmented social space, with different groups of residents and fledging nonprofits working at odds with each other, creating as much of a challenge as political fragmentation. And most attribute this fragmentation to the residents themselves. We see it differently: social and political fragmentation has been produced by the same forces discussed earlier, particularly by the scale and speed of disinvestment, public neglect, gerrymandering, and Democratic machine politics prioritizing City Hall's agenda over the neighborhood's. Whereas white Englewood counted on a strong business district to lead, unite political representatives, and provide funding for civic activities and organizations, black Englewood lost this in the transition. Whereas a more affluent white Englewood could support ethnic organizations and clubs, a much-lower-income black Englewood can barely support its large number of churches. Interviewees from local organizations emphasized the tremendous difficulty of securing the funding that would be necessary to make a dent in improving this environment, and some pointed to a sense of cynicism emerging from the lack of responsiveness to their plight, which, coupled with the structures of racism, have frustrated their efforts over the years.

Still, what remains has been held together by a multiplicity of small and large, formal and informal actions, organizations, networks, and other less visible but numerous initiatives. Haines (2000) estimated 300 block clubs and 160 store-front churches, each with its own civic associations or committees and services.[6] Resident trust in religious figures have made churches the principal anchors and the most consistent convening entities and spokespersons. Yet this too has added to the fragmentation. In the words of a resident, "there are too many factions and churches without a mother ship organization. Many Baptist churches are run independently by men. . . . It is their place, their kingdom, and they aren't willing to share it with anyone" (Haines 2000, 27). Such churches operate out of storefronts largely as independent quasi-businesses rather than as local branches of larger institutions synchronizing their work. The income of their leaders is a function of the size of their membership and the resources they can attract from funders or from income-producing services and ventures. Under these circumstances, they compete against each other for members and resources. Lay organizations, which have also been small, are often dependent on individual leaders who most often are religious. Many fold with the departure of the leader. Relationships between church leaders and parishioners and between lay leaders and constituents tend to be top down. Competing political loyalties further pull people in different directions. The same can be said for different organizations in Englewood that provide social services (e.g., the local office of the Department of Human Services and the Salvation Army), plan (e.g., Englewood Community Conservation Council), and provide advice (e.g., Advisory Councils of local parks).

In short, black Englewood has been and continues to be pulled and pushed in all directions by many different forces. This, however, is not because the Englewood neighborhood is a dysfunctional ghetto or a culture of poverty. To the contrary, we find many people and organizations that seek to improve the neighborhood and the lives of the people in it.[7] It's true that crises and major issues do generate togetherness and cooperation. As Haines notes, "The people in Englewood will not come out en-masse unless something sensational is happening" (2000, 29). But so do overlapping interests. Cooperation exists and has been successful many times. One example of this is the New Communities Program (NCP), which, as described in the previous chapter, was funded by the MacArthur Foundation and run by the Local Initiatives Support Corporation (LISC). NCP made Englewood one of its sixteen priority neighborhoods and appointed newly formed Teamwork Englewood as the lead agency.[8]

Teamwork Englewood was led by a charismatic and experienced leader with recognized skills and outside contacts. Nearly seven hundred resident and non-resident leaders and agency representatives engaged in a process that produced a holistic quality-of-life plan, *Englewood: Making a Difference*.[9] This process incorporated ninety-five different local and external, public and private groups and institutions and focused on physical improvement, business attraction, retail development, employment and training, housing, health, safety and security, education, recreation, civic engagement, services to special needs populations, and internal communications and networking. Launched by a powerhouse of funders, technical assistance providers, and City Hall, NCP put on the table some resources and support. Teamwork Englewood brought forces in the neighborhood together and facilitated a process that made many believe in a new beginning and a promising future. For the first time, four of the six aldermen came to the table and agreed to sit on the board of Teamwork Englewood; City Hall, which had formed a special cabinet of department heads to target selected neighborhoods, added Englewood to the list.

Despite many skeptics who felt the plan was ultimately about gentrification (D. Williams 2005), people in the neighborhood responded by actively participating in the different programs (contrary to assumptions about a culture of poverty). Yet only a few years into the plan, the board of Teamwork Englewood decided to shift its focus from developing opportunities for residents through community building, support services, and institutional improvement to a real estate agenda, apparently enticed by a booming market in the city. The charismatic leader left and much of the momentum was lost. Pursuing a real estate strategy continues to be important for those who see neighborhood development in terms of new for-sale housing and retail development.

Redeeming Englewood through Creative Destruction?

Creative destruction has been widely accepted as a necessity of accumulation. We prefer calling it *for-profit destruction*, which is mediated by existing social factors and, in the case of Englewood, by race. The main urban expression has been disinvestment associated with white flight, redlining, and public neglect.[10] In this context, Englewood has become a land reserve for much of the labor of last resort. For-profit destruction in this case refers primarily to real estate activity that allows a neighborhood to be destroyed through disinvestment, and then in turn using poverty to justify further devalorization and stigmatization. The final demise is to declare an area as unfit, dangerous, socially disordered, and out of control, a wasteland in need of drastic intervention. This circular reasoning turns a socially produced outcome into a representation of space that obscures the harsh reality of racism that, if in plain view, could be seen for what it is: unfair and immoral. As it is now, however, it's hard to know who or what is immoral here: the processes leading to Englewood or Englewood itself. From our vantage point of for-profit destruction, causality has been reversed so that the blacks who moved in, rather than the forces responsible for the disinvestment, are now the villains. Meanwhile, value depletion and real estate destruction set the grounds for a new round of for-profit redevelopment that brings in "the right people"—the deserving—along with the right real estate that can "redeem" the neighborhood.

We label this form of development *redemption* because the underlying logic formulates the process as a matter of redeeming the people and the neighborhood through real estate development and using discipline and punishment to reinstate order and rescue both people and place. It can also include an aesthetic component: rescuing and preserving "aesthetically valuable" architecture through historic preservation efforts. However redeemed, the result sought is an orderly, rational, for-profit city neighborhood regardless of whether Englewood residents can actually afford it. Underlying the moral rhetoric is the "potential" of the neighborhood associated with its location, which was also enhanced by the tear-down of public housing across the expressway and grandiose plans for nearby Bronzeville. All contribute to the potential value that could be extracted from Englewood's redevelopment in some proximate future.

A discourse of redemption led the city of Chicago, developers, local nonprofits, institutions, and even residents to once again pursue redevelopment of Englewood's former shopping district, which required both eliminating resistance and reintroducing capital investment but also controlling crime. This is where the powers of government (police, resources, budgets, and sheer power) make the difference. Englewood's rescue drive started in earnest in the 1990s, with the efforts to discipline residents described above. As already discussed, discipline was the responsibility of the police. Paradoxically, aggressive police action actually drew attention to the issue of crime and away from the potential benefits of redevelopment. Underscoring this point, an alderman pointed to the media's lack of interest in local events other than crime, "but the local ABC affiliate has a truck roaming Englewood with a police scanner, just waiting" (Interview with alderman). While the reporting of crime was a likely deterrent for many middle-class investors, it also produced real third-party casualties: residents and bystanders hit by stray bullets, police harassment of males and youths, intimidation, and so forth.

City Hall used each crime as yet another justification and opportunity to do more of the same. The state of siege, meanwhile, added to the minimal levels of mobility and opportunity as many residents became imprisoned in the neighborhood. Once criminalized and contained, Englewood is available for development forces to take. Serious redevelopment began in the late 1990s when Mayor Daley designated two tax increment financing (TIF) districts and announced in 1999 a $256 million plan to establish an anchor of revitalization on the east beginning with the intersection of Sixty-Third and Halsted including relocation of Kennedy-King (completed), commercial development (now in progress), a new police station (completed), and residential development (only a few units completed).[11] This project was to produce a ripple effect of private-sector investment. Adding to the push, in 1999 President Bill Clinton went to Englewood and pledged support through his New Markets Tax Credits initiative to attract private investment. Clinton, joined by Representative Dennis Hastert (R-Ill.), then Speaker of the U.S. House, announced this bipartisan plan in a highly publicized event, but no actual interventions followed.

Enthusiastic reactions reinforced these announcements and took success for granted. A millionaire professor born and raised in Englewood announced prophetically that "something extraordinary is about to happen," believing "there is gold in the blighted Englewood community" and "envision[ing] the area becoming a new, gentrified neighborhood of mostly middle-class blacks, similar to neighborhoods like Bronzeville and the South Loop" (Robinson-English 2007). The alderman of the Sixteenth Ward joined his voice: "Fourteen years ago we ended up on the front page of the *New York Times* for being the murder capital of the world. Fourteen years later, we hope to end up on the front page of the *Sun-Times* or the *Tribune*" for positive things happening (Spielman 2005). And an article in the *Chicago Sun-Times* announced with fanfare, "After decades declining into a crime-ridden social and economic wasteland, Chicago's Englewood neighborhood is poised for a comeback. Spurred by a $200 million, relocated Kennedy-King College campus that Mayor Daley described as a 'beacon of hope,' the Southwest Side Community is all set for a boom in commercial and residential construction" (Monroe Anderson 2006). Lastly, a broker for a realty group echoed, "Englewood will see soon the trend of continuous development and growth that other Chicago neighborhoods have seen. There are a lot of developments driving the area."

Wishful thinking? Apparently everybody at the top was for redevelopment. One alderman explained that "elected officials in the Englewood and West Englewood areas actually have a major focus to try to re-gentrify or revitalize them but do it in a way that keeps as many long-term residents as possible." A few housing clusters went up, mostly on the east side. This initiative, however, came principally from churches and nonprofits.[12] Much of the development relied on TIF subsidies rather than private investment. Institutions such as the Salvation Army and the Department of Children and Family Services also built new facilities in the neighborhood.

The ensuing rush of speculative buying and flipping (often without rehab) did further damage to Englewood. But the actual culprit was the Chicago Housing Authority's (CHA) Plan for Transformation that would demolish thousands of public housing units nearby. Prior to the plan's approval in 2000, CHA staff members contacted local real estate agents and visited Englewood to explore potential sites for relocation of potentially thousands of high-rise residents to be displaced from nearby public housing scheduled for demolition. Eventually Englewood and South Shore became two of the neighborhoods with the largest number of public housing relocatees. Interviewees claimed that this expectation and the actual relocation enticed speculative acquisitions often through suspicious or fraudulent financial schemes, in some cases to quickly fix up and rent to voucher holders or to sell to the CHA. A longtime Englewood resident we interviewed described it in these terms: "The CHA was trying to find places to buy, so they [speculators] flipped them, sold them to CHA, and made a profit. HUD and CHA are still a part of the problem of how these properties are not being used to the best advantage of the community." And based on research by Calvin Bradford (2008), some investors even bought homes from HUD that the agency had already repossessed from other investors who had used HUD money to rehab but then either walked away or foreclosed.

The quick and easy gains of these actions enticed more and more real estate opportunists, many of whom engaged in "creative" and at times illegal schemes. It also brought along the predatory and subprime lending industry, as speculators also created a non-CHA market profiting from the expectation of high returns on investment. When we asked one interviewee why Englewood had become a target for such activities, he explained that "[they] were doing it, using this whole game as well to probably flip it. And so it became pretty popular.

Well, you had properties that were pretty affordable. So you can get a better property, do some basic rehab, and flip it to $200,000, when most of them were worth only $60,000 . . . it was just a private market that was into flipping properties."

Depicting Englewood as a "real estate market of opportunity" and "a place for the taking" was akin to the men of the American western frontier grabbing available land. The city's announcements for different development projects and the CHA's plan produced this gold rush that encouraged borderline practices and fraudulent schemes. The representation of Englewood that justified increased policing and social control was that of a place to be colonized and appropriated, a land reserve temporarily housing disposable people. Largely dismissed by these representations of their deficits and criminality, residents are no different than the land; they are to be controlled and contained. And everyone was getting into the game. As one resident described it:

> Now see, you can get the property and still come back with your own appraiser who is crooked too and appraise it down. So, "give me the mortgage for that." So they were working all sorts of side deals so just they could get that loan again. . . . Eventually it got to the point where the blacks were doing it using this whole game as well. . . . At the same time, we had a lot of gangbangers become appraisers and brokers. Remember there was a moment when it was so loose that anyone could become an appraiser. . . . They weren't regulating the industry, anyone could become a broker. There were laws covering appraisers but even they were pretty loose too. . . . Professionals were coming in only to buy and flip; they weren't living there. (Resident and member of an ad hoc local group monitoring development in the neighborhood)

Ultimately, the strategies of speculator-developers, landlords, and brokers backed by financial institutions, predatory schemes, and government explain how the built environment and residential neighborhoods are produced (Harvey 1989) and destroyed. Speculation ran rampant up until the 2008 recession, when many investors simply defaulted, went bankrupt, and walked out, leaving behind what they called "opportunity properties." For example, Smith Rothschild Financial Co., a Chicago lender, acquired forty-nine properties in Englewood that had defaulted. Then, in 2010, in response to a lawsuit by Citigroup, Inc., over a debt, the company sought bankruptcy protection, which amounted to a de facto second default. In a deposition, their attorney testified that an employee had told him that they were not maintaining the properties. "Multiply the situation at 5964 S. Lowe by a couple of thousand and the devastation to

Englewood and West Englewood is clear" (Glanton, Olivo, and Mullen 2011).
Still, a local alderman expects that investment will continue since "there is a
growing number of investors buying up land in Englewood because they see the
potential. They are not doing anything with it but they're buying up the land and
in five years you'll see a rush to development." Along these lines, she advocates
"keeping the soil warm."

The 2005 NCP plan was launched in the midst of all this turnover and tur-
moil. Looking back at the NCP process that included City Hall and so many
organizations and institutions and the private sector, each bringing its own
expectations, the question posed in the aftermath of all this speculation and the
loss of nearly ten thousand people in a decade is: what will happen now with
the plan, which was based on a belief in a new era for Englewood?[13] It is not just
about keeping the soil warm, but also about tilling it and producing real results
for the remaining residents if the NCP plan is going to fulfill expectations:

> Our neighborhood is ready for a new period of prosperity and hope. We've lived
> through many years as a poor and downtrodden South Side neighborhood, where
> community improvement efforts haven't always produced results. We believe
> that era is over and that we, the residents and leaders of Englewood, are pre-
> pared to make a difference in the quality of life in our neighborhood. (Teamwork
> Englewood 2005)

In this context, different parties viewed the NCP effort differently. Inspired
by state-of-the-art comprehensive neighborhood initiatives, the plan pursued a
holistic intervention. But implementation was in the hands of multiple parties,
many acting independently to address an aspect of the plan and each relying on
its own resources. Institutions such as the police and the Chicago Public Schools
and the private sector did not transform their policies and approaches or add
resources to fit the spirit of collaboration that fostered the plan; instead they
continued to promote their own agendas. And despite their commitment, local
nonprofits, which are small, overstretched, and competing for the same sources
of funding, continued to work independently at very low scales. Although most
of the people we contacted shared in the initial enthusiasm it brought, they
pointed to the enormity of the task and the challenges created by foreclosures,
gang activity, public housing relocatees, bad schools, crumbling infrastructure,
and poverty. Many expressed concerns that are common to planning efforts
of this magnitude: resources and power, staff changes, poor communication,
competition for resources, and leadership. In their words:

> It's going to take all of us working collectively to do this. You eat an apple bite by
> bite. So it's whittling away at it piece by piece. Sometimes it feels like what you

did amounts to nothing at all but, when you find families that it has impacted, you know that was the right thing; when you find children that it has impacted, you know it was the right thing. (Director of development nonprofit)

It took record time to put the plan together following with monthly meetings and strategy sessions. . . . It brought aldermen together, got the mayor to pay more attention to Englewood and aldermen to deliver services, put a slew of programs in place. . . . What took place during those seven years was unexpected: you cannot underestimate the power of people's involvement once they are properly motivated and understand that they have some options and can in fact engage in some change. The plan had a brilliant start but petered out. . . . We created a sense of responsibility to deliver services to people and brought new ones. . . . But there was a sense of dismay after Teamwork Englewood decided to go in a different direction. (Local organizer)

It was the promise for a better life; people could come together and be a part of not just putting together a plan but being a part of the resources. But them saying "we don't have funding," that lost some people. We had all our committees in place. . . . Everything was going smooth but then a problem came up with the board. . . . So people get tired of that mess; but that's what's happening to us in Englewood: we are not connected; we have listservs but we are not connecting to people and people are losing faith. . . . And then people feel that they are fighting over the same dollars. . . . Everybody is out for themselves. . . . Even Teamwork Englewood, they are just starting up . . . but there is nothing going on . . . the vision has now dissipated. (Director of social service agency)

Putting aside these issues, a major challenge came from the task itself: not only do local organizations lack the scale, power, resources, and standing to resolve issues accumulated through the years and maintained by structural forces, they are not in a position to address the root causes. Their interventions have made a difference and continue to do so for some. Although going further than previous interventions in black Englewood, the process could not be sustained long enough or reach the scale that would be necessary to make the significant changes residents sought. Most important, though, real estate redevelopment can really only redeem the neighborhood (i.e., the physical space), not the residents. As the millionaire mentioned earlier said bluntly: it's about putting a new economy in place that will likely displace current residents, sending them "mostly to the South suburbs with Section 8 vouchers or dispersed among those that are not doing well" (Robinson-English 2007). In other words, the latest iteration of creative destruction in Englewood would shift the black "underclass" into new spaces of last resort, creating new opportunities to extract value from their neighborhood while concurrently blaming them for their continued poverty, resulting in new spaces of reserve.

Conclusion

For the most part, writings on Englewood have treated the neighborhood as a homogenous, natural, and rational totality. In contrast, we find a rugged, fragmented, and contingent reality in which individuals or groups negotiate their life, tracing different paths on the ground that do not necessarily fit neatly in the various theoretical frameworks. Within these rationalities, which act to flatten out experience, so-called users/consumers stubbornly elude discipline in the practices of everyday life (de Certeau 1988) trying to carve out their own autonomous spaces of self-determination and survival.

Neighborhoods like Englewood are produced by disinvestment, which in this case was introduced and then accelerated by racism. Under profitable destruction, they become places for the poor and destitute. The end of the neighborhood cycle is its final destruction to make room for a new cycle of accumulation. For some residents, redemption may be available, while others are condemned to the discipline and punishment they allegedly deserve. Along the way, inequality—as mediated in this case by racism—is obscured by games of power. Neighborhood advocates attributed the situation to the lack of opportunity. But accumulation trumps community when strategies rely on market-based or market-supporting discourses to achieve their ends. Meanwhile, redevelopment is displacing residents from so-called opportunity communities into yet other disinvested and racialized spaces, repeating the cycle. Under the circumstances, another path is necessary if development is to both improve their conditions on site and allow them to stay. Plans such as NCP, however, cannot do this as long as they rely so heavily on real estate strategies. In fact, they may actually facilitate gentrification and displacement. The next chapter brings together the stories of Pilsen, Bronzeville, and Englewood to show how representations of space, race, and class power were manipulated in the processes of creative destruction and destruction for profit to produce specific sites for consumption and accumulation.

CHAPTER 5

Constructing Flexible Spaces of Accumulation and Social Reproduction

> "Real property" (along with construction) is no longer a secondary form of circulation, no longer the auxiliary and backward branch of industrial and financial capitalism that it once was. Instead it has a leading role, albeit in an uneven way, for its significance is liable to vary according to country, time or circumstance. (Lefebvre 1991, 335)

The two previous chapters illustrate the trajectory of creative destruction in the production of two extreme types of neighborhood space—ghettoized and gentrified—and the ways dominant forces interacted to produce a different and highly complex experience in each case. This is the production of space under the new societal regime of accumulation. In this new regime, space is the industry and a major engine of accumulation. We explore in this chapter how in more general terms this shift has redefined neighborhoods and social reproduction.

Like Lefebvre, we believe that "everything converges in the problem of space . . . in the urbanization of all space" (1991, 222–23). In this way, the process of becoming urban moves to the core of human experience. Equally important, the production of space has moved to the core of political economy. Connecting space and political economy transforms both, and as a result our analysis of capitalism now must expand to include land as well as capital and labor. But land is not simply an input for production, it is also now a commodity. No longer tied solely to the production of things, space is "the thing" that is produced and, like consumer products, it must be continuously reinvented to expand demand in order to generate profits. Furthermore, Lefebvre reminds us that beyond suburbs, towns, and agriculture, new sectors are being created to facilitate this process of producing new space. This includes producing leisure space such as vacation homes and spas, but also tapping underground resources (e.g., hydraulic fracturing to extract natural gas) and above-ground resources (e.g., transfer of air rights for development).

We believe as Lefebvre that this new industry of space has many possibilities and gives new life to advanced capitalism as it plays multiple roles:

> As a mix of production and speculation . . . the ["real property"] sector oscillates between a subordinate function as a booster, flywheel or back-up—in short as a regulator—and a leading role . . . it retains an essential function in that it combats the falling rate of profit. Construction, whether private or public, generates higher-than-average profits in all but the most exceptional cases. Investment in "real estate", i.e. in the production of space, continues to involve a higher proportion of variable capital as compared with constant capital. (Lefebvre 1991, 336)

Speculation, as Lefebvre suggests, is an important factor in shaping the mix of capital. Not only does it affect the price of land but it also shapes production costs. As a result, prices have become nearly independent of value and the cost of production. This variability—even uncertainty as Lefebvre notes—has expanded capitalism through different practices that now produce space. Evidence of this is the concurrent exponential growth beginning in the 1990s in the number of real estate agents, the rapid expansion of mortgage brokerage firms, and the explosion of investment in mortgage-backed securities in the financial markets. As noted earlier, a new collective industrial code was created to track job growth in the finance, insurance, and real estate (FIRE) sector and expansion of the economy related to the development of land and buildings. Made up of existing labor categories, the intentional combining across traditionally separated (though historically interrelated) sectors marked a significant shift in how the production of space was looked at in US capitalism. Furthermore, while the housing bubble may have burst in 2008, the apparatus that produced it is still intact, seeking opportunity in the foreclosure crisis and taking advantage of low prices in once hot markets. This makes sense given the close interdependence between capitalism and the production of space today. As Lefebvre observed, however, "Not that the production of space is solely responsible for the survival of capitalism. . . . Rather it is the overall situation—spatial practice in its entirety—that has saved capitalism from extinction" (1991, 346).

Innovations allowing for quick circulation of the value fixed in space made this shift possible. Value that previously was realized over long periods of time was now immediately available through such instruments as the secondary market and derivatives; in short, financialization. At the neighborhood level, these instruments allow for the packaging and sale of mortgages with the subsequent recapitalization and a faster product turnover. They actually transform the role of the neighborhood in accumulation. Deregulation, in turn, set off unfettered speculative schemes that allow for the ongoing valorization of such instruments, and the value of housing became a function of how much it could be traded for. This is what we call the production of "flexible" space. Thus, at the heart of contemporary gentrification and ghettoization is the accelerated creation and destruction of value in its multiple forms.

Several things helped to make the industry of space flexible, fast-moving, and free-floating. A new global division of labor was deindustrializing US cities (Bluestone and Harrison 1982) and turning them into service nodes for the global economy (Harvey 2005). Financialization, especially through securitization, provided the capital that set off a construction boom comparable only to the Industrial Revolution, while deregulation gave carte blanche to the new FIRE industry and allowed it to dictate the terms for exchange and extend its "reach to space in its entirety" (Lefebvre 1991, 325). Combined, these forces made space the engine of accumulation, and the need to circulate its value led to the drive to turn the entire globe into a commodity.

To become effective, though, all these processes have to sort through or be aided by existing structures, such as FIRE, to unleash the dynamics of speculation and value inflation, which then creates new challenges. They also have to sort through existing struggles in place. The housing bubble "burst" and the subsequent crisis challenged developers and the FIRE industry to find new means to produce and consume space. The temporary solution was to switch from condominium to rental housing production. While framed as a response to new demand, it was also an effective way to quickly get back into development given the resources available and limited credit for individual purchasers. And while there was demand for it, the rental housing consumer being targeted was the same prebust condo consumer seeking the same type of space but now without the long-term risk and commitment. In turn, this new footloose consumer base can now consume housing like fashion, moving to the next new neighborhood or building with little effort or transaction costs. Of course, the response from developers has been to build more luxury rental housing!

But how did we get here? In simple terms, the shift began in the 1960s when our socioeconomic structure began transforming from being relatively inflexible to becoming a much more nimble system of value production and circulation and of capital accumulation and expansion. Looking back at the "crisis of the former regime of accumulation known as Fordism" and ensuing efforts to address it, restructuring via new forms of creative destruction and subsequent societal regime change fundamentally reshaped the relationship between capital and neighborhood, with deep effects on the process of social reproduction. This was and still is a process of trial and error in which resistance by existing formations and their corresponding agencies (e.g., workers and unions) was as important as the forces advancing flexible accumulation. Capital's first reaction to the crisis was to pull the floor out from under existing worker relations. As manufacturing jobs disappeared, many neighborhoods went into a tailspin, with high unemployment rates. Deregulation in the 1980s transformed work and started removing social protections (e.g., health insurance, welfare support, unions) and placing workers at the mercy of capital. The rise of the service sector largely polarized workers into either high-skill (e.g., financing, accounting, lawyering, advertising, and product development) or low-skill (e.g., fast food, sales clerk, and cleaning) positions. Along with this, the industry of space incubated by suburbanization moved center stage and the new FIRE industry formed. Combined, these forces provided the flexibility, mobility, scale, and speed that has been seeking to make the entire globe a spatial commodity and to make cities the leading sites to invest mobile capital. In this way, restructuring generated gentrifiable neighborhoods and the gentrifiers (Beauregard 1986), but also the ghetto and its expendable residents.[1] The *postindustrial neighborhood order* was born.

This Is Not Your Parents' Neighborhood . . .

In the industrial city, neighborhoods generally conformed to a hierarchical mosaic of spaces differentiated by class, ethnicity, and race, each of them more or less held together and supported by institutions (e.g., savings and loans, schools, churches, and associations) and social bonds (e.g., kinship and ethnicity). Real property played a limited role in the circulation and accumulation of capital. Residential space, while bought and sold in the market, was primarily the site of social reproduction; its use value was more pre-eminent than the exchange value, especially in working-class neighborhoods. Ethnic enclaves were "homes away from home" for immigrants and operated as launching platforms that they defended as quasi-nations.

Industrial city neighborhoods generally followed the rhythm of the workplace. It was common for working-class neighborhoods to be associated with nearby employers or employment clusters and for their ethnic workers to organize by trade, occupation, or politics. This order was supported by a long expanding period in which manufacturing provided mass employment and social mobility, at least for whites. As the University of Chicago sociologists observed, after moving up the income ladder, people often also moved into other residential spaces that gave them the symbolic distinction corresponding to their new and higher rung on the ladder. This made room for a new group of people from the lower rung to then take their place. Generally excluded from the mobility ladder, racial minorities were confined to interstitial spaces of containment—black belts, ghettos, and barrios—which, as discussed already, the Chicago School read as a natural order rather than as a form of containment, isolation, and discrimination.

The new postindustrial regime weakened and dissolved the industrial era order of space, revealing just how contingent these residential formations were in reality. Race played a major role in the breakup of the existing order, as many white middle-class families moved to suburbs that were more racially and socially exclusive, while minorities were confined in spaces that were disinvested in order to finance suburbanization. Not only did this shift maintain and reinforce class separation, it also moved a lot of "white power" out of the city while at the same time devalued the city neighborhoods left behind and now inhabited by the lesser races and classes.[2] In turn, the destruction of value turned these areas into land reserves—opportunities for later redevelopment—providing spaces for gentrification but also sites in which to contain lower-class families and racial minorities. While some ethnic neighborhoods remained intact, others eventually morphed.

The resulting new order of neighborhoods was a distinct dialectic of ghettoization (disinvestment) and gentrification (investment) in central cities surrounded by a sprawling middle class expanding into the surrounding suburban space. When first studied, gentrification was attributed to relatively affluent new households (so-called yuppies) moving into disinvested neighborhoods with unique architecture and advantageous locations in or near the center of the restructuring city. But as political economists like Neil Smith (1996) suggested, gentrification was really an industry in which the state subsidized and promoted the production of gentrified spaces for consumption, allowing higher-income families to take neighborhoods back from lower-income families at great gains for the industry, creating exclusive spaces of distinction.

Neil Smith (1996) characterized these dynamics as *revanchism*, the revenge of the (mostly white) middle-class against the (mainly minority) lower classes that had "taken the city" from them. As a Bronzeville gentrifier explained why he should get to live close to downtown and near the lake instead of near public housing and low-income residents: it is about class entitlement; contributing to the growth of the economy entitles him to live there. But this isn't a conspiracy, as Smith suggests. Rather than revenge, it's a continuation of the urbanization process, producing space for accumulation through creative destruction so that the capital of dominant classes can continue to generate value and capture rent while concurrently pushing disinvested spaces on to the lower classes, all in order to assure that the investment-disinvestment cycle continues. While the gains of the wealthy occur at the expense of the poor, this is more than revanchism; it is a whole process that produces and destroys value while concurrently creating space *wherever it is*, from which value can then be extracted. In this sense, no class is completely safe from the cycle of neighborhood destruction.

Gentrification as we have come to understand it certainly shows this yo-yo effect of value extraction vividly through the recolonization of the city and its neighborhoods, turning them into spaces of extreme consumption. From the first definition introduced by Glass in 1964, what ultimately differentiates gentrification from other forms of value production and appropriation is class displacement and replacement. In Chicago and other cities in the United States, urban renewal more so than individual investors led the way by forcefully taking strategic locations primarily occupied by lower-income blacks and Latinos to then pass on to private concerns for higher-end users who were primarily but not always white. A deeply subsidized process, urban renewal helped to unleash a middle-class rush into the inner city, producing spillover gentrification and benefiting the gentrification industry that built on the demand for new capital colonization opportunities. In these spillover-effect neighborhoods, real estate agents and individuals benefited from the demand generated by high-level service employees such as consultants, lawyers, and investment bankers moving in as the city transformed with the new and expanding corporate global economy.

But was this a deliberate act by the state? Yes and no. Following the initial state-led urban renewal and ensuing pioneering inroads into the inner city, gentrification came to operate as an industry on its own right, further capitalizing and expanding by the day. Paradoxically, the Community Reinvestment Act (CRA) that residents put on the books in the early 1970s that required banks to invest in their inner-city neighborhoods may have fueled gentrification in some places rather than generating resident-based development (Miller 2011). Independent of CRA, speculation pushed deeper and deeper into the inner city as the FIRE industry refined its practices of buying low, rehabbing, and flipping, as well as resident harassment, solicitation, code reinforcement, and historic designation. Still, gentrification followed a different trajectory in each city and produced a different outcome in each neighborhood, depending on local conditions, levels of resistance, players, location, prices, mixes, and so forth.

Bronzeville, Pilsen, and Englewood illustrate the full movement of immigrants coming to the city, beginning with manufacturing, the establishment first of the Black Belt and then the Latino barrio, the mass disinvestment following white flight, and the dislocation triggered by the latest production of space under the new postindustrial regime. While each generally followed the trajectory of ethnic settlements, the Black Belt, although apparently fitting the succession process, was a clear departure from it as it became an intentional community of racial segregation. In response, blacks within these communities formed a multiclass community of resistance, advancement, and identity. Similarly, Chicago barrios like Pilsen formed in response to repeated displacement, providing different Latino groups a space of their own from which to struggle for advancement, recognition, and respect.

When white flight landed in the suburbs it did not reproduce the ethnic segregation found in Chicago neighborhoods. Families merged increasingly into a single white race regardless of country of origin. The few remaining truly ethnic neighborhoods in the city, such as Bridgeport just south of Pilsen, remained intact, keeping nonwhites out until the 1990s, when many residents moved out either directly to the suburbs or to predominantly white middle-class neighborhoods in northwest and southwest Chicago next to suburbs occupied by families of similar ethnic heritage.[3] This pattern of white flight followed by disinvestment as capital left and banks redlined these new black and Latino neighborhoods was creative destruction en masse. As a result, Chicago became a *majority minority* and moderate-income city. In consort, deindustrialization launched the dual-service economy of high and low services that now defines the local economy and presides over the new neighborhood order that concurrently results in gentrification and ghettoization.

Bronzeville was the site of government-led creative destruction twice: first when it became a ghetto due to its high concentration of public housing and poverty, and then when government advanced gentrification by tearing down thousands of public housing units. Creative destruction of Englewood came first in the form of property devaluation, which caused mass real estate deterioration and tear-downs (with the ensuing depopulation), and later with rampant speculation, which led to foreclosures and further abandonment and disinvestment. In Pilsen, creative destruction came in the form of race-based property devaluation and the same public neglect found in Englewood and Bronzeville immediately following white flight. For all three community areas, creative destruction depleted the assets and wealth potential of thousands of families as property values fell, which then justified new top-down and outsider-designed plans and actions to "save" the communities, which then opened each up to investors, developers, and speculators. Each also illustrates a form of creative destruction generated by so-called public-private partnerships and the unnatural processes that tie them to flexible accumulation: value depletion, production, and extraction.

Making Space for New Neighborhoods: Public-Private Partnerships

Harvey argues that a major role of government today is to produce markets for the private sector and to generate the proper business climate for them to prosper. The primary form this work takes is public-private partnerships (PPP), in which government and the private sector work in concert around the new priorities of accumulation. Public-private partnerships are the staple of contemporary urban redevelopment efforts in the United States and elsewhere. With growing concerns in the 1970s and 1980s over the level of public debt and decreasing federal funding for cities, local governments began to seek out private capital to invest in infrastructure. The strategy assumed that the public benefit produced through the partnership would be at no or little cost to the public. While this assumption has been proven wrong in many cases, there continues to be thousands of such arrangements actively in use. For the most part, each PPP has its own unique origin that reveals the particular relationships driving the partnership as well as the formal structure it takes.

In Chicago, the PPP mechanism of choice is the tax increment financing (TIF) district. TIFs allow the city to subsidize developers on the premise that development would not occur "but for" the TIF. City intervention in the market is justified by the lack of investment, which has reduced quality of life and has limited opportunities. People have been disciplined into accepting this premise and the subsequent development on the basis that it will generate employment opportunities, higher housing values for homeowners, and improved infrastructure for all. Overall, TIF has been a mixed bag in Chicago. Regarding the productive TIF districts, some have argued (O'Toole 2011; Dye and Merriman 2000) that the transformation would have likely occurred without the incentive, and in some cases the results have actually harmed existing residents by pushing up rents and taxes.

After twenty-five years of TIF, Chicago has produced some successful economic development projects (e.g., see Hudspeth 2011). Despite rerouting more than $1 billion in taxes to spur development and generate jobs for Chicago residents, however, the downtown lost nearly twelve thousand jobs between 2002 and 2008, most of them held by African Americans living in Chicago's South and Southwest Side (Caputo 2011). In the meantime, the community area known as the Loop increased its population by more than 80 percent following a significant growth in high-end residential space downtown and the community areas surrounding it. With the median income in 2010 at about $78,000, it is just below Lincoln Park—one of Chicago's wealthiest communities—and $30,000 higher than the city as a whole (Voorhees Center 2014). As mentioned in chapter 3, one can argue that the 1958 *Plan for the Central Communities* and the follow-up *Chicago 21 Plan* of 1973 developed under the first Mayor Daley were finally implemented thanks to his son.

In Chicago, neighborhood redevelopment usually begins with a plan. The transformation of Bronzeville was engineered in two steps. First, the Mid-South Planning Group developed the *Mid-South Strategic Development Plan: Restoring Bronzeville* in the late 1980s that gave shape to a long-standing dream of restoring the area to an earlier grandeur imagined by a group of local notables. Long concerned about the low-income black area surrounding them and the inability of urban renewal to take over the adjacent black communities, several large white-led institutions subscribed to the idea of developing a mixed-income, black-pride destination neighborhood. Initiated from the inside by residents, this vision actually gave an entry point to the outside. The next step was a takeover by City Hall, which in taking stewardship reformulated the plan to fit its larger agenda that many argue was first articulated in the 1958 *Plan for the Central Communities*. This included strategies to entice investment by black and white developers associated with the mayor's growth coalition. Banking on the gentrification of the South Loop adjacent to Bronzeville and looking forward to a continuum of development between downtown and Hyde Park, the partnership moved fast to generate momentum and scale in order to turn the area into a commodified marketplace that would be a local, national, and international tourist destination.

In Pilsen, the growth coalition controlling City Hall began pushing plans on the community to entice outside investors in the early 1970s. Despite opposition that held development at bay for a while, many of the community's notables were seduced into helping open up their neighborhood to gentrification starting in the 1980s. While not a formal plan to change the physical space, the vision of a culturally focused, mixed-income community sold to both white and Latino gentrifiers opened up Pilsen to developers pushing south from the Near West community. This too began with plans, starting with the 1958 *Plan for the Central Communities* followed by the 1979 proposal for a World's Fair and a plan to transform the Pilsen Triangle into el Zocalo in the tradition of the Mexican town center, and most recently Pilsen's *Quality of Life Plan of 2000*. While the last plan included the preservation and production of affordable housing, when it was updated in 2006 it also included the 391-unit Centro condominium development, the so-called workforce housing to be developed by a PPP that included former HUD secretary Henry Cisneros, a well-known Latino face. This development deal fell through after the limited liability corporation filed for bankruptcy, and as of early 2016 no development has taken place and the lot sits empty. All these plans, however, reflected the strong commitment to transform Pilsen into a middle-class community through the machinery of gentrification.

Englewood also is experiencing the spillover effects of gentrification, but in a negative form. The City Hall–led external engineering that helped produce further deterioration after blacks moved in produced *a neighborhood of last resort*, and its real estate was there for the taking. Investors bought up houses in the late 1990s in anticipation of thousands of families that eventually would be displaced by the Chicago Housing Authority's *Plan for Transformation*. Before the plan, the CHA had already begun demolishing public housing high-rises and closing low-rise projects next door in Bronzeville, claiming they would eventually be redeveloped. Supported by Englewood's *Quality of Life Plan*, the possibilities of tapping into the housing choice voucher market, along with a plan to redevelop the east side of the neighborhood, unleashed unfettered buying of properties at basement prices. Encouraged by the possibility of a renaissance, flipping and speculative acquisitions jacked up prices briefly in 2002–2004 to levels that made some believe the area really was on its way up. This environment made room for creative schemes, some outright illegal, that turned Englewood into a free-for-all market and that, relatively speaking, led to little actual development despite many real estate transactions. What happened in Englewood exposed new forms of unregulated practices and new value-extraction schemes used to stir up the production of space via creative destruction across the board. Englewood shows how money is also made in the destruction of value. These processes illustrate the ways creative destruction produces different markets for different populations and the underlying forces teaming up to produce them. These processes appear to be merely economical and driven by the real estate industry, but the city enables them by providing the platform on which they operate while using its powers to remove obstacles and halt the opposition.

Together, these three cases demonstrate how government can create a market in a neighborhood by subsidizing private investors to develop in it while also controlling, often through community leaders, how residents within the space respond. These three neighborhoods also show the investment-disinvestment cycle of capital moving from one geography to another, extracting value through processes of creative destruction in which "[t]he 'truth of prices' tends to lose its validity" (Lefebvre 2004, 337). In other words, the price of a property depends less on value and production costs and more on what it—and the space it is located in—can get in today's highly financialized market. Acting independently within the larger real estate scene, disinvestment brings property values to the bottom in some neighborhoods, producing areas of reserve for possible future deals, while investment brings new areas to the market or restarts the cycle in disinvested spaces. This process frees up capital for investment by extracting value and it creates demand for other spaces to lure that capital. Either way, capital picks its target based on the value that can be extracted through the manipulation of real estate. This includes adding value without having to actually invest in the neighborhood (e.g., Pilsen becomes a hot commodity because it is being talked about in the *New York Times* and the *Guardian*).

Even though they are independent forces, disinvestment and investment work in combination to continuously produce neighborhoods for both lower- and higher-income families, each with its own dynamics of value production and extraction and differentiated social reproduction. But it is neither an even process nor necessarily in balance. In Chicago, the number of hyper-ghetto community areas has grown faster than the number of gentrified community areas, yet the gentrified spaces have more people living in them (Voorhees Center 2014). In part, this is the result of population loss and replacement. Between 2000 and 2010, Chicago had a significant loss in population (200,000 people, nearly 10 percent of the total), and 90 percent were African American, of which most were children (130,000). The community areas where the population decreased were predominantly black and poor. The communities that retained their populations were the few long-standing upper- and middle-income communities, which are for the most part majority white.

Looking at these changes in terms of the production of space, neighborhoods with lower-income families, particularly African Americans with school-age children, appear to be expendable. But so too now are neighborhoods for the middle class given the decrease in the number of people in this income bracket and the decrease in community areas for them in Chicago since 1970 (Voorhees Center 2014). Suburbanization and gentrification belong to the same regime of accumulation. But while this class is generally wealthier, the geography of class has shifted nationwide with the increasing suburbanization of poverty (Kneebone 2014). With the city-suburban divide breached, a small but growing body of evidence suggests the question: is suburban gentrification next?[4]

The 2008 recession appears to have sped the cycle up, as deflation of property across the board has created the next path of investment-disinvestment (see Niedt 2006; Charles 2011). Whether a neighborhood is in a city or a suburb, the postrecession rebound is uneven, with values rising quickly in areas that had been relatively stable and above average while slow to rebound in areas that had been below average (Keely and Bostjancic 2014), creating new challenges for those at both ends of the gentrification-ghettoization spectrum as well as all in between. These dialectics in the city and the suburbs speak to the increased importance of space under this regime, which was unleashed first by white flight and then by policies and partnerships that encourage gentrification and ghettoization. In fact, the suburbs are using the same types of public private-partnerships to induce reinvestment (e.g., TIF). But all this work, as our analysis of the representational dynamics accompanying these processes shows, could not happen without the power to define, characterize, and represent space, and specifically to shape and reshape it by using class and race to determine winners and losers in ways that appear natural and deserved.

New Challenges for Social Reproduction

Fast-paced accumulation for the sake of accumulation poses a particular threat to social reproduction through the intense commodification of daily life. The removal of supports and high levels of male incarceration, employment insecurity, and stagnant wages further compounds these circumstances for lower-income families. The response from government over the years has been to withdraw and shift its assistance to the private sector. Neoliberal in nature, these changes in the name of privatization and social austerity also tie to the production of space. To start, welfare reform that began with Ronald Reagan and then solidified under Bill Clinton removed the guarantee of some form of ongoing support for families and individuals by setting time limits and forcing them "to make it on their own" regardless of their ability to do so. For people of color who historically have had much higher rates of unemployment and underemployment than whites, increasing dependence on the market was not an even-handed policy. Furthermore, cutbacks in federal support meant strains on local tax bases, which in turn resulted in even more aggressive efforts to "keep the rich and powerful in town" (Harvey 1995, 977), on the premise that they directly contribute more to the tax base but also because indirectly they are expected to create jobs from the services and goods they consume.

Producing markets for private investment that will attract and retain higher-income consumers—whether as residents or tourists—has absorbed an increasingly higher proportion of the public budget at the expense of services to the poor and even the middle class. To this end the city of Chicago has shifted an estimated $600 million from public schools to support private investment through its nearly 180 TIF districts. And when the schools faced a $100 million shortfall in 2013, instead of pulling money from this pot of funds, which could have been used to improve school conditions, the mayor committed that same amount to build a basketball stadium for a private university that plays only eighteen games a year in Chicago (Spielman 2013). It will be near the McCormick convention center in the expanding South Loop, which is part of the mayor's billion-dollar effort to boost tourism (Brennan 2013).

Around the same time, the mayor announced the closing of fifty public schools affecting twelve thousand students. Nearly all were in lower-income African American communities that had lost population the previous decade (Kunichoff 2014). While the justification was declining enrollment levels, these communities still had a higher proportion of children than the city average and definitely above the rates in higher-income white communities. So where were these children going to school? Many attended the charter and contract schools that opened as the result of an aggressive campaign to privatize Chicago public schools in order to turn them around, although research based on test scores has shown that this is not happening (Orfield 2014). At the same time, CPS invested millions of dollars building several select-enrollment high schools, some that now are in the top rankings statewide and nationally. While there are about the same number of buildings distributed north and south, there are about twice as many slots in schools in middle- and upper-income community areas on the North Side.

The uneven development of educational opportunities matters in a deindustrialized economy. Higher-wage jobs that have been created require a higher level of education, which many either cannot access or cannot afford, leaving many more people condemned to low-end jobs with nonlivable wages. Complicating all this is continued discrimination in employment, which further limits access to jobs with mobility opportunities that often are created using tax dollars. While this in no way justifies extra-legal informal activities and illegal businesses, many have resorted to these while trying to scrape out a living. This is not to say that only lower-income people resort to such activities; higher-income people do too, but usually in more sophisticated and invisible ways that are more likely to avoid prosecution and criminalization. As described in chapter 4, extreme policing, small and confined markets for income-producing activities, and other aspects of poverty make informal and illegal businesses far more risky and visible in already struggling communities. This results in high levels of incarceration and felonization that take them (and their families) out of the game. As Lowenthal (1977) explained it, in addition to the monetarized market system, the lower classes also rely on the "social economy," which he defines as the "non-monetarized, non-market systems of production and exchange" in which "many goods and services are provided through an economic system that is based on the network of social relations" (312–13). For many now the social economy is their only economy, which opens up even more opportunity for predatory behavior within their own neighborhood and which can be amplified further by the dislocations and disturbances occurring in the economies of other neighborhoods.

The intensified efforts to commodify neighborhoods and social reproduction have ejected many lower-income people from spaces of opportunity into residual spaces of reserve, confining them to the carceral neighborhoods described in chapter 4. In this way, the new regime sinks more city residents deeper into poverty and undermines their critical pillars of survival. If we add failing schools and socioeconomic isolation to the picture, we can see the new challenges of social reproduction that are complicated further by a regime that justifies deep cuts in public support and services in order to build sports stadiums.

The Ebbs and Flows of Neighborhood Life Today

Historically, neighborhoods have been conceived of as sites for social reproduction that should be filled with the necessary elements to support families and sustain life, which Lefebvre described as "a secondary form of circulation" (1991, 335) in the flow of industrial and financial capitalism. While Harvey (1989) added more nuance by pointing out the role neighborhoods play in separating groups through a class-differentiated social reproduction process, Lefebvre pushed us to see how this also varies depending on the societal regime it occurs in. So in our current regime, while neighborhoods continue to retain the primary function of differentiated social reproduction, they also now have an added significant new role: they are a major means to reproduce capitalism itself. Furthermore, the people living in neighborhoods also contribute to its production as a commodity, whether as active participants or not. As Katznelson reminds us:

> Most people live on the margins of history. They experience its flux, their lives are shaped by inherited and shifting limits, and their daily behavior testifies to the constraints on their lives. And yet, people are never merely passive agents of structural imperatives. Within lives whose definitions and possibilities are largely created for them, they create—families, symbols, solidarity ties, beliefs, friendships, institutions, rebellions. In short, people create a culture, which in all its dimensions composes a set of resources for living in society and for affecting the contours of society. (1981, 1)

In Pilsen, for example, the space is occupied by a variety of people now, show-ing evidence of gentrification and resistance. Gentrification has (so far) settled in clusters along the east side and is expanding to the middle of the neighbor-hood. These census tracts have significantly smaller households, fewer chil-dren, higher incomes, and a lower percentage of Latino residents than to the west. In part, the majority Latino tracts to the west may reflect resistance, but it also may be that investment over time has raised the value of these homes and therefore the price of gentrification, making it harder for others to enter the market. Longtime residents—owners and renters—have continued to produce their own spaces in the midst of this restructuring. There is the coexistence of a shared identity in a few spaces (e.g., a community garden, the farmers market, a couple of bars), but most other spaces are either off-limits to one group or the other or are only sites of temporary interaction and exchange.

The tumultuous ups and downs produced by wheeling and dealing and the uprooting of people in Bronzeville, Pilsen, and Englewood are both manifesta-tions of and responses to the restructuring associated with the new role neigh-borhoods play in American culture. In the current regime, in which it is often development for development's sake, the accumulation-neighborhood relation-ship has assumed a new, uneasy form. As local governments have lost much of their ability to provide the basic services that foster social reproduction, they now rely heavily on higher property taxes that development along with land sales and spillover effects can generate. Government now helps commodify its neighborhood space, joining the fray as a gentrifying force by welcoming the creative class and marketing culture. Now house trumps home, symbol trumps reality, commodified culture trumps lived culture, poverty is criminalized, and the poor are made disposable. In short, when space becomes overcommodified, the ability to stay in the neighborhood is an absolute function of the ability to pay. This is playing out differently in all three neighborhoods and across the city.

The dual character of commodity and community—commudity—makes neighborhoods into sites for opposing interests that at times may converge or accommodate. But even when they coexist, they always represent "perhaps incompatible values" with a "strong but asymmetric and ultimately antagonistic interdependence between accumulation and community" (Mollenkopf 1981, 320). Looking at this relationship over time, Mollenkopf argues that "what works in a period can frequently become an impediment in another" (1981, 324). Along these lines, we agree that the accumulation-community relationship also changes over time, from regime to regime. As regimes change, however, the responding production and appropriation of space does not necessarily eradicate and replace all pre-existing marks. After all, these pre-existing social spaces are the raw material for the production of new ones. Space, then, is appropriated in different ways as dominant forces work to remove what is not needed but also to retain, accommodate, or tolerate what fits in or can coexist with the new regime. This appears to include families with children, which are accommodated by privatizing public schools and by appearing to give parents a choice in where they send kids.

As representations of space, neighborhoods too have been appropriated in specific ways in this new regime. One example is the means by which the neighborhood itself and the change that occurs within it is represented. As we saw in Bronzeville, Englewood, and Pilsen, categories of identity are linked, decoupled, and relinked in different ways with the value of real estate, sometimes helping to sell it and other times hindering sales. The same holds for ideas, values, and political systems, which can often shape the space of a neighborhood independently of the experience of its occupants. Whether it is the image of a vibrant Latino community that attracts middle-class whites to art galleries in Pilsen or a black heritage that attracts black investors to buy in Bronzeville, representations of neighborhoods are produced through sets of relationships that are neither one-sided nor simple to interpret or categorically explain.

Re-presenting Neighborhoods

Looking across the details of change in the three community areas examined so far, we find structuring forces and conditions affecting all and shaping each in different ways. We do not intend to produce an absolute or totalizing explanation of neighborhood change. While there are spatial concentrations of low-income populations, we know that neighborhoods are highly differentiated internally and that social relations within, between, and outside each span a wide range of experiences and points of view. Still, the nature of residential development and segmentation does bring together households of similar incomes around their habitus, resulting in spatialized social reproduction by different class segments. In Bronzeville and Pilsen, the presence of a wide variety of incomes translates into differentiated purchasing power, differences in lifestyles, and struggles between the structures in place and those being introduced by investors and public agencies.

Both Pilsen and Bronzeville are still majority low-income communities. In Pilsen, some longtime residents are holding on to their social fabrics and histories and are resisting gentrification. In Bronzeville, there really is no visible antigentrification front other than a small group advocating for affordable and public housing. Yet despite the support of the city and fairly aggressive gentrify-ing forces in action, not a lot has happened in this neighborhood. Investors have had a hard time redeveloping empty lots, finding a profitable reuse for many disinvested structures, or establishing an upscale retail and cultural destina-tion. Some link this to the fact that it is a majority black community (Hwang and Sampson 2014), while others point out that until the people and their behaviors that intimidate gentrifiers are gone or at least significantly reduced, the neigh-borhood will not change (Anderson and Sternberg 2012).

Rather than a homogenous community shaped by the forces under discus-sion, Englewood is also more diverse than most believe, with homeowners, renters, squatters, homeless people, households making livable wages, public employees, businesses of different kinds, formal, informal, and illegal econo-mies, various institutions with a range of volunteers, community-based orga-nizations, and churches of multiple denominations. There is a wide range of incomes, educational levels, social capital, roots, and so forth. There is a level of community ownership among some groups and individuals working sepa-rately and collectively. Rather than a single community, there are actually many subcommunities brought together in space by the forces shaping and reshaping neighborhoods and the practices of everyday life.

We contend that these are *hybrid spaces* in which different forces produce and fight different struggles, sometimes parallel, sometimes overlapping, some-times diverging and sometimes converging. Similarly, although pushed by the power of capital often working in tandem with government, gentrification and ghettoization are not a fait accompli even when plans are made and apparatuses put in place intended to produce that outcome. Many contradictions shape and reshape the social relations that produce the space of a neighborhood. Most of the displaced and downtrodden, for instance, are not passive actors sitting idle and helpless as chaos ensues, but instead use what resilience and power they have to appropriate space, create openings, and make their own markets where the marketplace has failed. In other words, they take charge despite their dispossession and perceived disposability, something we will illustrate more in the following chapters.

The new centrality of space converging in urban areas, but also dispersing urbanization outward, has pushed residential space from a subordinate role in social reproduction into the primary sphere of accumulation. The actors work-ing in neighborhoods, however, are not all driven to commodify space, and in fact we saw groups that fought against it. Still all are affected by this drive to commodify space since it is a key component of contemporary capitalism. And while each case has a different trajectory, common threads also connect them.

As the previous chapters demonstrate, the production of uneven power rela-tions in neighborhoods, no matter how seemingly fixed or veiled, unleashes different forms of resistance. History also suggests that the power relations embodied in neighborhood space have to be re-enacted on an ongoing basis and that managing resistance takes different forms: violence (symbolic and actual), displacement, concealment, or postponement, holding opposition at bay and remaining dominant even when unable to completely eradicate it. This dynamic is examined next in the formation and subsequent struggles and resistance in three highly commodified spaces, one based on cultural identity, one based on sexual orientation, and the last based on poverty. All are in the space between the extremes, moving toward gentrification but in very different ways, and each demonstrates challenges for neighborhoods as sites for social reproduction.

CHAPTER 6

Selling the Neighborhood

Commodification versus Differential Space

> A new space cannot be born (produced) unless it
> accentuates differences. (Bourdieu 1992, 52)

On June 15, 2013, the Puerto Rican People's Parade (aka the neighborhood parade) and the 34th Puerto Rican Parade (aka the downtown parade) merged for the first time, holding a single march along Division Street between Western and California. For Puerto Ricans (PR) in Chicago this is Paseo Boricua, the heart of the PR community. Having the parade there reinforced efforts to make the area a permanent home. Two weeks later, on June 30, the Chicago Pride Parade marked its forty-fourth anniversary by marching down Broadway and Halsted North (HN), the core of Boystown.[1] Participants hailed Supreme Court decisions that had gotten them closer to their goal of equal marriage rights while at the same time criticizing the Illinois legislature for failing to pass the gay marriage bill.[2] Both parades are yearly milestones of these two "communities" in Chicago, but whereas the gay community has been able to establish an identity and a place, Puerto Ricans continue to struggle.[3] Each group also has a neighborhood retail strip that has become a political, cultural, and economic stepping stone, reflecting efforts to gain recognition and physically locate their community.

Lefebvre argues that "space is political" (2009, 170) and that "groups, classes or fractions of classes cannot constitute themselves . . . as 'subjects' unless they generate or produce a space" of their own (1991, 416). This chapter focuses on the spatialized dynamics associated with the two communities' struggles and the ways the forces of capital and the state redirect their efforts. Starting with the establishment of Paseo Boricua and Halsted North and the role each played in the dynamics between community and accumulation, we argue that while forces within these communities carved out differential spaces, commodification has worked to turn them into spaces for sale and what they represent (i.e., gayness and Puerto Ricanness). These cases reveal the contradictions between building spaces of recognition and the flattening effects of commodification and repression.

Paseo Boricua: Spatializing the Puerto Rican Struggle

On Three Kings' Day, January 6, 1995, Mayor Richard M. Daley (1989–2011), accompanied by Latino leaders and elected politicians, officially recognized the PR community through the naming and designation of Paseo Boricua and the inauguration of two fifty-nine-foot-tall metal Puerto Rican flags, each weighing forty-five tons, at both ends of the strip. Following decades of struggle against Puerto Rican displacement and racialization in Chicago (F. Padilla 1987), this recognition was neither city-initiated nor did it compensate for the racial policies and practices of the first Mayor Daley (Richard J.). It did, however, introduce a form of commodification that was contrary to the community consolidation that Paseo Boricua proponents envisioned, and it pitted the Puerto Rican community against the administration.

The presence of PRs in Chicago dates back to the late 1800s, but the first large waves arrived in the 1940s and 1950s as a result of coordinated efforts between Operation Bootstrap, an initiative of the PR administration to ease unemployment in Puerto Rico, and the efforts of Castle Barton Associates to bring recruits from the island for nonunion foundries, domestic work, and other job openings for which there were no domestic takers (Maldonado 1987). Initially placed in temporary housing near their assigned workplaces, PR recruits eventually rented properties made available by white flight in Woodlawn, Garfield Park, Near West Side, Lincoln Park, and Lakeview (F. Padilla 1987).

Led by the Catholic Church–sponsored Caballeros de San Juan to embrace assimilation, PRs turned to activism in the 1960s, joining the coalition against urban renewal in the Near West Side and confronting urban renewal in Lincoln Park under the leadership of the Young Lords, an organization akin to the Black Panthers, which City Hall attacked relentlessly through its infamous Red Squad (F. Padilla 1987).[4] Displaced from their first settlements, PRs moved next to West Town, where they ran into the same police harassment, media stereotypes, and landlord abuse they had experienced in their previous settlements. Tensions came to a boiling point when in June 1966, as PRs gathered in Humboldt Park for their annual patriotic celebrations, the police shot a PR bystander, which set off a riot that lasted three days and left behind major property damages, injuries, and further rancor. Police brutality and hostility, mostly from whites, continued and peaked again in June of 1977, producing a second riot that city officials and other power holders blamed on a violence-prone, unruly, and inassimilable mass instigated by leaders of the Puerto Rican independence movement (see E. Padilla 1947; F. Padilla 1987; Maldonado 1987; Cruz 2007).

Unlike most European immigrants that came in groups, PRs came individually to Chicago, each under a job contract assigning him or her to a low-wage job and a temporary shelter. Despite this, many brought their families and formed rich networks and self-help associations. Over time these efforts produced one of the densest ethnoracial organizational infrastructures in the Humboldt Park and West Town communities and in the city (interviews with elder leaders; also F. Padilla 1987). Organizations ranged from social services and advocacy to lobbying, both to help themselves and gain the recognition and respect European immigrants had secured. The difference for PRs was that they were citizens who were operating in opposition to colonialism—both in the US-PR relationship and in the space of a city that greeted Puerto Rican immigrants with racism. An old-timer interviewee explained,

> We are citizens, we are not like any immigrant, but we are not treated like citizens. That leads us to the conclusion that the Puerto Rican migration is a change in space but not in condition. Anyway we [concluded that] we were an internal colony in the United States, that we were like immigrants but we were also like black people, Native Americans and all the people that the US had some form of colonial relationship to but has never literally integrated into the greater society.

Displacement has never really stopped. Recent racialized gentrification has unleashed a bitter process of contestation (Betancur 2002), with gentrifiers pushing PRs west, first out of Wicker Park and then expanding into the entire West Town neighborhood. Today, the only remaining large PR concentration in Chicago is along and around Division Street in Humboldt Park to the west (Betancur, Domeyko, and Wright 2001; F. Padilla 1987; Cintron et al. 2012).

Unlike Europeans and even other Latinos that had come earlier to Chicago and the United States, the combined forces of colonialism, racism, urban renewal, and gentrification had prevented PRs from establishing a neighborhood in which to anchor. Inspired by anticolonial and civil rights movements, many defined their quest in terms of liberation and self-determination while also pursuing economic opportunities, access to public services, and entrepreneurship. They were also seeking respect and equal treatment. In this context, consolidation in place was an urgent and challenging task: *urgent* given their experience of repeated community dispersal and destruction of place-based systems of support (Betancur 2002; F. Padilla 1987, and interviews) and *challenging* because a majority lived in rented apartments, which made their ability to stay put dependent on the decisions of (mostly white, non-PR) property owners. In this context, any success against gentrification was due to their ability to hold the line using any means possible.

An advantage of being a citizen was that compared to other new immigrants, PRs had a ready-made and large voting bloc. Resorting to political power, they began running candidates in the early 1970s and electing their own representatives in the 1980s. In 1992, the local alderman brought residents and decision makers together for a summit to develop a comprehensive plan. Attended by the mayor, members of his cabinet, and nearly a thousand participants, the summit advanced strategies by issue and formalized the idea of an anchor that would allow PRs to stay put while it operated as their headquarters and point of convergence:

> One of the things that we realized was that of all the areas Puerto Ricans were moving into along Division Street between California and Western, there were more or less 120 buildings and out of those 120 buildings . . . somewhere around 80–90 were Puerto Rican–owned properties. And that is when we said, we need to create something that is going to be established as an anchor. . . . That's how Paseo Boricua came into being. (Interview with an organizer of the summit)

Leaders and politicians pressured City Hall to dedicate this stretch of Division Street to the PR community and to anchor it with two gigantic PR flags to signify peoplehood, identity, and pride. The flags were made of steel to commemorate PR recruits working in foundries. In exchange for this good will gesture, they offered to rally the community to vote for Mayor Daley, and he agreed. Once Paseo had been established, the Puerto Rican Cultural Center (PRCC) and the Division Street Development Association (DSDA) joined forces to establish a restaurant district to enhance it. Along with this, PRCC opened new programs while organizing a yearlong agenda of cultural events along Paseo "to create a place of encounter of Puerto Rican culture" and to holistically address community challenges (community leader interview). Other leaders and organizations embraced the initiative, which enticed new businesses, nonprofits, and institutions to locate along the strip. As a result, the number of PR restaurants tripled and health agencies and nonprofits occupied vacant storefronts. Many in the neighborhood supported these efforts.

While it appeared as though PRs were being given space to settle, Paseo Boricua was part of a gentrification-inducing agenda for the city. Expanding on its characterization as a city of [ethnic and racial] neighborhoods, City Hall had begun marketing this "difference" via neighborhood festivals, "theming" selected business strips, organizing trolley tours, and promoting arts and culture. Whereas Puerto Ricans sought an anchor, City Hall sought tourist destinations. Now Puerto Ricanness was a motto for business development and tourism. The Puerto Rican Agenda (PRA), an established group of leaders, saw Paseo as a means to solidify the staying power of PRs against displacement and gentrification. In short, PRs were building community while the city was selling it. This tension has marked Paseo Boricua from the beginning and has been the source of many skirmishes between the outside and the inside and even within the PR community.

The early success of Paseo Boricua was challenged by the 2008 Great Recession. As some businesses moved and closed, the strip's real estate destabilized and stalled. The leadership via the PRA sought to deepen the PR presence through campaigns directed to their own people. This included cultural events such as "Celebrate on Paseo" or "Boricua come back to el barrio," a walk of fame featuring outstanding Puerto Ricans, naming businesses after Puerto Rican towns, murals featuring community pride and struggles, façades imitating Old San Juan, establishment of *La Voz del Paseo Boricua* newspaper, construction of senior apartments featuring San Juan architecture, and plans for an arts building with performance and exhibition space. The alderman downzoned residential areas to gain concessions from developers requesting zoning changes in the area, making sure building permits lined up with the PRA's goals. This included requiring 30 percent affordable units in large condominium developments and attracting subsidized and nonprofit housing development. Topping off this work was the opening in 2013 of the Institute of Puerto Rican Arts and Culture in an impressive historical building immediately west of Paseo in Humboldt Park. These strategies were based on the belief that a critical mass of Puerto Rican-centric activities would deter gentrification and consolidate Paseo as the heart of the PR community while sending a strong message to the outside that "this is our space," "a counter reaction to our lack of resources" (Puerto Rican Agenda member), and "an attempt of our community to remain relevant" (interview with youth leader). A local politician simply described it as "a community stand."

Most developers resented these actions. The alderman was sued multiple times. In their words, "what right does the alderman have to tell me what I can do, where I can build?" Contention had the features of a race and class war that continues today (Betancur 2002; Betancur, Domeyko, and Wright 2001). An interviewee spoke of actual meetings of real estate agents and developers to "plot" against PRs. When we asked about the reaction of developers to the antigentrification strategy, a real estate agent operating in the neighborhood responded:

> I know nobody was happy about that; these guys are in the business of making money. Basically when you come into a bump or a fence the only way to go ahead is to jump over; they are figuring, "this sucks." They don't like the idea but this is what it is and this is the only way to do it, so they have to do it. . . . You know, they find ways: they may price this unit this much but then they are going to make it up with the other units; there is always ways.

Then, with the change of aldermen, the environment changed: "Today I haven't seen that type of stuff; I don't hear that there is a percent; I do hear from the developers that are doing the new homes and haven't heard them having an issue with the current alderman."

Paseo did not deter real estate agents, developers, and speculators from pursuing deals within the Paseo Boricua even with efforts such as a grassroots campaign warning that "Humboldt Park is not for sale." While resistance appears to have delayed displacement of the remaining PR concentration, Paseo is surrounded by gentrification. The housing crisis has significantly slowed the pace of gentrification but a local real estate agent indicated that the crisis merely screened out flippers and small-time gentrifiers; large-scale developers continued to develop upscale condominiums and pricey homes, and with cash in hand, they were acquiring and renting short sales and foreclosures. Meanwhile, supporters of Paseo Boricua continue to strive to retain those that remain and to recruit others to return.

THE VIEW FROM WITHIN: PASEO AND PUERTO RICAN COMMUNITY FRAGMENTATION

While generally sharing the racial "minority" experience, Puerto Ricans had specific issues in different localities in the United States and in Chicago, particularly as the PR community developed its own affluent segments, which was a relatively small proportion of the total. Class differentiation translated into divided loyalties and visions over the direction of the community's struggle and its aspirations as well as the broader PR cause. Still, as was the case for many other minority groups, their advancement was largely a function of their ability to stick together and fight:

> For us, it's about claiming who we are and having a space that doesn't erase us . . . we don't want to be erased like we were erased from Lincoln Park, like we were erased from Wicker Park; it's really about utilizing the community to be that oasis of "this is who we are" and "this is what we have given." . . . What has

been the habit or perception of these folks was that you were disposable, you were just a temporary feature . . . and what we are saying is, "no, we are not, we have the roots here." (Interview with PRA member)

Hence, it made sense that the PRA focused its energies on retaining a place they could control and use as a platform for their struggles. But not all agreed or felt the same level of commitment to the space itself. Interviewees explained their differences as follows:

[T]he only way you fight is by having a loud voice, by taking a stand, by planting some big flags on the ground and saying, "they cannot be removed!" . . . What would be a victory is seeing more development on Division Street creating real ways where we can access capital that helps build the entrepreneurs who are not only thinking about money but also about community. (Interview with PRA member)

Businesses on Division benefit but also the Puerto Rican Cultural Center scares white people away; some young [PRs] who moved their businesses there encouraged by the Cultural Center are frustrated. Who can own businesses there? Only PRs. Do businesses have to be PR? Yes, or at least hang the PR flag in the window and say "we are going with it." (Interview with business owner)

Questioning the identification of leaders in the concentration around Paseo Boricua as *the PR community*, one ex-PRA member noted, "The community is bigger than the neighborhood." Generally, this question revealed an "old" and a "new" guard with some "in between" and others unconcerned.[5] The old guard was loosely united around the need for a spatial anchor to preserve PR culture and identity and as a statement against colonization and discrimination. The self-proclaimed new guard viewed wealth creation via entrepreneurship as the only feasible strategy to pull the community out of its current condition. Whereas the former have been movement-oriented, the latter view Greektown or Chinatown as the prototype: "what matters is money, economic development . . . [In Greektown] the leader is money; [in contrast] the leaders here [in Paseo Boricua] believe in preserving PR roots" (local politician). Accordingly, the former seek a systemic political struggle headquartered at and reflected in Paseo, while the latter view becoming part of the mainstream as the way up. Both are about capital, but different kinds of capital, as one PRA member reflected in an interview with us:

It [Paseo Boricua] needs major [financial] capital. . . . In lieu of this centrality of capital, you have the attempt to substitute culture in some fashion or other: so, if you don't have real capital, you try to create cultural capital, to create social capital, whatever. . . . I think [there is] one way to split the problem: is it capital itself or is it cultural capital? At the moment it is cultural capital. Paseo Boricua functions as metaphorical ownership under conditions in which actual ownership cannot be granted.

And a local businessman countered,

I think if you don't [focus on business development] it [Paseo] is not going to remain PR. . . . What happened here was that the area became so saturated with public [subsidized] housing and blah, blah, blah that a lot of the PRs that were left were low-income and more and more of the PRs with kids started leaving and that actually caused a lot of gentrification because as they left (they were the homeowners and they were the ones that sold and actually did very well). . . . But they didn't leave just for the money; it was all about resources for the poor; but there was no focus on crime or bringing in more police because that was politically incorrect here. . . . Of course, there are PRs with capital but they are more conservative, they are less likely to come into a situation in which you have to work with that political ideology that they strongly disagree with; they are not going to come . . . the only thing that can move this thing [Paseo Boricua] forward are entrepreneurs. (Interview with PR businessman)

An additional dimension shaping the debate was the relationship between the United States and the island of Puerto Rico, with some wanting Puerto Rico to sever ties with the United States while others want things to remain unchanged. This debate has been a major factor in constructing Puerto Rican identity and spatial disenfranchisement since Puerto Ricans' arrival in Chicago. For some, independence and the Paseo were tied; both represented a genuine Puerto Rican spatial identity. For others, they were Puerto Ricans living in America as Americans with the same dreams and aspirations as Americans. Here too class appears to be a factor as we heard more affluent PRs supporting strategies that fit within the American Dream framework. Mobility allows them to leave the barrio, and graduating out of it is a sign that they made it in the white world just as other immigrants to the United States aspire to. For them, the Paseo Boricua was a point of entry, not a permanent home.

These dilemmas bring back the classical debates between Booker T. Washington's advocacy of black capitalism and W. E. B. Du Bois's call for social change, or between acceptance and resistance. For those tying the PR condition to US colonization of the island and their reduction to colonial subjects, the struggle against race-based disadvantage and oppression is the priority. For those who don't, equal opportunity and mobility has been extracted from the white experience, making assimilation and entrepreneurship a logical direction. These are two fundamentally different viewpoints and strategies. Both, however, involve real estate and who owns the community. Looking at the debate, it's social change versus capital investment; the former raises awareness and challenges oppressive powers that can push people out, while the latter aims to attract affluent PRs to invest in Paseo Boricua, promote entrepreneurship among the youth, work with the police to rid the neighborhood of gangs, and attract PR homeowners:

> Honestly, I believe the only thing we can do to control gentrification is to convince PRs and other Latino professionals to appreciate the beauties that professional whites see that make them buy into the community.... The middle class is the only one that can maintain and preserve a community ... the one that can move here and hold the push of displacement.... You asked if fomenting the move of middle-class PRs is also going to cause gentrification; that is almost impossible because we have a superabundance of CHA housing and other affordable housing developments. (Interview with elected public official)

> It's not like we didn't want other people here; it was like "we are inviting you in but you also have to give something back to the community that is already here." ... A lot of real estate people, a lot of developers went away and said, "Oh, they don't want anybody in this community, they don't want development!" But that wasn't it at all; they just saw it in a different way ... people want to get into business and want to make every dime they can; they don't want socially responsible development. (Interview with former local politician)

Despite its clear demarcation along Division Street, many Puerto Ricans and non–Puerto Ricans prefer to stay away from the debate about whether or not it is important to have a clear physical PR presence in Chicago. Others view the Paseo and its events as something for lower-income people but not for them. A real estate agent made this distinction,

> [I]f it is PRs, they love the idea [of the flags], "Oh my God." But if it is a white it's going to be like, "they are nice, beautiful," but they don't care. [laugh]. They are thinking about the area; that's what they buy. They think about the area and how close it is to the Blue Line, how close it is to the parks and then as far as PRs. They only care about these things, that there are restaurants, that there are bars, that's what they look at. (Interview with PR real estate agent)

Still some laughed when we asked about the importance of the Paseo to PRs. From their perspective—whether they were for it or against it—the Paseo was a hole to fill in the current map of gentrification in Chicago and it was just a matter of time before it happened.

Interestingly, nearly all the Puerto Ricans we interviewed described gentri-fication as blatant speculation. As one PRA member described it to us, "The problem exists with the folks that have that pioneer settlement mentality who are just waiting us out and who treat us like we are the Indians on the reserva-tion." Furthermore, while gentrifiers loved the neighborhood's diversity, we heard how some newcomers went after PR cultural markers such as the flags, corn vendors in the park, and neighbors who *didn't fit their standards*. Many of *those people* did not patronize Paseo businesses or festivals and organized their lives around doing things outside the area of the Paseo Boricua. An elected official described how "this [gentrifier] wrote me a four-page e-mail about the nice places he visited in the community but he was totally oblivious to all elements of the local culture including in his list only white places."

Some we interviewed floated the idea of a mixed-income community of Puerto Ricans and other Latinos, claiming that it would be different from the mix induced by gentrification since, as one PRA member described, "our middle class is not really middle class" but actually closer to the less affluent in the neighborhood. Unlike the white middle class moving in, it was assumed that PR middle-class residents wanted to be in the neighborhood for what it has to offer and not simply the location. Of course, this also presumed the PR middle class in the neighborhood wanted to stay even as gentrification created an opportunity for property owners to finally make some money off their homes, which some did but found it hard to do. As a former PRA member explained:

> As the neighborhood was changing, the housing market pushed people out; there was no choice and homeowners cashed in and moved to the Brickyards and then there are PR vultures who actively participate in gentrification but it was really white Realtors who came in to gentrify . . . an ally of NN who was in real estate told me of a meeting she was invited to with other real estate people to discuss how they were going to take over the neighborhood; they talked about using CAPs and other tactics; that to me makes gentrification so ominous . . . there was also an alderman saying that it was NN tenants who were the problem. (Interview with former PRA member)

All these views reflect the fact that in Chicago and most of the United States, gentrification has a primarily white face, which is supported by the facts but also reproduced as the dominant narrative evident in the perceptions recorded throughout this book. As with Bronzeville and Pilsen, interviewees across the spectrum assumed that gentrification would not occur until whites were part of it en masse (some went as far as saying "only if"). In a way, they harked back to Homer Hoyt's 1933 hierarchy that privileged white Anglo-Saxon over other

Europeans, with Negroes and Mexicans at the bottom of the real estate food chain. This was assumed to be the case for PRs too. In other words, even if Puerto Ricans wanted to gentrify the Paseo, they did not have the market position to do so. Clearly racialized markets in which class and race reinforce each other (e.g., Betancur 2002; Cohen and Taylor 2001; Feagin and Vera 1995; Berry 1979; D. Wilson 2007; Anderson and Sternberg 2012) have created these conditions for PRs in Chicago. In this context, it's understandable why Puerto Ricans perceive gentrification as white invasion and colonization, especially when you hear stories about real estate agents conspiring to take over the neighborhood.

UNDER SIEGE: COMMODIFICATION, PROPERTY, OCCUPATION, AND COMMUNITY BUILDING

Historically, in the United States, white privilege has controlled the distribution of people, wealth, and opportunity and has limited the ability of nonwhites to own (Jensen 2005; Kinchelow et al. 1998; T. Allen 1994, 1997; Frankenberg 1993). Most Puerto Ricans in Chicago are less affluent and largely limited to renting apartments in disinvested areas or, less frequently, buying properties often purchased with subprime mortgages. The ability of the PR concentration in and around Paseo to stay in the area depends on those who control the real estate, unless something else roots them in place.

As already described, gentrification moved center stage in Chicago as real estate became a major core of value creation, capture, and circulation under the current societal regime and became a major force of urban change. After migrating to Chicago when the economy began shifting in the 1950s, Puerto Rican recruits started in low-wage jobs in declining industries and lived as temporary occupants in prime locations opened up by white flight that soon would be targeted for redevelopment. While spatial concentration allowed PRs to organize and elect local political representation, many were soon dispersed into other areas of disinvestment, only to hold these spaces until the next wave of speculation.

Was there an alternative? The PRA sought stabilization through intense occupation that included a strong cultural, institutional, and political presence and identity to "keep the vampires out," as one PRA member said to us. Another PRA member explained it as an effort to create cultural capital in order to make up for the lack of economic prowess. The combination of a PR restaurant district with institutions and nonprofits was to produce a critical PR concentration that could be a base for struggle while offering programs and services to the community and outlets to keep the city and others accountable. Initiatives have included the Humboldt Park Empowerment Partnership, the

Community of Wellness, and the Community as Campus to reorganize local education.[6] Seeking an alternative to overt commodification, all these actions were to be combined with nondisplacing, socially responsible businesses such as the Puerto Rican restaurant district. Developed incrementally in response to threats and opportunities, the combination of resistance and community building was a sharp contrast to the top-down approach based on containment and neglect that Chicago had employed in similar neighborhoods.

Has it worked? Has it prevented the commodification of ethnicity advanced by the growth coalition in control of City Hall? Has it stopped gentrification and can it? Paseo Boricua and all the associated community-building strategies are all a work in progress. Along the way, many of the challenges posed by commodification and racialized markets have been exposed. Resistance and some level of neighborhood control have made a difference despite racialization, limited economic resources, and development pressure, and despite being threatened by political shifts and internal divisions, PRs have grown roots in the Paseo that at least for now have prevented another round of displacement and erasure.

Control may be the key to what the future holds. Interviewees agreed that the strip is far from being an economic development success by orthodox standards. Yet it has offered hope to many in the PR community, who are concerned about holding their ground long enough for these strategies to produce lasting effects. Business development seems to have stalled, which has opened up the possibility of reaching out to other consumers or even opening up non-PR venues as long as it does not play into the hands of gentrification forces. Effective occupation and perhaps the recent recession has allowed PRs to stay longer than in other locations, despite their limited property ownership and financial capability. Still the siege continues.

Looking beyond property ownership, the PRA's approach tested the possibilities of pitting cultural capital against gentrification. According to Bourdieu and Wacquant (1992), economic capital can avail itself to other forms of capital; each is relatively autonomous and thus can be used to acquire others. Just as gentrifiers rely heavily on symbols and symbolic power to make places desirable and to add value to them, development of the Paseo suggests that symbolic capital can be a formidable force for low-income people as well, providing a means to partake in place making through symbolic occupation, culture, resistance, intimidation, and other tactics. Both are struggles to commodify space. Whereas the city and the marketplace are commodifying identities and lifestyles, the PRA and others are trying to guarantee their cultural survival while also providing a launch pad for recognition and advancement. Unlike Greektown in Chicago, which has long been without a critical Greek population, the area around Paseo is still relatively Puerto Rican. As Joan Didion stated, "A place belongs forever to whoever claims it hardest, remembers it most obsessively, wrenches it from itself, shapes it, loves it so radically that he remakes it in his own image" (1979).

Halsted North: Spatializing Gayness

Chicago has been at the forefront of the gay movement in the United States, dealing with its own struggles while connecting with others in New York City and San Francisco, following at times and leading at others.[7] Although Stonewall has been consecrated as the milestone of the movement, Chicago had its own Stonewalls. This includes Illinois being the first state in the nation to remove the sodomy law from its books in 1961, thanks to the initiative of city lobbyists, and the emergence of Halsted North (HN) as a gay hub and destination on par with the Castro District in San Francisco and Greenwich Village in New York, a community that shifted from seclusion and exclusion to visibility and defiance.

As with Puerto Ricans, spatialization gave the gay community permanence and legitimacy, and it facilitated self-expression. Still this oppressed and outlawed group of people confronted unique challenges when trying to establish a place for themselves. Historically, gays have been forced into hiding, producing spaces of identify and encounter in the shadows beyond the gaze of the commons (Baim 2008), finding each other "in the closet," which included parks, public washrooms, baths, and bars.[8] Bars emerged as the pre-eminent places of encounter, but they were also used for strategizing and organizing for defense; police raids were common and politicians used them to secure votes at election time. They were usually located in dicey parts of the city that helped their anonymity such as red light districts and bohemian neighborhoods. Often on the periphery of downtown, these bars were accessible but also less visible. From these spaces came the first organized actions and campaigns and the informal guilds of bartenders and transgendered, those with the least to lose and the bravery to dare, because when identities were revealed (e.g., newspapers listed names of those detained in police raids), careers would likely be over.[9] Some were driven to suicide.[10] Over time, gay bars and gay patrons moved near each other and formed loose, anonymous communities.[11]

In Chicago, the northward trajectory of urban renewal that started in the mid-1950s priced bars and gay residents out of the Gold Coast just north of downtown, pushing them along Clark Street into Lincoln Park, which was also gentrifying. Continuing north into Lakeview, the burgeoning gay community established itself at the convergence of Clark and Broadway on Diversey Street.

The city's largest concentration of gay bars and businesses opened further north along Halsted from Belmont to Grace—hence the name Halsted North—and continues moving north to the border of the city (Blackie 2013).

The HN concentration began with two or three gay bars on Halsted in the 1970s followed by others in the 1980s. A bar owner recalled,

> When we opened, Halsted was a neglected area, but since it was on the edge between West and East Lakeview, it was always left out. . . . There were all these fringy things and craftsmen. . . . Gays discovered this neighborhood frankly by coming to the bars; there were a lot of rental properties from Broadway to the Lake . . . they were cheap rentals. . . . We are talking probably about the 1980s. . . . People would come to the bars and discover these nice side streets, good housing stock, relatively untouched . . . they started buying real estate . . . this may be anecdotal but I am convinced that during the 80s to early 90s, 60 or 70 percent of my clients walked here. . . . Halsted was this kind of no man's land . . . it was our ghetto; we lived by ourselves. (Interview with bar owner in Halsted Street)

> The solidification of this neighborhood happened because this was the first place that gay businesspeople invested in the properties themselves and were not renting. That was the big difference. This was the first neighborhood where there were a lot of invested gays in residences as well as in business locales. (Interview with business owner)

But gaining ground was not a simple matter of concentration and ownership. The civil rights movement gave the community the courage to respond with ever-bolder actions against police raids and homophobic attacks. Some suggest that it was the raids of the Fun Lounge in 1964 and of the Trip in 1968 that launched the local gay movement (see also Baim 2008). Responding to the 1964 raids, gays organized a local chapter of the national Matachine Society that connected them through a widely distributed newsletter.[12] The forceful closing of the Trip resulted in the first ever court challenge and augmented the community's pressure on the police and the city to end the raids and harassment. The Pride Parade that started in 1970 grew annually and brought gays and their causes out in the open. Gay newspapers started circulating in the 1970s, increasing their coverage and reaching out to more gays while further politicizing them. In 1973, a black alderman introduced the first gay rights ordinance in the City Council. Although tabled in committee, it was introduced again and again until its approval fifteen years later. Activism in university campuses further expanded calls for gay rights. A massive 1977 rally at Medina Temple when former beauty queen Anita Bryant brought her national antigay campaign to Chicago spoke to the determination and momentum of gays at the time. But what seemingly galvanized and widely exposed the gay cause was the AIDS epidemic, depicted as Silence = Death (Baim 2008, 145). Gays mobilized as never before, and a mass coming out showed the ubiquity and bravery of the community, provoking homophobic attacks but also creating widespread support:

> People came out of the closet because the ugliness of the epidemic outraged so many, straight and gay, that they mobilized to take care of strangers, and in that common cause community was born, because community is born over the common belief in someone, in something that we galvanize for. (Interview with director of gay organization in the area)

> AIDS was one of the impetuses why people finally understood that they had to take a chance, they had to come out and let everybody know that gay people were all around you. . . . They were all over the place and everybody knows somebody and there was somebody in your family; that all came out; it was a national movement . . . there was a wonderful unit . . . it was just awful to watch people suffer in that way. (Interview with nongay resident)

> Out of adversity you have strength: that unfortunate epidemic actually solidified the community; at the time of where we were in the struggle that was the epicenter. (Interview with local politician)

Because there were no real formal services and support for people with AIDS, new organizations and leaders emerged to fill the void (Baim 2008, 145–46). Halsted North became a site where gays could now find much more than bars and entertainment; they could also gather, organize, and march forward.

INSTITUTIONALIZING THE GAYHOOD

As the first openly gay neighborhood, one indeed with a sense of permanence, Halsted North is a culmination of these developments and the symbol of a new era. A series of factors helped it become the official gay destination in the city despite the existence of other clusters in Uptown, Edgewater, and Rogers Park, as gays continued moving north to reach the edge of the city.

- White flight opened Lakeview to others who gave it a second lease on life, in part due to lower rents and property prices and in part to the lack of demand from traditional households. Although Latinos had formed a cluster that included HN, landlords preferred small gay households to large Latino families.
- Progressive churches, a liberal lakefront, and an expansive arts community provided a relatively tolerant environment.

- Struggles and advances in the movement made gays a force in politics and businesses.
- Changes in politics led to the prohibition of raids under Jane Byrne (1979–83), political organization under Harold Washington (1983–1987), the 1988 Human Rights Ordinance under Eugene Sawyer (1987–89), and the designation of HN as the city's official gay strip (1998) and appointment of the first openly gay alderman (2003) under Richard M. Daley (1989–2011).
- A shift from nongay- to gay-owned bars and real estate gave gay businesses control of the HN strip, which allowed them to resist displacement.

A journalist explained, "Halsted North was possible because it was the next geographic area in the northern push of the gay community." Although some bars opened on nearby Broadway Avenue, HN was zoned commercial, a category that allowed for bars with liquor licenses next to each other. Also, storefronts were not available on Broadway, which was a well-established retail strip catering to Lakeview residents.[13]

Gay households grew with the strip as some bought homes and others rented. The residential presence supported gay bars while also increasing demand for other gay and gay-serving establishments. A nongay local activist observed that "it wasn't just entertainment: for a lot of people it was a lifestyle," and a pioneer added, "one reason gays liked to be in Lakeview was at least you could get an apartment; they would not rent to two men living together in other places in the city . . . at the beginning we were here by ourselves, we were like a ghetto" (Interview with resident).

Halsted North became the gay neighborhood of choice, an entertainment gay hub and a concentration of gay-oriented services, politics, and culture where being gay was safe.[14] It was a refuge from the homophobia of the larger city and the familial orientation of neighborhoods and suburbs. While not necessarily an intentional neighborhood, it materialized the dream of many: "there was always a sense that things were going to get better, that we could have a critical mass, that we actually could have a community of our own" (interview with businessman). Although the gay movement itself was much larger than HN, the gay hub reinforced it. In the late 1980s, *Advocate*, a major gay publication, put HN on the short list of gay hubs in the country along with the Castro District in San Francisco and Greenwich Village in New York, causing many to exclaim joyously, "My God, we've arrived" (interview with bar owner). The 1988 Human Rights Ordinance outlawed discrimination against gays in housing, employment, and public accommodation, which strengthened the community and made it and Chicago more attractive. It also made HN gay safe, which brought in gays from the Midwest and beyond, who then formed new hubs elsewhere. As one researcher described:

> HN serves the function of providing visibility and seeming stability, a location for a group of people that in the generation before had to keep hidden . . . it provides a set of businesses and socializing locations that are openly gay, where people go because they are gay, where some of them move because of that and, unlike in the past, it's happening free of harassment . . . there is this visibility, permanence, a sense of respect of the fact that we have the right to be here. (Interview with academic researcher)

But success brought other problems. Gentrification started pushing out less-affluent gays. Others preferred to move to more quiet environments, while some decided to cash in their property appreciation. As a result some of the most affluent gays in the city were living alongside traditional, nongay households. To add to the frenzy, zoning changes brought in a flurry of condominiums, which unleashed new tensions and broke old alliances:

> Everybody believed that he [the alderman] was too close to developers; the rumor was that if a developer could find a way to help him out that you could get anything you wanted approved. He started approving buildings that were basically going to push gay bars out of business. (Interview with businessman)

Clearly, Halsted North was changing. On the one hand, it was the iconic landmark for gay Chicago and a tourist destination for gays from the city and beyond. On the other hand, it was rapidly becoming a high-end, predominantly white, heterosexual community with gay bars, shops, and symbolic markers of a community that was fast disappearing.

COMMODIFYING GAYNESS

In 1998, on City Hall's initiative, HN was added to its list of themed business corridors, making it "the first sanctioned gay destination in the country if not in the world" (journalist). Still, the city's $3.2 million offer to mark the neighborhood with gay icons brought out old fears and raised new issues, reflecting the changing population:

> In some of the hearings there were even gay people who said they didn't want this because they were afraid that it was going to attract antigays. Those were real fears that people had. Some straight people didn't want it because they thought the neighborhood was already changing to be very straight . . . there was people on both sides of the issue and ultimately people even thought that it might hurt

property values while others thought it would help; so people really had questions about it, but Daley always got what he wanted and he went through with it and it really helped people and helped Chicago's visibility as a gay destination. (Interview with journalist)

After some modifications, the city "erected eleven pairs of 23-foot-high art deco-style pillars with rainbow rings" (Gelman 2005) along with major streetscaping along the strip. These pylons identified HN as a gay district while demarcating the shifting social space that was creating new territories within the neighborhood: "It's like people were saying 'we are going to stay in this community' even though the community kept moving on" (interview with local social service agency director).

Designation transformed HN from a gay community of pride and self-determination to an officially sanctioned fetishized space of sexuality for sale:

[NH] is kind of similar maybe to what Greektown is to Greeks: not a lot of Greeks live there anymore but it's the place they go to and have their culture and have entertainment, and a lot of out-of-towners also go there for the same thing; it's one of those things that out-of-towners really know about Chicago because of the pylons that are really contributing to anchoring the area and for out-of-towners especially to know that that's the demarcation. (Interview with journalist)

Like Greektown, HN was becoming a gay-themed space without gays as more gay residents were priced out. Still, businesses of all kinds started catering to gays, and the Pride Parade became the focal point. Along the way, many felt that commodification and becoming mainstream threatened to make HN irrelevant as a gay community:

My perception is that the gay community is more and more like the rest of society . . . if you are gay or not is no longer important. . . . There is less and less of a community because the thing that binds us is no longer important. . . . Gay people no longer feel that the only place they can go to is Side Track and Roscoe's [two of the largest bars in HN]. (Interview with businessman)

COMMODIFICATION AND FRAGMENTATION

In general, our sources viewed HN as successful in bringing recognition to the gay community. A few actually described it as a diverse community of sorts.

HN is what people make of it: if you want to be in a bar dancing until two in the morning, yes, that's what you can get on Halsted. But you can get also education, you can get sports. . . . The Community Center made it more friendly for the whole gay experience, not just the bars, but there have always been restaurants and shops, and I really feel like it is not like the whole gay community is centered there, but it's still a very important part. (Interview with journalist)

But recognition and gentrification actually brought to light the challenges of other diversity issues, especially race, class, and gender, that were previously veiled by the struggle and most certainly by anonymity:

> There are certain elements of the community, particularly many of the young people who are coming who don't live here . . . and they are loud and they are crude and a lot of them are people of color and they are parading and are not civil to one another or to others who are on the street, and that behavior is offensive to people, no matter who you are. (Interview with longtime resident)

> There is lots of sexism and racism [in HN]. . . . There is a level of discomfort between these groups of people that is in part race and in part class; it's a boiling pot in HN that from time to time will erupt into problems; it's surprising that actually relatively few things have happened . . . if you are a white gay man walking on Halsted at midnight on Saturday and you have racial issues you are going to see the [nonwhite] youth as threatening, but if they were white they would not be threatening at all. . . . There have been [public] meetings that were very racial; I have seen comments on blogs that are atrocious. (Interview with journalist)

> This community [HN] didn't speak to women. It was not like, "let's break out the Champagne and celebrate!" There was not that celebration that some people thought they would receive. (Interview with director of a nonprofit organization)

Many described how the realities of race, class, and gender progressively came out with the gay community and intensified in the past decade in HN:

> [The life of minority gays] is so far away from the reality of wealthy white gay men who live in condominiums on Lake Shore Drive. I think that the distance between people in our community is greater than it used to be. . . . [The Gay Pride parade] is now just another Chicago parade and like the Black Hawks victory parade it is a reason to get drunk and disorderly in public. (Interview with local businessman)

> On the one hand, there are gentrifiers whether gay or not gay who have class status and privilege and live in that neighborhood, and then there are kids who are looking for a place where they can hang out and not get in trouble either in their own neighborhood or with white police. . . . So, you have these clashes between race, class and age and gender just displaying themselves on the streets of Boystown, and it kind of illustrates that we may share an identity called gay but in a lot of ways what we need in our lives and what we want in our lives is

different and those differences have to do in the case of Boystown with class and racial identities. (Interview with HN researcher)

An interviewee pointed out that even the writing of gay history has been skewed to focus principally on the white North Side, dismissing the black South Side. As with other movements, the story is told as the universal story of gays rather than one that is nuanced by race and other dimensions such as space. A researcher who studies gay issues noticed that early maps listing gay sites in Chicago included only those in the white North Side. Perhaps complementing this was the image of a homogeneously homophobic black community, which many of our interviewees believed made gay blacks conceal being gay. Still, we heard how many young people and transgendered persons, as well as nonwhites, carried the weight and actually took the risks. Like the feminist movement, minorities and the less affluent were generally left behind, while race- and class-advantaged gays profited the most from the movement. As with the Puerto Rican community, many interviewees emphasized class over race while pointing to the dominance of whites and their agenda in the movement:

> There are black gay people who are rich and there are black people who are poor and there are white people who are rich, etc. There is no one single gay person; there is probably people who are black who were forced out because of the higher rents and it's not because they are gay; there is no way to say that the community is one way or the other. (Interview with journalist)

> When people from the African American community come to areas like this, it is very noticeable. . . . They are coming here to party because bars say "this is where you come to party but you don't have the money to come in our bar because you cannot pay four dollars for a bottle of beer"; but they come anyway. (Interview with resident)

> Racism is a fact of life and this is the most racially segregated city in the country. . . . I hope there is nothing specific about white gays that makes them more racist. (Interview with businessman)

In general, whites and to some extent affluent minorities are in the best position to make gains and shape their environment, move to areas of choice in cities, have jobs that are more gay-tolerant, and have their rights enforced:

> The benefits of identity movements are unequally distributed. . . . There are people who are privileged and people who are not; so inequality gets piled up

on top of inequality. . . . What we are and how we are able to live in this world of gay liberation has to do with what else we are. . . . One of the other things that has popped up that should be said and that is obvious is that gay is not like gender crossing or queer or transgender: gay is not a visible marker, [but race is]. (Interview with HN researcher)

HN is now a primarily white, heterosexual, gentrified neighborhood, and being gay in HN is not a source of exclusion or discrimination for affluent gay residents. But it is for gay youth of color, poor aging gay men and women, runaways, and others visiting the neighborhood to escape homophobic oppression at home and at work, whether for an evening out or even to make a living on the fringes of the entertainment world.

Through the pioneer organization, Horizons, gay activists have tried to mitigate this tension and extend a hand to outsider gays through the establishment of the Center on Halsted. Attached to a Whole Foods, the center is a safe haven in the middle of HN that offers services and a gathering space. Many gay and nongay residents and visitors, however, have actually blamed the center for attracting "characters" that they consider a threat to businesses, residents, and quality of life. An exchange with a staff person at the center provides a sense of the tension between "insiders" and outsiders:

Q. So this is considered a safe space for the LGBTTQ community but apparently not for the black community, the Latino community, and others. Despite gains, the community's lifestyle is not accepted everywhere, and the kid from the South Side coming here gets this kind of reception?

A. They get this reception and there are people who are not informed, who say, young people came into Lakeview when the center opened . . .

Q. You are the draw . . .

A. We are the draw and I say to them, "Thirty years ago this corner was the hustler corner for young people . . . we have these major donors who give lots of money to the center who came when we opened and said, 'You have homeless people here?' and I was like 'Yes, isn't that wonderful?' 'What do you mean wonderful?' 'What do you think we were going to do? Although it is a beautiful building we are still going to serve our vulnerable community.'" (Interview with staff of local social service agency)

The stabbing of a black youth by another black youth on Halsted Street in 2011 brought the issue to a boiling point with the organization of a group, Take Boystown Back, demanding zero tolerance against "outsiders" and adding fuel to the fire, as a flurry of hate comments in blogs and in mass meetings illustrate. These excerpts present the two sides:

> They [black youth] happen to be very noticeably out of place!! So, why are they not questioned and asked to leave by the police is amazing! Check their IDs and if they don't live there ask them to enter an establishment or leave!! . . . They travel from all over the city to infest Boystown with their ghetto mentality and violent attitude. . . . It is what it is and they were all black. (Anonymous blogger, *Huffington Post* 2013)

> Last year Take Back Boystown events highlighted the extreme racial and ideological segregation in Boystown, when a community was no longer fighting to exist as a space where the oppressed and the marginalized could find refuge; rather, the community was fighting against itself, mobs forming to exclude those seen as outsiders and threats to the received Boystown "in group." This group included the predominantly white, gay patrons of the neighborhood bar scene, a group which claimed that they were "Taking back Boystown" from the queer youths of color seen to be the source of violence and conflict in the community. The Center on Halsted, which offers resources and programs to at-risk youth, quickly became a symbol in this perceived menace, as if the Center were a Trojan horse, ready to explode. (Lang 2012)

Although white privilege and economic affluence help mitigate and potentially wipe out the negative effects of gay sexual identity, homophobia is still a major source of disadvantage. When asked whether the gay community had come to the point where it no longer needed a spatial concentration, interviewees indicated that although affluent and educated gays, especially whites, had far more options than their counterparts, homophobia continued to reduce gay lifestyles to ghettos and nonfamily environments.

> I think we still need LGBT spaces for those who need them, but I think fewer people especially in cities like Chicago feel they can concentrate only in gay areas. . . . There are still people who need gay places; there are others who don't need that anymore and will live openly gay lives in Oak Park [a liberal suburb] and in other places and just feel fine about it and not feel threatened. (Interview with HN researcher)

> The white gay man in effect can move through the world invisible, but young black men cannot move through the world invisible; they are targeted all the time; sometimes overtly by the police, sometimes by the way in which whites civilians look at them, it's like "why are you here?" I believe the gay community will always be a semi-reviled minority; at the end of the day, straight people will always be scared about gay people. (Interview with businessman)

I think there is still a long way to go in terms of acceptance: we live in a ghetto in the sense that people are accepted. . . . Now we have a problem in terms of perception that there are too many people of color in Halsted Street and how that affects mostly white tourists or white patrons of the gay bars. . . . We have to realize the diversity of our gay culture: it's not just about white gays and lesbians. . . . I call it what it is: if it's racist, it's racist. (Interview with local politician)

The gay struggle spatialized in HN is both a milestone and a reflection of the challenges of race, class, gender, age, and other sources of inequality. Its trajectory shows how the gains of the movement and the benefits of HN are mediated by societal inequalities and unevenly distributed. Even when the community as a whole apparently had arrived, white gays (males in particular) were able to recover more privileges and position. Perhaps most importantly in our discussion of neighborhood change, commodification turned gayness into a product for sale, screening out or marginalizing many and weakening the ties that had been the original basis of community.

What Do Paseo Boricua and Halsted North Say About Neighborhood Change?

We selected these two cases to investigate the spatialized struggles of two different "minority" communities in order to shed light on how such formations produce space in the current regime of accumulation. While the analysis could have focused only on the change triggered by gentrification, we wanted to call attention to how identity was used to spatialize each community against oppression and to demonstrate ways to cut through the veil of homogenizing interpretations of neighborhood change. Allowing the story to reveal its complexity and contradictions, we were able to identify the openings, dynamics, and contradictions involved in neighborhood change, demonstrating its nonlinear and multidirectional nature but also capturing the multiplicity of stories taking place simultaneously in the same geography.

Both groups produced spatial formations in response to and as a basis for their struggles. In common is the use of boundaries and symbolic markers to put down stakes and declare turf, a ground on which to stand and even to stand out from in a display of pride and defiance. They also gained control through cultural and symbolic spatialization. Protest and parades were declarative gestures inviting the outside in but also providing parameters for participation. Both profited from the discarded spaces created by white flight and disinvestment. In turn, converging their own condition with place produced neighborhood change of sorts. To put down roots, members of each group invested in the place and tried to gain control by opening businesses and buying property. Commodification started from the inside as commercial space was transformed to cater to community demand. But over time, bars, restaurants, and shops further opened the neighborhoods to the outside, bringing in potential allies and revenue but also hostility and, in HN, extreme commodification.

Common strategies and pursuits, however, do not lead to the same trajectories or outcomes. In both neighborhoods, gentrification has been a threat to each community's spatial roots. While many described the change over time for the gay community as moving toward a "happy ending," it was at a cost, and while the PR community has managed to stay so far, many have been displaced and those remaining continue to face uncertainty. HN continues to be a major tourist destination and gay hub even though many gays have left. In part, we attribute this to affluent whiteness, which appears to have the ownership and capital needed to keep Halsted North as a gay destination and a safe haven though with some pushback. In Paseo Boricua, however, the Puerto Ricanness of the space has not reduced the racial disadvantage or the threat of gentrification.

Ultimately, both groups were fighting for the recognition and standing that could put them on par with the rest of society. To this end, they branded, named, and obtained formal recognition for their spaces. As Bourdieu explained, the act of naming is "a symbolic act of imposition which has on its side all the strength of the collective, of the consensus, of common sense, because it is performed by a delegated agent of the state, that is, a holder of the monopoly of legitimate symbolic power" (1991, 239). Still the gains and recognition are precarious for those weaker segments in each community. In Halsted North, while property ownership anchored the gay community, it also helped to push out the most vulnerable, many who had assumed the most risk initially in the struggles to get the community off the ground. Meanwhile, cultural occupation made Paseo a social and political instrument of recognition that also mobilized internal differences and struggles for control often characteristic of oppressed communities.

An important difference between the two communities was the role of race in gaining access to and shaping a space to call home. Puerto Ricans ran into a wall of blatant racism and white gentrification. Although members of the white gay vanguard were forced to operate underground for a long time, race was an advantage for them. Meanwhile, class played a confounding role as the well-off in both communities profited from property ownership and the ability to choose where to live, while the less affluent struggled to stay as renters. Another major difference was the relationship each had with the outside. The Puerto Rican cause depended primarily on PRs themselves to sustain the Paseo and the surrounding neighborhood. In contrast, outside support, legislation, resources, and recognition helped to entrench Halsted North as a permanent gay space in the city. As a site for consumption, HN has effectively commodified gayness with its shops, restaurants, and bars, while Paseo Boricua has tried to balance culture and commercialization as a means to advance the struggle and avoid displacement. And although gentrification continues to change both hubs, many believe this is not as much of a threat for commodified HN, which has been successfully positioned as a local, regional, national, and even international destination. In contrast, Paseo Boricua has not attracted the crowds and visibility of HN although it has been pitched as the one and only PR-themed strip in the country.

Does it matter that gays live in Halsted North or Puerto Ricans in Paseo Boricua? As a symbol for their communities, the answer is likely yes since they make the group "visible and manifest, for other groups and for itself attest[ing] to its existence as a group that is known and recognized, laying a claim to institutionalization" (Bourdieu 1991, 224). Once each community achieved recognition, people worked to safeguard it by amalgamating the sites into anchors, *homes*, and safe spaces. Controlling this space—the neighborhood—is important in preserving this symbol. As a local elected official said about Halsted North:

> The guys that are my age said, "We are not going to be kicked out of here, we are going to try to own our business, our real estate." The struggle is now to keep it gay because if some of these properties turn over and they are not gay bars anymore, then we might have a struggle. . . . Obviously the feeling of comfort is very important for the community and now serves the entire city. . . . People from all over the city . . . come because it's safe, a safe space for them to understand their history and sexuality in a nonthreatening environment. (Interview with HN politician)

Still, the permanence of the space can be metaphorical and transient given capital's need to remain mobile, particularly in today's regime. The space of each can easily be reduced to a sanitized commodity. While these neighborhoods face the same tension between the flow of gentrification and efforts to fix the space for a community, they also have the added pressure to assimilate while trying to retain identity. Perhaps most important is the real possibility of losing what already has been gained:

> Is the point to ghettoize the gay community? No, OK? If you are looking at enclaves, "Oh, we need to have our space." I am not exactly sure that's the goal. Yes, we want cultures to be respected, whether it is Puerto Rican, whether it is gay, and so on . . . so, I am not sure what the end game is but I wholly believe as a gay man that I want to be welcomed in every community and I also want to

contribute to the entire city. Whatever our goals are, there is a question about a city of neighborhoods: is that a positive thing? For someone who grew up in a neighborhood that was all Irish Catholic and when someone came in that was Italian or Puerto Rican, that could be a dangerous situation. What is happening in the city of Chicago is this idea of neighborhoods being all of one type. I think that is negative. (Interview with HN politician)

Why this obsession with land? What I have thought about in this relationship is that Paseo Boricua . . . functions as a metaphorical ownership under conditions in which actual ownership cannot be granted. So property ownership in the US is what rules the day and therefore grants all rights to gentrification to say "who are you to stop me?" . . . Paseo Boricua as an entity I think is metaphorical ownership . . . what brings everything together is land, land that has to be owned metaphorically or land that has to be owned in real terms. (Interview with PRA member)

The efforts of making the community is not just in terms of money or property; it's a lot broader; it's more inclusive . . . for us it's about claiming who we are and having a space that doesn't erase us. . . . For me space is important; others may not need that or may have found that through their institutions or their churches or whatever [they can achieve what they want] but I think we need that. . . . In Chicago, the only way we could have access to power was through the concentration of people. . . . The more we disperse, the less access we are going to be able to have. . . . Even if we disperse, we need a space to call home. (Interview with PRA member)

Clearly, the population segments within each community are differently represented in the neighborhood spaces they occupy. Reflecting Harvey's claim that different groups "construct their sense of territory and community in radically different ways" (1995, 370), gays and Puerto Ricans in Chicago produced different territories for community, each with different significance for those within and outside the neighborhood. Yet so far both remain critical for the disadvantaged members of their community, even if from outside the neighborhood in the case of HN. Interestingly, Paseo is playing this role for PR gays, providing place-based formal and informal support networks to those with limited income.

[Paseo Boricua plays] I think a very important role. When you look at the dropout rates in the community, if you look at how the system is set up, the resources that are given to communities like HP [Humboldt Park], LV [Little Village], and some of the AA [African American] communities, there are very little resources. So we ask, "Why is that the case and what can we do, what resources can we provide to young people?" So this is a counterreaction to that situation of lack of resources. . . . [Paseo] allows me to be involved with building the community . . . looking at the possibilities of a better, a just world; a place where we are working not only about the situation of PRs here but the people that are marginalized, the people that are oppressed. (Interview with young PR leader)

For the well-off in either community, class appears to mitigate the effects of their primary identity—race or gayness—detaching them from the lower classes. As Bourdieu explains:

Those who occupy dominated positions in the social space are also situated in dominated positions in the field of symbolic production, and it is not clear whence they could obtain the instruments of symbolic production that are necessary in order for them to express their own point of view in the social space, were it not that the specific logic of the field of cultural production, and the specific interests that are generated within it, have the effect of inclining a fraction of the professionals engaged in this field to supply to the dominated, on the basis of a homology of position, the instruments that will enable them to break away from the representations generated in the immediate complicity of social structures and mental structures and which tend to ensure the continued reproduction of the distribution of social capital (1991, 244).

In this sense, those without the financial resources to assimilate need the space for identity but also for the social capital it offers and can generate. What is less clear, however, is what will keep those that generate social capital within the gay and PR communities connected to the space if not economic capital. So far, it is much more symbolic, and that could disappear with time. Yet both Paseo and Halsted North are spaces that have been able to maintain their identity while in a continuous flow of creative destruction. Change over time pushes and pulls each in different directions without completely eliminating what came before and without eliminating specifically important symbols and markers of the community. But despite the feeling of permanence conveyed by the flags and the pylons, the intensified commodification of both spaces keeps them under siege, with gentrification threatening to consume the identity that remains. In contrast, the transformation of public housing, which is discussed next, is promoting a controlled form of commodification to intentionally erase its identity and promote gentrification.

CHAPTER 7

Reinventing Neighborhood?

Transforming Chicago's Public Housing

> If there is no resistance, there are no
> power relations. (Foucault 1982, 29)

On December 19, 1998, four high-rise public-housing buildings in the Lakefront Properties on Chicago's South Side were imploded. The whole process, from the initial explosion of dynamite to the still pile of rubble, took less than five minutes. The strong winds out of the west quickly carried a large dust cloud over a closed section of Lake Shore Drive, scattering the crowd of a couple of thousand people who had gathered to watch. Like the dispersion of the seven hundred or so families who had lived in these buildings more than fifteen years earlier, most of the observers were quickly gone from sight. The demolition, a concrete destructive act, was an important symbolic gesture to Chicago and the world that this was the beginning of a new era in public housing in Chicago.

This chapter examines the transformation of two public housing developments into mixed-income "communities" and the neighborhoods in which they are located: Cabrini Green, located in Chicago's gentrifying Lower North Side,[1] and Lakefront Properties on the South Side in the North Kenwood-Oakland neighborhood adjacent to Bronzeville.[2] Both are still in the process of redevelopment, so the outcome is still to be determined. But that is not the focus here; rather we are interested in how each was transformed over decades into a space of flexible accumulation in which to build these new mixed-income communities. Like Englewood, both public housing developments have been officially classified as ghettos, places of no value "as is" and in need of complete reconstruction. The arguments for redevelopment hinge on this particular representation to justify demolition but also on an imaginary future space that is mixed-income and stable that will lure private investors. Contrary to the homogeneous communities conceptualized in theory, these new neighborhoods will allegedly somehow perform differently because of the context in which they are located and the circumstances under which they were created.

The two cases presented here are a little different than the previous ones. The change in public housing is a result of targeted policy and decisions made at both the federal and local level, as well as serving the interest of capital. Because so much is in the public record, we have more evidence of the forces that drive policy decisions that continue to shape the space of these sites in Chicago and around the United States, which can be useful for others trying to make sense of what is happening in their cities. As this chapter demonstrates, policy implementation controlled to some extent the market forces that normally shape the cycles of creative destruction over time, but it also made accumulation and commodification more surgical and calculating in these neighborhoods. Furthermore, this current regime has given the private sector the authority to shape how the space is commodified, determining who can accumulate it and who can consume it. We begin by retracing the US housing policy that made transformation necessary.

Creating a Space for Hope

In the 1990s, the United States significantly changed its public housing policy with the intent to transform large-scale developments, particularly those with "severely distressed" high-rise buildings, into smaller-scale, economically integrated housing communities. This was facilitated by the HOPE VI program (Housing Opportunities for People Everywhere). Announced soon after President Clinton took office in 1993, HOPE VI offered Public Housing Authorities (PHAs), through a competitive grant process, up to $50 million to "turn around" distressed developments. These funds could be used to rehabilitate, raze, and rebuild units to produce lower-density, high-quality public housing. Beyond improving housing quality, social services were also expected to help transform the occupants of public housing. As Andrew Cuomo, former secretary of HUD (1997–2001), described, there was a broader agenda for HOPE VI: "This program is about much more than rebuilding housing. . . . We will give them the chance to work their way out of poverty and out of public housing." This particular representational space—poverty as something that can be "worked out of"—was a powerful trope, paralleling the administration's framing of welfare reform. Both public housing and welfare were holding poor people back, preventing them from getting out of poverty. The underlying logic was that once free of these federal programs, the poor would get out of poverty, but if they did not then they likely had a character flaw that made them "hard to house" (Popkin et al. 2008). The former demonstrated that the poor did not need public housing and the latter that they did not deserve it.

Equally important was the aspiration to transform public opinion about public housing or at least the government's role in it. Public housing was emblematic of a long-running failed urban policy that had negatively impacted communities. The HOPE VI demonstration program was designed to help PHAs tear down those developments with high vacancy rates and rehabilitation costs that were deterring private revitalization of neighborhoods, which generally is what qualified them as severely distressed. The primary target was the modern high-rise "projects" built in the 1950s and 1960s, including Chicago's Cabrini Green, Henry Horner Homes, Robert Taylor Homes, and Stateway Gardens. Many of these developments were in need of significant repair, which was costly due to years of neglect and the way they were designed and constructed.

Congress made it easier to tear down the projects by passing legislation in 1995 to no longer require PHAs to replace "one-for-one" demolished public housing units; instead, displaced tenants could be given vouchers to subsidize rent in the private sector. Then, in 1998, it required all PHAs to remove from their inventory any development with 250 or more units with high vacancy rates (10 percent or more) if modernization was more costly than providing tenants rental assistance in the private market. In Chicago, more than eleven thousand of the thirty-eight thousand total habitable units were slated for demolition, the highest proportion in the United States. Furthermore, if the housing was rebuilt, it had to be mixed-income (see Smith 2013).

Income integration appealed to many planners and policy researchers even though most scholarship on neighborhoods still questioned the viability of income mixing. Research did suggest that economic segregation of the poor created and sustained a culture of poverty that prevented residential mobility (J. Wilson 1987). Also, it was believed—though not explicitly stated in HOPE VI—that income mixing could help break the cycle of poverty by connecting public housing tenants to the middle-class and their values and ethics about work, as well as their network in the labor force (Khadduri and Martin 1997). While limited, evidence from the Gautreaux program, which moved more than seven thousand African American families from segregated public housing in Chicago to predominantly white middle-class suburbs, suggested that living in a low-poverty neighborhood could improve employment and education outcomes for some public housing residents (Rosenbaum 1994).

This new approach to public housing redevelopment was also shored up by a general shift in the United States initiated by the Congress for New Urbanism, which supported mixed-use development as opposed to single-use and segregated land uses (e.g., Duany, Plater-Zyberk and Speck 2000), and by groups promoting smart growth and compact development to encourage people to use public transportation, reduce urban sprawl, and build stronger sustainable communities. In fact, the Congress for New Urbanism (1996) worked with the US Department of Housing and Urban Development to produce design guidelines for HOPE VI projects. This included guidance for designing spaces for community interaction to assure that mixing actually occurred. It also presented a more suburban middle-class image of public housing, with front porches and private access to individual units along with small parks and play areas for kids.

Public housing transformation had bipartisan support because it did not rely solely on public funding. Instead it sought out private investment and even allowed private developers to own and operate the replacement housing, assuming that privately built and privately managed communities could attract higher-income owners and renters whose presence would make the development economically viable. Of course, this approach was not without its critics, especially among public housing tenants and advocates (J. Smith 2006a, 2006b). A primary concern was the loss of a permanent supply of publicly owned housing that was not tied to or subject to the volatility of the private market. The foundation laid in the 1930s was meant to keep public housing and the land it occupied out of the speculative hands of the market to assure long-term affordability and availability (Bauer 1951; Stone 1993; Hartman 1998).

Making Stable Mixed Neighborhoods Possible

Many attribute public housing transformation to a broader neoliberal agenda (e.g., Hackworth 2007). A more nuanced explanation is found, however, when this policy framework is examined through the lens of creative destruction and flexible accumulation. From this perspective, public housing transformation is the result of a particular form of ghettoization that has morphed over time. Initially a space that protected the poor from the speculative hand of the market, public housing has changed to one that is destructive and harmful to the poor because it is outside the market and, more importantly, because it can only be saved if the market intervenes. Specific representations of space justify both forms of the ghetto, making each transition possible. The first is the policy that made the development of high-rises possible and the second is the policy research that supported deconcentration.

THE DESTRUCTIVE GHETTO: BUILDING UP

From the start, national policy set the stage for the destruction of high-rise projects even before the first one was built in the 1950s. Up to this time, public housing was relatively low-density walk-up apartments and row houses, much like the private rental housing stock at the time it was built. It also was often of a higher quality because it was new construction and built to relatively good standards. The 1949 Housing Act proposed building more than 800,000 units of public housing in ten years. Grossly underfunded and generally unsupported in most communities, the act itself did not specify developing high-rise public housing; rather it was the conditions at the time that led housing authorities in this direction. In Chicago and elsewhere, it was highly political to site public housing because not all agreed it was needed. The now famous debate in the city council on where to build public housing resulted in suggestions of sites considered to have no value (e.g., in the middle of an expressway) or ones that did and would therefore challenge white segregation (e.g., a golf course) (Hirsch 1998).

The push for high-rise construction was also controversial among architects, planners, and developers. Some believed that high-density, high-rise living was the wave of the future for cities, while those in opposition, including Catherine Bauer, who championed the legislation that created public housing in the United States, believed low-density housing was best suited for families with children and also would blend in better in most neighborhoods. High-rises, however, assured that many units could be built on a smaller footprint, thus requiring less land to produce the same outcome. In Chicago, the result was poor-quality buildings often built in isolated and undesirable locations (see Hirsch 1998). Still, for many families, the new units were better than the tenements and cold-water flats they had moved from.

As time went on, investment in upkeep lagged, which led to an estimated $25 billion backlog in deferred maintenance in the 1990s for America's 1.4 million public housing units (Kimura 2011), most in large developments like Chicago's Cabrini Green, Henry Horner Homes, Robert Taylor Homes, and Stateway Gardens. High rates of crime and violence, which was often drug-related, coupled with high rates of unemployment, teenage pregnancy, and gang activity, and public housing in most cities was deemed a disaster. For the most part, its failure was attributed to the residents living in the developments, much like the demise of Englewood was attributed to the blacks who moved in and not to the racism and uneven development occurring around it. Unlike Englewood and other ghettos constructed by private disinvestment, however, there was also a sense of public responsibility to at least help the families with children to escape these neighborhoods before another generation was trapped. At the time, specific representations of the space via public narratives and national media justified this intervention, partly on moral grounds but also because it was assumed that the mix of people "as is" was incapable of transforming the situation.

The nationally acclaimed book *There Are No Children Here* (Kotlowitz 1991) provided an up close and very personal account of two brothers growing up in the Henry Horner Homes on Chicago's West Side. Coming from a perspective that was inside the projects rather than from outside like so many reports of the time, their story was broadcast in a 1993 movie that starred Oprah Winfrey. It provided graphic images that made their lives real for people outside of public housing. A few years later, Sudhir Venkatesh published *American Project* (1998), which was based on his dissertation completed while studying sociology at the University of Chicago with William Julian Wilson. Revealing similar conditions, Venkatesh showed how despite the disinvestment and neglect that allowed gangs to settle in and that concentrated the poorest of the poor together, people managed to form communities of survival via extended networks and families. In fact, when it was time to move out of their development, a group of families asked the CHA to allow them to "stay together" rather than disperse since they were an extended family that took care of each other and their kids (Venkatesh 2008).[3]

During this time, the Chicago Housing Authority was under the leadership of Vince Lane (1988–1995), who had been trying for several years to turn the organization around but also advance the notion that private investment and mixed-income development was the future (Terry 1995). In 1995, the federal government took over the CHA, claiming the agency was mismanaged and that many of its developments were at a point where rehabilitation was infeasible. This was the first time in US history that HUD had stepped in to manage a PHA that it regulated, which required congressional approval. Under the new management, HUD began cleaning house within the authority and its high-rise developments, using eviction to move out thousands of tenants. Some (Rogal 1998) have suggested this was a means to reduce its obligations in the future, especially after the federally required viability test determined that much of its stock would have to be demolished.[4]

THE DECONCENTRATED GHETTO

Transforming public housing into mixed-income communities required a particular representation of space that ran contrary to how stability had long been presented in hegemonic theories of neighborhood change and reproduced through federal policy. But this did not necessarily render all homogenized communities unstable. It applied only to those that had a high concentration of poverty; high concentrations of wealth were not a concern. Based on mounting research about presumed "neighborhood effects" of living in concentrated poverty, public housing ghettos were assumed to breed and sustain a culture of poverty and would continue to do so as long as so many poor people lived together in such isolated conditions (e.g., Galster 2010).

Perhaps most influential was research by William Julius Wilson (1987) on the "disadvantaged" black communities on Chicago's South Side, which drew attention to the lack of middle-class role models in these developments. This research did not necessarily justify mixed-income communities, but it did suggest that poor people would benefit from living with middle-income people and their values. While there was no clear evidence that mixed-income communities would produce the social and financial goals sought (Schill 1997; Schwartz and Tajbakhsh 1997), the Gautreaux study found evidence that moving poor people into middle-income communities had some positive benefits (Rosenbaum 1994).[5] The promise of deconcentration helped to justify the displacement of public housing residents in the redevelopment process. Proponents of deconcentration supported moving tenants out into communities because it would benefit them (X. Briggs 1998) and, by deconcentrating the ghetto, it was possible to produce the space needed for higher-income people to move in. In other words, it was no longer displacement; it was part of an overall strategy to benefit the poor by purportedly providing opportunities throughout the region.

Still, moving middle-class families into former public housing developments is not the same as moving a small number of poor African American families into a white middle-income neighborhood. Meeting social goals meant creating a development that would attract higher-income families to rent or even buy a house in a mixed-income community, something that at the time was highly unusual for consumers and investors. Taking this into consideration, the Federal Housing Administration (FHA) created underwriting criteria in 1996 to use federal funds to develop mixed-income housing, cautioning HUD that a sufficient number of higher-income families must be part of the mix. Rather than provide a formula, the FHA outlined what was "critical" to develop viable mixed-income and mixed-tenure housing:

- Ratio of public to market-rate housing units: While there is no standard ratio for the mix of income and housing types and tenure, the surrounding income mix will help determine the ratio of market-rate to low-income units. It is assumed that a higher proportion of market-rate units is needed in a predominantly low-income neighborhood to "successfully attract" the market rate tenants.
- Design: Mixed-income developments need to have adequate amenities and good design in order to "compete against" conventional market-rate

units, and the prices must be "very competitive with or, at least initially, even below what the competition is offering for the same level quality and amenities."

• Tenant selection and management: Successful marketing requires careful screening of all tenants, and successful projects will have strong, "even-handed" management that is "customer driven" (US HUD 1997).

HUD did not provide specific ratios or screening criteria. Instead it allowed PHAs and developers more flexibility while removing caps on total development cost to assure quality housing was built under what HUD believed was the sound judgment of market-oriented developers. HUD also crafted new policies to privatize property management by moving it out of public housing authorities.

Congress proposed a threshold of 35 to 40 percent extremely low-income families when rehabbing existing public housing. The HUD secretary commented that this approach "seeks to improve public housing by excluding poor people" (Cuomo 1997, 1). It was a different story in new mixed-income housing developments, however, as HUD opted to follow the FHA's lead and let developers read the market conditions and determine the mix. In other words, it was up to developers and not federal policy or even the need for affordable housing to determine what ratio of public to market-rate housing made a heterogeneous "community" stable.

Mixing It Up in Chicago

The redevelopment of Cabrini Green and Lakefront Properties illustrates how public housing residents—the presumed beneficiaries—are contained and diminished in both the physical and social space of Chicago. Each is a contrast in community engagement and resident resistance, some of which stems from their place in the racial spatial segregation of Chicago, including the Black Belt and places of urban renewal. Both are in very different housing submarkets, with Cabrini Green surrounded by high-end housing and within walking distance of major shopping districts, the Gold Coast, and Lincoln Park, while Lakefront Properties is in the "gap" between the expanding South Loop and Hyde Park and between Bronzeville and Lake Michigan. At their beginning both projects were developed to contain the ghetto. Forty years later the same reason was given to justify their demolition and redevelopment.

CABRINI GREEN: GENTRIFYING THE GHETTO

Located within walking distance of some of the most expensive real estate in the city, Cabrini Green is in the Near North Side community area. Initially this area had been in the Chicago School's zone of transition in the 1920s and was the site for ethnographic research that went into *The Gold Coast and the Slum* (Zorbaugh 1929). By the 1990s, the Cabrini Green development site was truly an "island of despair in a sea of prosperity," a label given to other public housing developments around the country that were now being encroached by gentrification (Wyly and Hammel 1996). The space of Cabrini Green today has been transformed from slum to a gentrifying/gentrified community area, but it did not happen overnight or without a fight. Outlined here is the sequence of events and strategies that moved this forward, beginning with efforts to contain the ghetto and then conquer it.

GHETTO CONTAINMENT Cabrini Green was a combination of four development projects built over twenty years that began with the Frances Cabrini Rowhouses (586 units in 1942), followed by Cabrini Extension North and Cabrini Extension South (1,925 units in 1957) and the William Green Homes (1,096 units in 1962) (Bowly 1978). Before the projects were built, this was "little hell" on the concentric zone map in *The City* and included "Death Corner" according to the 1931 map of Chicago's gangland (Bruce-Roberts 2004). Because it was seen as a threat to the Gold Coast, Mayor Kelly had seven hundred units in old tenement buildings demolished in 1941 on the grounds that the unsanitary conditions were a health hazard. In its place, the CHA built the Cabrini rowhouses. The new housing was an improvement and was welcomed by the first families that moved in.[6] In the beginning, it was a mixed-race settlement with poor Italians, Irish, and African Americans together in one space, most working in nearby factories. This changed as the factories closed and most white residents moved, leaving behind unemployed blacks and many single-parent families. The surrounding area too was struggling.

Since the area was still a threat to the Gold Coast as well as to the north Michigan Avenue shopping district, city planners decided to take a different tack. Employing a military approach, the planners decided to establish a stronghold space, one that after invasion they could use as "an anchor from which the offensive could be launched" (DeClue 1978). That anchor was Sandburg Village, an urban renewal site that pushed out several thousand first-generation Puerto Ricans to build a 2,600-unit middle-income rental development with townhouses and low- to high-rise buildings. A vision of Arthur Rubloff, a "make no small plans" developer, Sandburg Village was Mayor Richard J. Daley's first effort to retain and lure the white middle class back to Chicago (DeClue 1978). This was no small task. The newly formed Chicago Land Clearance Commission (CLCC) had to be convinced to speed up its investigation and report, and the alderman Paddy Bauler had to be convinced it would be all right to lose a substantial portion of his voting constituency. Mayor Daley took care of both (DeClue 1978). At the same time, the CHA expanded Cabrini Green north, building nearly 2,000 high-rise public housing units just west of the CTA Brown Line.

Sandburg Village was an expensive venture compared to other land clearance projects at the time. The CLCC spent more than $10 million to buy the property, relocate 854 families, and demolish 1,053 dwelling units. Rubloff also spent twice as much as other interested developers to acquire the land (about $6 million). Of course he envisioned a good return on his investment, and he was right.[7] The planners and Rubloff's goal was to "set the renewal urge spinning off on its own" with this new development (DeClue 1978). Wells Street in Old Town was still a home to peep shows and prostitution, but the area was also home to artists, hippies, and homosexuals and was ripe for gentrification given the housing stock and the location, which was now "protected" by the new Sandburg Village.

By the 1980s, Cabrini Green still had industry flanking its west side along the river, but that changed when the long-time catalog and retail department store Montgomery Ward closed in 2000. This freed up several buildings along the river west of Cabrini Green that were converted to condominium and office space. By the mid-1990s, Cabrini was becoming an island surrounded by prosperity. Cabrini residents understood the situation. Rumors had long been circulating that the CHA wanted to tear down these projects. As Congressman Bobby Rush said at a meeting with residents, "This is some valuable land . . . you have people salivating to get their hands on it." But they could not just take the land; the seizure had to be justified. To this end, specific representations of the space and its people as well as real events made it easy to invade the island. Residents, however, also resisted, which is why the offensive launched fifty years ago is still not complete.

DEMOLITION JUSTIFIED As Cabrini Green became more isolated, its representation in the public eye became more "notorious" and emblematic of what was wrong with public housing in the United States. Cabrini Green was exposed to the country through different media that put the spotlight on the violence in the development. One such event was Mayor Jane Byrne and her husband occupying an apartment in 1981 to show Chicagoans—and the world—that public housing could be managed and the violence tamed. They left in less than three weeks without much impact. Ten years later, the movie *Candy Man* (1992), which featured a mythical serial killer in Cabrini Green, was released. The same year,

Dantrell Davis was shot and killed by a gang member from a vacant unit high up in a Cabrini building as he was walking with his mother to school. The shooter had intended to kill a rival gang member.

Dantrell was the third and youngest child at nearby Jenner Elementary to be shot and killed, and it triggered national media attention. Mayor Daley ordered the police to sweep Cabrini Green for weapons, drugs, and gang members, but he did this only after being publicly criticized by residents and black community leaders (Dumke 2012). CHA's leader, Vince Lane, ordered four "underused" high-rise buildings to be sealed up, including the one the shooter used, which meant moving tenants out quickly. At the time, Daley suggested that these and other buildings might have to be torn down as part of a "long-term master plan for public housing in Chicago" (Dumke 2012).

RESIDENT RESISTANCE The image of Cabrini Green as an extremely violent space was real but was also hyper-realized through the media. Missing from the narrative was the neglect, and, most likely intentionally, the community space created in order to survive living in the projects. As with Englewood, Cabrini Green residents found ways to cope with disinvestment and racism. While fictional, the sitcom *Good Times* (1975–79) gave Americans a glimpse into life in the projects. Set in Cabrini Green, the show focused on a family—which included two parents—and the larger community of people in the building who helped each other out. While it included some violence, it mostly dealt with real issues like racial discrimination in the workplace, machine politics, and the poor management of public housing, with comedian Jimmie Walker helping to lighten the heaviness of watching a show about poor black people in Chicago. In the real world, Cabrini residents facing these same problems had a long history of standing up for themselves and protesting the CHA for not responding to their requests to improve the living conditions (Wright, Wheelock, and Steele 2006).

A year after Dantrell was shot, the CHA made an agreement with the Local Advisory Council (LAC)—the elected tenant leadership—to demolish 660 units and build 493 new units of public housing and issue 167 housing assistance vouchers for the remaining. In 1994, HUD awarded the CHA its first HOPE VI grant of $50 million to redevelop this small portion of the 3,600-unit site. A Request for Proposals was issued to replace what was going to be torn down. None of the responses fully met the minimum criteria of reducing density and providing the appropriate number of replacement units on site, and the city and CHA declared all the plans inappropriate. Soon afterward, the city and CHA entered into "private" meetings to create an alternative strategy: the Near North Redevelopment Plan and the corresponding tax increment financing district.

The plan was to demolish 1,300 public housing units and produce 2,300 new units in a larger geographic area (340 acres compared to 10 acres in the original proposal). Only 700 units would be public housing and half of those were for "working poor." In response to this plan, residents filed a lawsuit against both the city and the CHA on the grounds that the plan was prejudicial to their interests. Residents were outraged because, besides violating the previous development agreement with the LAC, the plan was to demolish more buildings and move more residents permanently off-site. A short documentary, *Voices of Cabrini* (1997), directed by a Columbia College graduate student, shows a couple hundred residents at a public meeting that they had not been invited to attend but should have been. In reviewing the plan, many residents were convinced that it was just a land grab. As one woman described it, "They're crooks every one of them . . . we have been dealing with [public] housing too long. Give us a piece of paper that says we'll get us one of those houses" (Bezalel 1997).

In the spring of 1997, a federal judge stopped CHA from demolishing anything more until the conflict was resolved. This injunction eventually gave tenants legal standing and power in the redevelopment process. The judge ruled that the LAC would be a codeveloper with CHA and that firm plans for replacement units had to be in place—and preferably built—before existing buildings could be demolished. They also negotiated to expand the number of units available to public housing residents.[8] While controversial in Chicago, the city's decision to create a TIF district in the area also was an important factor in the lawsuit, as the court ordered the CHA to build 895 public-housing-eligible units in the HOPE VI planning area, which was now defined by the boundaries of the TIF district and not just the public housing site. It also meant that any development that utilized public funds to produce housing in the TIF district would have to include some public and affordable housing.

GENTRIFYING THE GHETTO? Producing a TIF district requires evidence that the space is blighted, which officially made the entire space of the Near North Redevelopment Plan area a slum. While this designation provided the city a means to get a lot more funding for redevelopment, it also meant that families buying into new high-end housing around Cabrini were now officially living in or near the slum, and the city needed to clear it quickly. Since things were tied up in court, though, the CHA land was off-limits. The city had to create the impression that the space was changing quickly, so the city decided to start development of the first phase using land it owned. The area was rebranded as North Town Village. Residents were involved in the process of selecting the developer, and before ground was broken, banners were hung declaring the new space North

Town Village. The map produced to sell homes and attract market-rate renters surgically excluded Cabrini Green while including the assets nearby. The development, which truly mixed public housing into the market-rate and affordable development, sold out in a matter of weeks. A segment on *60 Minutes*, which began by showing demolition of a public housing building, featured a young white couple who described the buying frenzy (Kohn 2002). It also featured a public housing tenant who decided to move her family in without her husband since she worried he would not pass the annual drug test. All these representations conveyed an image that Cabrini was gone even though most of the buildings were still standing.

The second phase did not launch as well even though most of the high-rise and mid-rise buildings were gone, literally erasing from the site any image of public housing. While development around Cabrini was continuing to fill in, the new mixed-income condominiums on Division Street were not selling, in part because of the recession but also, unlike in the first phase, there were more options. In early 2010, the city "bailed out" the developer when it was unable to begin repaying a $32 million construction loan from J. P. Morgan Chase (Corfman 2010). As described in *Crain's Business*, a default "would be a punch in the gut to the ambitious plan to remake the city's public housing projects" (Corfman 2010). After paying $3.4 million to the bank, about two months later the city gave the developer about $8 million from the American Recovery and Reinvestment Act so he could continue building his mixed-income community (Corfman 2010). The new phase, however, is market-rate and affordable rentals instead of condos.

CONQUERING THE GHETTO? The last high-rise was demolished in the spring of 2011. It was the building that a group of residents had tried to convert to a resident-owned limited-equity co-op. After that demolition was completed, the perception was that Cabrini Green was completely gone and the space transformed. But the original Cabrini Green rowhouses at the south end of the development site are still standing. All were to be rehabbed according to CHA's 2000 plan. To date, about 146 of the 584 units have been refurbished. The current status is uncertain since "[a]fter numerous stakeholder meetings and deliberate considerations, CHA has concluded that it will no longer support 100 percent public housing at the Cabrini Rowhouses property" (Chicago Housing Authority 2012, 17). Alex Polikoff, the lawyer who fought the CHA and won the Gautreaux case and supposedly represents the interest of public housing residents, sent a letter to elected officials and HUD stating that "to house nearly 600 exclusively public housing families in a single location (as this development did at the outset of the Plan for Transformation) would similarly ignore what we should have learned about the effects of concentrated urban poverty" (McConnell and Polikoff 2012). And while the letter goes on to note that the surrounding neighborhood is gentrified, rather than support for development of public housing, it states that "a thoughtful plan that includes unsubsidized housing for families of moderate means should be the objective" (McConnell and Polikoff 2012).

As of 2015, residents are still occupying about 125 rowhouse units. A judge recently determined that if the CHA demolishes the remaining units, then at least 40 percent of new units in the redevelopment area must be public housing. Others have returned to the approximately 600 replacement units built. New market-rate development is filling in the patchwork of vacant lots in the larger TIF district. Still, the space is a work in progress. Following the arc of its history, the Cabrini case illustrates how public housing can function as a site for reserve, anticipating a future state of intensive investment. As a flexible space for accumulation, it could be cast as a ghetto even with gentrification surrounding it by using TIF to declare it a slum and then using representations of space to reimagine it as a gentrifying neighborhood. The site, however, is not completely gentrified or transformed; rather it is an illusion that appears to rely heavily on the private sector but in reality requires deep public subsidies to work, not to support the low-income tenants but to subsidize development of the market-rate apartments and condominiums. This also is the case for the redevelopment of Lakefront Properties, which actually was the site of the first mixed-income public housing development in Chicago and in the United States. An experiment in the late 1980s, its mix then was about half public housing residents, and all tenants were lower-income renters.

LAKEFRONT PROPERTIES: GENTRIFYING THE GHETTO IN A GHETTO

Lakefront Properties was a compilation of six high-rise buildings along Lake Michigan on a narrow strip of land just west of Lake Shore Drive straddling the Kenwood and Oakland communities between Thirty-Ninth and Forty-First Streets. They were built in the 1950s and early 1960s as part of four public housing projects: Victor Olander Homes (150 units), Victor Olander Extension (150 units), Washington Park Homes (150 units), and Lake Michigan Homes (457 units) (Bowly 1978). While lakefront property in Chicago is generally considered prime real estate, this was not the case in the 1950s in Kenwood and Oakland, which like many communities on the South Side saw a rapid shift from white to black as the Black Belt expanded after World War II. As described in chapter 3, poor families were being pushed out of Hyde Park by the University of Chicago and from the west, where the massive Stateway Gardens and Robert Taylor Homes were built along several miles of State Street.

As with Cabrini Green, development of the Lakefront Properties was a means to contain ghetto expansion along the lake down to Hyde Park (Hirsh 1998). Of the two communities, Oakland was poorer than Kenwood, though North Kenwood is more like Oakland while South Kenwood with its large homes and proximity to the University of Chicago is usually associated with Hyde Park to the south.[9] Today, the data on Kenwood suggests that both Kenwood and Hyde Park are "stable" middle-income communities while Oakland is still low-income. This shift appears to have begun in the late 1980s around the time when the first proposal to redevelop Lakefront Properties was being considered. Unlike Cabrini, where planners established a stronghold site from which to transform the larger space of poverty, the developer proposed simply to launch his invasion.

MARKET INVASION In 1987, Ferd Kramer, a major developer in Chicago, proposed to transform Lakefront Properties and the area around it by demolishing four of the towers, rehabbing the other two for seniors, and filling in surrounding land with low-rise townhouses and apartment buildings that would include a scattering of public housing for families. The full vision of Kramer's North Kenwood–Oakland Redevelopment Plan was for up to 3,500 units on three hundred acres in what was described as "housing for people of all income levels" (Ziemba 1987). Kramer had developed Lake Meadows and Prairie Shores, two large high-rise rental properties north of the site in the 1950s with the aim to "shatter the notion that urban cities were destined to be racially segregated" (*Chicago Tribune* 2002).

Ferd Kramer's vision was big and intended to be transformative, much like Dearborn Park, which helped launch massive investment into the South Loop in the early 1980s (Wille 1998). His plan for North Kenwood–Oakland projected a representation of space that did not erase the past per se—it still had low-income people and blacks—but instead repackaged the space in a way that the presence of poor black people in public housing was not the dominant image. It was unclear from his proposal, however, just how much public housing there would be in the mix and how and where it would be scattered in the space. Whether intentional, the lack of precision produced a "fuzzy" representation of space that was open to interpretation, which was to Kramer's advantage and disadvantage. While he was not obligating himself to a specific racial or income mix that could deter investors or worry the neighbors, it also left the future open to the imagination, allowing space to be more or less homogeneous, which, depending on a person's point of view, could be more or less threatening to the neighborhood.[10]

The downside of being fuzzy about the mix was that it meant an uncertain future for the public housing families that had already been displaced. At the time, families from three of the buildings had been relocated and a fourth was being emptied so the CHA could renovate them, but it was taking longer than planned because funding was not secured to cover the full cost of rehabilitation. Mayor Harold Washington and the CHA opposed Kramer's plan because he made no firm commitment to replace the seven hundred public housing family units that would be lost if the four towers were demolished, and HUD's regional office supported rehabilitation of what were considered sound structures (Ziemba 1987). Reports at the time, however, said that what really stalled Kramer's proposal was the lack of support from the local alderman, who was concerned about the political repercussions from forty thousand voters in public housing units (Ziemba 1987).

Support for the project came from outside the neighborhood and specifically from people and entities that could benefit from a larger share of middle-class families living nearby. This included the University of Chicago and the Amoco Corporation. The university was landlocked—an island of prosperity surrounded by a sea of despair—and in need of residential space for students and faculty members. The CEO of Amoco, along with other CEOs sitting in corporate headquarters downtown, was looking for something that would reverse the loss of middle-class families in the city (Wille 1998). The only significant support from inside the neighborhood came from Harold Lucas, a major voice of the Kenwood Oakland Community Organization (KOCO), which had been leading the charge to redevelop the neighborhood for more than twenty years. Some claimed he did not speak for them because he did not live in the neighborhood (he lived further south in Beverly). Some also thought Lucas was pushing for the development to be primarily low-income housing. In an interview, Lucas suggested that perhaps people did not understand that he and KOCO were in support of infill and new development of housing and businesses for a wide income range (Joravsky 1988). Clearly, the fuzziness of the proposal produced a space that could be filled many different ways depending on one's point of view.

As opposition remained entrenched and the four public housing buildings sat vacant as the CHA awaited funding, another supporter surfaced: Alex Polikoff, the lawyer responsible for the Gautreaux consent decree, which in addition to vouchers to disperse families from CHA housing included about $50 million for scattered-site infill public housing. These funds could not be used to rehab existing public housing buildings in concentrated poverty areas, but they could be used to build new units in mixed-income communities. Kramer told the *Chicago Tribune* that Polikoff "is willing to use the funds for replacement public housing in North Kenwood" (Ziemba 1988). In reality, this part of the consent decree had been challenging to implement, as even small developments were met with opposition. The Lakefront Properties and Kramer's plan represented a potential "win-win" situation in North Kenwood–Oakland because it permanently eliminated concentrated poverty on the site—the goal of the Gautreaux consent decree—and replaced it with mixed-income housing—the goal sought by Polikoff (2006). This did not necessarily align with the goals of all the public housing residents who were waiting to return to a renovated Lakefront Properties.

COMMUNITY RETRENCHMENT Running counter to Kramer's vision was a planning process under way that in his words would produce an "emasculated" plan that would simply rehab the CHA buildings and not take on the larger development needs, including retail investment. Critical of the city, Kramer said, "They would have us make little plans, instead of big plans, just the opposite of what Daniel Burnham wanted us to do" (Ziemba 1988). Planners from the city saw things differently: "We thought that the planning process should involve the entire community, and that it could be done without demolishing any CHA buildings. We come into this with no preconceptions, no plan of our own. We simply want to help the people" (Joravsky 1988). The process was slow going (Joravsky 1988). While the planning process was presented as being neighborhood-driven rather than from City Hall, many involved did not believe this was the case (McGlory 1993). Still, more than two hundred people gathered for many meetings over six months, all with different expectations and ideas. Some of the lower-income participants feared being displaced again, while middle-income homeowners, some long-term residents and others new arrivals, did not want to see conditions preserved (Boyd 2008). In the end, public housing was safe, though not necessarily because residents wanted it or the high-rise version of it.

CHA ADVANCEMENT By 1989, Kramer's plan had been tabled and the North Kenwood community area plan had been completed. The CHA had secured the $14 million needed to rehabilitate at least two of the four vacated buildings, and the newly hired head of CHA, Vince Lane, was preparing to implement a new model for public housing redevelopment, the Mixed-Income New Communities Strategy (MINCS), in two of the Lakefront Properties buildings. As the first mixed CHA development, it was to be a pilot for more to come. When the renovated buildings reopened in 1991 as Lake Parc Place, which was owned but not managed by the CHA, Lane described the mix in this way: "The working residents (will) provide a role model, at least in the minds of families on welfare, that is achievable: bus drivers, plumbers, medical technicians.... They're not doctors and lawyers, but if the goal that's set for you looks so far out that you don't believe you can achieve it, you won't even try" (Johnson 1991). In a way, he was describing the mix some Puerto Ricans envisioned for the neighborhood around Paseo Boricua with a narrower income range than might occur from gentrification.

Before Lake Parc Place opened, the city designated North Kenwood–Oakland a conservation area and appointed a fifteen-member Conservation Community Council (CCC) to guide redevelopment and, to a certain extent, move the neighborhood plan forward (Joravsky 1988). The CCC publicly supported lower-density residential development—infill and rehabilitation—and not the high density that would be sustained when CHA remodeled its remaining towers. As described in chapter 3, the CCC was powerful and, as Boyd (2008) describes, determined the fate of Lakefront Properties. In 1998, after sitting vacant for more than ten years, the rest of Lakefront Properties were demolished and the commitment made to the displaced families was unfulfilled.[11] Any vision for replacement housing was still to be determined since it was "subject to" funds being available.

Around this time, research was published on how the mix was working in Lake Parc Place. The data suggested that most residents were satisfied with the living situation (Rosenbaum, Stroh, and Flinn 1998), particularly public housing residents because for the first time they had good management that responded to problems and good quality housing they actually could maintain (Nyden 1998). A key finding, however, was that there was little mixing of the lower- and higher-income people and that higher-income families were more mobile than public housing families (Rosenbaum, Stroh, and Flinn 1998). Despite these findings, HUD and the CHA continued to promote this model as they advanced redevelopment plans across the city. A key difference moving forward was the shift to market-rate for-sale and rental housing to make the mix, promoting income levels that were higher but also tying people to the site with a home purchase.

Ferd Kramer died in 2002, the same year the development team of Draper and Kramer got the CHA contract to redevelop the fifteen acres of land from the cleared Lakefront Properties. The initial plan approved by the CCC had 510 units, half of them "affordable" and the rest market rate, each group split evenly between rental and owner occupied. The affordable rentals, which made up one-fourth of the mix, were technically for public-housing-eligible residents whose average income was about $10,000. But the income ceiling was up to 80 percent of the area median (about $50,000 for a family of four). The "affordable" for-sale housing was priced for families earning up to 120 percent of area median (about $82,000 for a family of four).

When the first phase of the new Lake Park Crescent development went on the market in 2008, the "market-rate" units were priced more like the North Side than North Kenwood–Oakland, with rowhouses listed at $700,000 (Luc 2008). Nearby, another developer had just completed five new million-dollar-plus homes, which suggests there was a market. But then the recession hit. In 2009, the city also lost its bid for the 2016 Olympics; many of the venues and the housing for the games were to be built along the lake on the South Side. By 2011, with only half of the Lake Park Crescent units sold, Draper and Kramer reduced prices by 40 percent and offered incentives such as down payment assistance and free washers and dryers to lure people in who were sitting out the market (Zenn 2011). While they were able to sell out the rowhouses, it was slower going with the condos. Around the same time, Draper and Kramer also stopped plans to redevelop nearby Lake Meadows into a high-density, seven-thousand-unit, mixed-income development. Two years later, a different developer began the $51 million Phase Two of Lake Park Crescent, with about $10 million in upfront support from the city to construct 132 units of multifamily rental housing in a mix of mid-rise and three- and six-flat buildings. It was not clear how many were for public housing residents. Mayor Emanuel was quoted in the press release announcing this investment: "Affordable housing is essential to the diversity that makes Chicago one of the world's most livable big cities. . . .We remain committed to the building and preserving of affordable housing city-wide" (Studenkov 2012).

As with Cabrini Green, Lakefront Properties was a space of flexible accumulation that over time was transformed but never fully gentrified, even though gentrification advanced south from the Loop and north from Hyde Park and Kenwood along the lakefront. Unlike Cabrini, Lake Parc Place and the new Lake Park Crescent Homes have not (yet) been surrounded by gentrification, which may be why the developer had a hard time attracting market-rate buyers. This might change, however. Draper and Kramer still own Lake Meadows, which is north of the site. Recent buzz is that a request for proposals was issued to redevelop it along the lines of the 2008 vision, which included razing the apartments and building up twenty new towers along with townhomes and low-rise flats, doubling the number of families living there and adding more than 500,000 square feet of retail (Dunlap 2014). This may be their stronghold.

Changing Public Housing Neighborhoods

From the beginning, Cabrini Green and Lakefront Properties were a means to cordon off the poor from wealthy and usually white homeowners. Like containing a disease, the initial intent was to contain the spread of the ghetto and, more importantly, prevent the further loss of the middle class. Left to the market, it's uncertain if these sites would have been eventually rebuilt for higher-income families. Building public housing, however, clearly prevented it. Intended to be a permanent space for lower-income families to occupy, public housing in the United States and Chicago was to remain outside the speculative hands of the market. Based on a policy narrative that the public sector could intervene in the market under certain circumstances, the city, like others around the country, replaced tenements with public housing, which was justified by health and safety concerns. Furthermore, building these developments only for poor people was justified since economic spatial segregation was assumed to be natural and was the status quo.

Whether it was intentional or an unintended consequence, as it became apparent that the permanent ghetto that public housing had created was benefiting neither the tenants nor the surrounding neighborhood, a new policy narrative began to evolve. Cities in the 1970s were feeling the fiscal burden as industry and the middle class were leaving. Public housing, a product of public funding, was undercapitalized and lacked the reserves to improve it, and policy prohibited demolishing it. This left public agencies in a difficult situation, which was often made worse when corruption and politics were involved, as was the case in Chicago. Entering the current regime, the Chicago Housing Authority and the city had limited options: hunker down and deal with the conditions or retreat and leave residents to fend for themselves. To a certain degree, both tactics were employed, and in both cases the surrounding neighborhood—residents and those outsiders interested in CHA's land—became partners of sorts even if they were not on the same side. Rubloff was more of a silent partner, aggressively working with the city to make money bringing the middle class closer to Cabrini but not as part of its space, while Kramer was quite visible and a vocal outsider on a social mission to mix race and class in one residential space. Both were poised in different ways when the policy narrative changed and the mixed-income model was embraced.

These cases present two solutions that played out differently even though they were guided by the same spatial practices and representations of space. Lakefront Properties, which built the first mixed-development public housing that included working-class households, was not extended when the CHA introduced the full mixed-income proposal. While this decision was driven by market forces, it also was in response to the surrounding neighborhood, which wanted higher-income families and lower density. Having been long dispersed, Lakefront's residents were not active participants in planning or protesting the redevelopment. While there were advocates for public housing itself, the voices of actual residents were not heard. In contrast, Cabrini residents were—and still are—actively protesting the plans being implemented. They were firsthand witnesses to the siege and employed their own tactics to hold their ground, though that is becoming a smaller space within the larger development.

When it came to income mixing, even with million-dollar homes being built nearby, the plan was to make only about one-third of the replacement units in each development public housing. In Chicago, this is the default no matter the location. Despite evidence that justified higher rates—especially in the gentrifying area around Cabrini Green—developers have successfully argued for this rate, claiming this is the only way they can make the whole development deal work, and the courts have believed them (Bennett, Hudspeth and Wright 2006). Others admit it is based on a lingering fear of racial tipping (Ranney, Wright, and Zhang 1996), and to a certain extent it is because this has become the logical stasis for mixed-income communities and the representational space for public housing in Chicago.

The trajectory of these cases shows how a blend of social science research, public policy, and market mechanisms can gentrify the public housing ghetto, or at least its representations of space. But it relies on a specific image of heterogeneous space, one in which the space is relatively homogeneous and in which the mix is controlled. Even then it cannot guarantee that gentrification will occur. While policy made it possible for the CHA to clear and redevelop large tracts of land, it could not control the process completely. Resistance by different parties over time and for different reasons slowed the process. In the case of Cabrini and other developments in Chicago, legal protections have given residents power to stay, at least for now. While it is not a fait accompli, it's uncertain what each space will look like in ten years, especially given the fast pace of the development apparatus that just a few years ago was nearly bankrupt. Regardless of neighborhood, these representations and constitutive forces and conditions warrant different forms of resistance and approaches to community development, which we examine next.

CHAPTER 8

Building the Organization or Building the Community?

Community Development in a Time of Flexible Accumulation

> My own guess is that the only thing stopping riots or total social
> breakdown in many cities are the intricate networks of social
> solidarities, the power and dedication of community development,
> and the hundreds of voluntary groups working round the clock
> to restore some sense of decency and pride in an urbanizing
> world shell-shocked by rapid change, unemployment, massive
> migrations, and all of the radical travails inflicted by capitalist
> modernity passing into the nihilist downside of postmodernity.
> But community has always meant different things to different
> people and even when something that looks like it can be found, it
> often turns out to be as much part of the problem as a panacea.
> Well-founded communities can exclude, define themselves against
> others, erect all sorts of keep out signs. (Harvey 1996, 55)

Although well-established and universally hailed, community development is among the most concocted, ambiguous, and contested concepts. Still, it is a fundamental part of urban life and plays many roles: associations that defend neighborhoods against outsiders; strong, place-based ethnic or racial platforms for advancement; a quasi-welfare "shadow state" helping disadvantaged people; spaces for innovation and social change; and co-opted institutions operating as middlemen. Whatever they are, many agree that community development initiatives have had a tremendous impact on US neighborhoods. Most of this work is done by people employed or volunteering in financially strapped organizations continuously facing the possibility of extinction, caught between the pressures and needs of their communities and the priorities and agendas of funders and outside forces. And most, but not all, recognize that government, corporate largess, and foundations will not fund the revolution, and that neighborhoods are probably not the optimal sites for advancing some of the changes needed to transform inequities. Still, they can make a difference, and they do.

In this chapter, we critically examine a trajectory of community development in Chicago that generally reflects what has occurred in US cities since the 1970s and is now driving change in neighborhoods as well as defending them. Our reflections here come from experience working in and with organizations challenged by "damned if you do, damned if you don't" conditions and through observing different strategies used to survive and fight another day. Focusing on such ambiguities and contradictions, we find community development caught in the trappings of flexible accumulation and in some cases contributing to the displacement of the people it claims to represent. Despite the wide range of organizations and approaches, many community development groups in Chicago (and elsewhere) have veered away from their social justice origins and have more or less transformed into extensions of the local governance regime.

Community Development: Real and Imagined

Lefebvre made the distinction between the space that is imagined (perceived) and the space that is actually experienced (lived) in order to show the disconnect between the two and to help us see how the former can mask or mislead our understanding of the latter. Community development is a vast and enormously diverse field of practice that advances disparate causes under the same general aspiration: to improve the life of the community. *Community* is a powerful term, evoking a wide range of positive images; practically anything can be and is advocated in its name. Marion Iris Young (1990) reminds us, however, that it is also a means of exclusion; in the process of distinguishing one community from another, we create a collection of "others" and a potential source of discrimination, segregation, or bigotry. We saw this occur to some degree in all the cases in this book. We also observed situations where placing all people under the same broad community umbrella ignores hierarchies within. Still, Young and others believe that the term is a powerful trope, particularly when informed by social justice and solidarity that is evoked when discussing community development.

Community development practice is a product of these divisions and of often competing interests, which at times cancel each other out and limit the field's ability to influence systemic forces. Narrowing community development to a single definition is problematic. In practice, it follows many different trajectories depending on who and what is targeted, who is driving it, and which principles are advanced. For example, efforts in poor neighborhoods may aim to alleviate the worst conditions by providing basic necessities (food, clothing, shelter), while community development in immigrant neighborhoods has generally helped residents transition into the United States.

By design, neighborhood-based community development is limited because it is literally grounded in residential, place-based, consumption, and social reproduction issues. Some argue that community development has evolved into a nonprofit industrial complex that can no longer question the status quo (e.g., Eick 2007). Others point out how its universal appeal and strategic location makes it a great vehicle to be co-opted by the forces it is actually trying to fight, influence, and even control. As Craig (2007) describes, community development is an integral element and extension of government and philanthropy "spraying on community as a solution to social problems" (337), often bypassing social justice issues.

A fundamental challenge for community development today is actually dealing with the failure of capitalism, which requires massive redistribution of resources and power to level the playing field. Clearly, social change of this magnitude is a big task! While some do not believe this is possible at all, others do, but they also recognize that it will not come through community development work alone. Occupy Wall Street reminded us that movement politics are needed to empower, raise awareness, and promote radical democracy. Even then, we cannot assume that social relations will be transformed in ways that might produce equality and opportunity for all or eradicate extreme forms of poverty in our society.

Creative destruction and the production of space for accumulation complicates our interpretation of community development practice. While the scale of intervention and change is rarely at the level where investment and disinvestment decisions are made, many believe that our neighborhoods and their occupants likely would be worse off but for the many community development actors and organizations out there. In practical terms, community development is always struggling with investors in some way, either trying to lure them in or fighting to keep them out. The challenge is finding a balance. In Chicago, we find many working in the field who have adapted their approaches to specifically respond to the creative destruction and accumulation taking place in neighborhoods, though not necessarily in ways that will stop it. Some are like the frog sitting in a pot with the water slowly being warmed up, unaware that the water is getting hot. Still others, while aware, are either unable or unwilling to jump out before it's too late.

Chicago's Community Development Mosaic

Chicago has long been a pioneer of neighborhood-based organization and action. Over the years, people from different neighborhoods have united to fight injustices caused by sustained levels of segregation and discrimination. Some neighborhoods have become platforms for action by those deprived of their civil rights and economic opportunities. When confronted with the self-perpetuating machine politics Chicago is so famous for, people have few alternatives but to fend for themselves, and their neighborhood is often where the struggle begins.

Contemporary community development in Chicago generally traces its roots back to several key moments and movements, beginning with Jane Addams and the establishment of settlement houses, and to Saul Alinsky, whose working-class neighborhood organizing model focused on putting demands on City Hall and corporations. At the same time, we find a long history of self-help and struggle against racism in the Black Belt, especially practices and policies that either constrain (i.e., restrictive covenants) or push out blacks. Beginning in the 1970s, some community-based organizations began joining citywide coalitions that cut across racial and ethnic divides, often to fight the mayor and other elected officials. This is how Harold Washington was elected the first African American mayor in Chicago. But as community development corporations and financial intermediaries grew substantially in number and size in the 1980s and 1990s, neighborhood planning and place-based development strategies became more common, and community coalitions subsided.

While not always working in harmony—or intended to—community development today in Chicago is a rich mix of civil rights struggles for equal opportunity and social justice, poor peoples' movements (Piven and Cloward 1978; Betancur and Garcia 2011), union-neighborhood partnerships, social service assistance, and political action as well as on-the-ground physical work to improve material conditions. These efforts fall into five community development approaches: (1) Alinsky-style organizing led for the most part by middle-class whites, (2) civil rights organizing principally led by racial minorities, (3) community economic development initiatives, usually business-oriented, (4) social-service-oriented community initiatives, and (5) state-directed neighborhood redevelopment initiatives. Many organizations have been established for some time. Some have changed orientation, while others have folded. We find patterns in the characteristics and behaviors adapted to survive in this current regime (though not in all groups), some more effective than others.

ALINSKY-STYLE ORGANIZING

A Chicago tradition, Alinsky-style organizing is a nationally and internationally recognized approach to community development that many continue to use. It includes focused campaigns that rely on mobilizing large numbers of people and public confrontation of elected officials and corporate leaders. Using the power of the people to change policy and systems, this approach to community development has been transformed over the past three decades from mobilizing large numbers of people to attend protests and rallies to focusing on lobbying and negotiating with elected officials at the local, state, and federal level.

United Power for Action and Justice (UPAJ) is an example of this new approach to organizing. Formed in 1997, UPAJ actually brought back to Chicago the Industrial Area Foundation (IAF), founded by Saul Alinsky. Following a couple of years of small meetings and "one-on-ones" along with extensive outreach to leaders and institutions in the region, UPAJ was launched at a public forum, where more than ten thousand people came together. As Tom Lenz, an organizer for UPAJ, described, "the talk was about building a politics of the common good, standing for the whole" (1998) and focusing on issues important to communities, such as gun violence, high housing costs, and health care. The approach was different from traditional Alinsky efforts in three ways: it was broad-based, it was multi-issue, and it was regional in focus. All were intended to bring people in Chicago and its suburbs together around common concerns about poverty and democracy. The UPAJ also sought to change the composition of people typically involved to include Jews and Muslims and to be multiracial and multiethnic, and if possible more economically mixed by engaging community-based groups working in lower-income neighborhoods (Lenz 1998).

UPAJ's membership is primarily religious organizations along with a few large membership organizations and coalitions. Leadership is an elected body of twenty to thirty people from the member organizations, who are responsible for bringing in dues and turnout when needed. Staying away from foundation funding and relying on minimal staffing (often graduates of training schools in the city such as the Midwest Academy, ACORN, and Jeremiah Foundation) has helped UPAJ survive the overall disinvestment in organizing of the past few decades. Since its launch, UPAJ and its affiliates, Lake County United and DuPage County United, have focused on specific legislation at the state and federal level dealing with affordable housing, gun control, and health care.[1] Still, while the target was different, the UPAJ organizing approach was much like the structure of past IAF campaigns. Whether large or small, each campaign had to meet the following criteria: "They must make a difference in people's lives. They must be specific and measurable. They must be winnable. They must help build our organization and move us forward" (United Power 2013). As in the past, the desire to win campaigns generally limited the scope of their work.

Organizing in Chicago and elsewhere—for the most part—appears to have shifted from the explosive and confrontational tactics of the 1960s and 1970s to permitted rallies that begin and end on time, pressure tactics, advocacy through the courts, political lobbying, and negotiation. Many factors have contributed to this shift: professionalization, limited resources, co-optation, institutional fatigue, zero-tolerance policies, an increasingly conservative political environment, the paradigm of terrorism, and a sense of impossibility instilled by all of the above. Today, it is more about speaking the institutional language in hopes of getting concessions than it is about "speaking truth to power" (Fisher 1996) to produce institutional change.

Today's context, which often uses a heavy hand—such as the police—to prevent mass outbursts and contain mobilization, has definitely influenced the change in strategy from conflict to negotiation. The initiatives of many Alinsky-style groups in the twenty-first century are often cautious, but they are also moving more toward gaining power by getting a seat at the table (e.g., being appointed to a commission by the governor) to influence decisions made within government. Others are working to openly shape elections, such as Take Back Chicago, a project of Grassroots Illinois Action, a 501(c)4 organization whose mission is "changing the face and focus of politics in Chicago." Their strategy was employed in the 2015 mayoral campaign to hold elected officials accountable for implementing key neighborhood-driven initiatives such as raising the minimum wage, expanding affordable housing, putting more money into public schools, and fair taxes.[2] If challengers to the status quo supported this agenda, the collaborative would back them. Working with other groups to get thousands of people registered and out to vote, Take Back Chicago helped several incumbents lose their seats.

Still, some organizations continue to practice the traditional confrontational approach Alinsky espoused. This includes mass grassroots outbursts in 2006 on immigration reform. These rallies and marches brought together various philosophies of organizing that both coalesced and clashed, and it eventually disbanded once the legislation was defeated because a concerted course of long-term sustained action could not be agreed upon (Betancur and Garcia 2011). Similarly, other ad hoc efforts disintegrated, such as the campaign for a livable wage ordinance after the ordinance passed and the campaign to oppose the 2016 Olympics after Chicago lost the bid. And while some membership groups (e.g., Illinois Coalition for Immigrant and Refugee Rights, National Council of La Raza, Coalition for the Homeless) have been able to maintain sustained actions, they are also cautious and seek to avoid alienating funders and institutional supporters. The same holds for civil rights organizing, which like immigration is based on a broader social justice framework even though focused on specific legislative gains.

CIVIL RIGHTS ORGANIZING

While some may not view civil rights organizing as community development, it was critical in the fight to change how African Americans and other now protected groups were treated in their search for housing; it literally affected where people could live and the quality of their homes and neighborhoods. Having a foundation in the civil rights movement makes this approach to community development a particularly important part of gains minorities have made in the city. Since the 1960s, African American and Latino neighborhoods have been platforms against racism and for affirmative action and collective advancement. Still, some (e.g., see Thorne and Rivers 2001) have deemed civil rights organizing inappropriate for our post-civil-rights era, and many groups have shifted their work to monitor and pursue legal recourse for rights violations. Meanwhile, challenges in the courts have undermined, discredited, and even dismantled civil rights gains, beginning with affirmative action in the 1980s and voting rights in 2013.

The fundamentalist turn in the United States has also transformed how many view civil rights issues. For example, the fight for racial equality has been overwhelmed by accusations of reverse racism. Similarly, some blame immigrants for US employment problems and their own misfortunes. While these conditions have to some extent helped to unite groups, most civil rights causes are on the defensive. The struggle around racial justice has been largely sidelined and in its place we find community development focused principally on social service provision and development.

Today, there are also fundamental questions about other rights, such as the right to housing (e.g., Bratt, Stone, and Hartman 2006) and the "right to the city" (e.g., D. Mitchell 2003). Both offer new directions for organizing communities to challenge disinvestment, displacement, gentrification, and privatization of public goods and services. In Chicago, several groups have focused on incorporating human rights into their work. For example, Heartland Alliance—a nonprofit that has provided services for poor people for more than a hundred years—has reframed this work, saying it is assuring that people get their human rights. The Coalition to Protect Public Housing invited the United

Nations' Special Rapporteur on housing to visit Chicago on the premise that public housing redevelopment violated their human rights (Bennett, Smith, and Wright 2006). While using a human rights framework in the United States is challenging, these efforts represent interesting variations on a rights-based approach to organizing, especially with respect to conflict triggered by creative destruction and space accumulation. An approach like the "right to the city," for example, aims to control the use and ownership of space, something traditional community economic development has struggled with for fifty years.

COMMUNITY ECONOMIC DEVELOPMENT

Initially building on grassroots self-help initiatives and promoted by the federal government in the 1960s, community economic development became a favorite in the 1970s. Community development corporations (CDCs) boomed in Chicago as they did in other cities, engaging in a series of projects to help retain industry, build low-income housing, cultivate and stabilize retail strips, and create credit unions. Over time, nonprofit housing development organizations came to dominate the field, as seen by the large number of them nationwide (Vidal 1989). While a few folded in the 1980s (e.g., Voice of the People in Uptown and People's Housing in Rogers Park), community development initiatives continued to receive significant institutional support and evolved into a solid infrastructure of developers, funders, technical assistance providers, consultants, and financial mediators.

Beginning in the 1990s, momentum shifted to partnerships, especially between the private and public sectors. Advocated by Porter in "The Competitive Advantages of the Inner City" (1995) and hailed by the Ford Foundation in *Corrective Capitalism* (Pierce and Steinbach 1987), community economic development was appealing because it did not rely solely on government funding. This is the case with the low-income housing tax credit, which has allowed CDCs to partner with private capital investors to develop more than one and a half million units of low-income housing in the country since 1986, more than the federal government did in sixty years of public housing development. This marks a shift, too, as some CDCs moved from developing low-income to so-called affordable housing and also focused on for-sale units over rental, which in Chicago and most of the United States benefits lower-middle-income people rather than the poor.

To date, most of the development in places like Englewood has been led by nonprofits, which proves that often they still are "the only game in town" in these neighborhoods. At the same time, driven by quick and profitable deals, the private sector has for the most part only showed interest in potential gentrifying ventures and land deals in strategic locations. Interestingly, the Community Reinvestment Act may be helping to advance private-sector development in some communities, as "greenlining" the inner city has opened floodgates to investors (Miller 2011). In communities like Humboldt Park, CDCs are literally losing ground to speculative investors and losing supporters who move out as rents go up or as opportunities to sell are too good to resist. And while the goal may be "development without displacement," some CDCs have been accused of contributing to gentrification simply by trying to improve the neighborhood, while others, seduced by the idea of mixed-income neighborhoods, are actually building housing for higher-income families.

Hailed in the late 1960s as *the* approach to turn neighborhoods around, nonprofit-led large-scale development projects were expected to spur further investment that would improve conditions in low-income neighborhoods and create opportunities for residents. To date, the results are complicated to interpret. While on the one hand, CDCs have built several thousand units of affordable housing in Chicago, on the other hand the city has lost nearly ten times that much to gentrification and disinvestment. The two top recipients of special federal grants in Chicago under the Office of Economic Opportunity demonstration program, Pyramid West in North Lawndale and the Woodlawn Organization (TWO) on the South Side, are both now defunct. Both ended in scandal after several decades and millions of federal dollars had been invested in the neighborhoods they served and after the organizations were accused by residents of contributing to blight rather than improving the neighborhood. The decline in either neighborhood despite the public investment not only raises doubts about what CDCs can actually do, it has further justified expanding support for public and philanthropic incentives to induce private-sector investment. This includes luring private dollars to support social services that either help people improve their own circumstances where they live or help them escape the ghetto rather than continuing efforts that simply "gild the ghetto" (Lemann 1992). It has also led others to support a more social-service-oriented approach to community development in order to mitigate the effects of poverty and racism or to help individuals and families escape declining neighborhoods.

SOCIAL-SERVICE-ORIENTED COMMUNITY DEVELOPMENT

Social-service-oriented community development really began with the settlement house, which provided residents in a neighborhood access to basic sustenance and support but also assistance that could help individuals to help themselves. Today it is the most common approach to community development in the postwelfare state and includes a wide spectrum of initiatives, from traditional popular education to business-like training institutes, from emergency food and shelter to preventive health and nutrition, from child to elder care, from a faith to a lay focus, from serving only single constituencies to at-large multiethnic coalitions, and from progressive to maintaining the status quo.

Expanding in times of crises or government budget cuts, social service community development efforts have gone from small organizations largely controlled by residents to a "shadow welfare state" that has assumed the responsibilities government has dropped, relying on meager resources and much lower levels of support. Today, practically any church and community organization has added social services of one kind or the other to its core of activities. Poverty alleviation has become the buzzword, and these organizations have become the "go to" places for some of the destitute. In contrast, more left-leaning perspectives believe that strategies that can only alleviate (if that) the effects of poverty and injustice are hiding the problems under the cloak of charity, much like Engels observed in Manchester more than a hundred years ago (Engels 1995 [1872]). Interestingly, this critique aligns with more conservative, market-oriented positions that think social services prevent people from actually struggling with and resolving their economic problems (e.g., see Porter 1995). So for different reasons, radicals and conservatives are both challenging the costs and benefits of providing social services. In the meantime the providers are struggling to keep food on the pantry shelves and clinic doors open as they see more people seeking assistance. Furthermore, many are being asked to participate in large-scale urban projects like HOPE VI, which is intended to transform the social and physical space of poor and disinvested neighborhoods. While the approach is more holistic, as we discuss next, the state's role creates even more challenges for community-based efforts to deal with the effects of creative destruction and accumulation.

STATE-DIRECTED INITIATIVES

A lot of community development is driven by federal policy. Looking back at the War on Poverty, neighborhood-based urban centers were among the forerunners along with the community economic development program in the Office of Economic Opportunity Special Impact Programs. In 1973, President Nixon consolidated federal transfers for community development into the Community Development Block Grant (CDBG) program, which was managed by local government to allow more targeted local strategies. Beginning in the 1980s, drastic reductions in funding turned the CDBG into a marginal community development resource for a decade until the federal government expanded it in the 1990s. At the same time, new initiatives were added, including empowerment zones/enterprise communities (EZ/EC) and HOPE VI. The federal government also included support for faith-based community development, public school reform, and comprehensive community initiatives. Since the 1990s, these types of initiatives have expanded as foundations and intermediate financial institutions have turned to community development to help implement their own top-down reforms. Primarily intended to shape civil society, these approaches often center on disciplinarian, responsibility-based concepts such as communitarianism and social capital (N. Rose 1999; Putnam 2000). Chicago has been experimental ground for many of these efforts. As described below, community-based development groups have either been subordinate, usually as a conduit or middlemen for different institutional actors, or have assumed an oppositional role.

Empowerment zones provided a limited opportunity to spur the economies of selected neighborhoods through incentives to promote job creation. In Chicago, coalescing around the Chicago Workshop for Community Development (CWED), a coalition of nonprofits especially from the Pilsen–Little Village community and the Mid-South put together a grassroots planning effort to draft the application; once it was approved, though, City Hall took over, deciding what and whom to fund (Gills and White 1998). Little or no benefit came out of this program in Chicago (US HUD 2010). Rather than coordinating their work around the plans they had crafted together, the organizations ended up competing with each other to get support from local aldermen and City Hall. This flurry of dollars strategically allocated to already threatened Pilsen and Bronzeville may have further contributed to their gentrification.

The HOPE VI program described in chapter 7 has been the largest land clearance program in Chicago's history since urban renewal, displacing thousands of low-income, mostly black tenants to other poor black communities despite its mandate to relocate people into low-poverty areas of opportunity (Voorhees Center 1996). The result has been more work for nonprofits in these neighborhoods as violence grew from new gangs entering and fighting over turf. While trying to reweave the social fabric of those displaced, community groups are trying to determine how to confront poverty that is even more entrenched. Furthermore, the communities that have been cleared remain unfinished. On the south side in Bronzeville, there are several hundred acres of grass and trees waiting for new development.

Often compared to HOPE VI, Chicago's version of school reform, in part triggered by federal policy, has transformed where children are educated in relation to their neighborhood (Smith and Stovall 2008). The No Child Left Behind act focuses on using test scores to place failing schools on probation.

It has led to nearly a hundred schools closing over ten years, nearly all of them in poor neighborhoods and many where public housing once stood. Along the way, a quasi-private system of charter schools became instrumental in bypassing the teachers union, dividing parents, and taking the best students out of the remaining public schools, further damaging them. As parents and residents of these low-income communities are challenged by yet another outside mandate, community development organizations of all kinds have been dragged into the reform movement. Some have opted to collaborate and actually develop their own charter schools, while others have chosen to design methods to cope with the change (e.g., safe routes to schools). Still others are fighting, to prevent school takeover or closure through neighborhood engagement and protests such as sit-ins and hunger strikes.

Finally, Chicago has been the testing ground for an initiative to develop and implement neighborhood "quality of life" plans, which, while not directly tied to federal policy, is now going nationwide. The New Communities Program (NCP), which produced plans for Pilsen and Englewood along with fourteen other community areas, takes the notion of public-private partnership to a different level. The Chicago Futures initiative, sponsored by the Local Investment Support Corporation (LISC) and the MacArthur Foundation in the 1990s, concluded that direct development activities could be best carried out by the private sector and that neighborhood-based nonprofits should focus on facilitating these efforts through comprehensive strategic plans they drafted together with residents. NCP is based on the assumption that neighborhood interventions had to be comprehensive to make a dent in local conditions and that strategic interventions would bring about neighborhood redevelopment. NCP chose sixteen "challenged" communities with the necessary institutions and organizations to carry out the work. The process started in each neighborhood with LISC's selection of a lead nonprofit agency and a planning process that, although participatory, included for the most part staff members from local and other nonprofits and institutions. Although each community area underwent a separate planning process, most plans contain the same elements and similar strategies in health, education, housing, the arts, and employment and training.

NCP operates as an umbrella for organizations and institutions with an interest or stake in the respective neighborhood. Generally, existing programs and entities are incorporated into a concerted five-year plan. LISC focused on neighborhoods with an appropriate organization and institutional infrastructure, though in a few cases it helped to create the lead organization. From the beginning, LISC sought a division of labor between the public, nonprofit, and private sectors. Community development organizations continued doing their prior work or used the opportunity to add new programs (e.g., home ownership and financial counseling or policy work), with LISC providing seed funding for some initiatives and technical assistance and mediating involvement of City Hall and other parties, particularly foundations.

NCP has been flexible enough to allow for local dynamics to continue, yet it also has influenced them to go in a certain direction, such as establishing centers for working families or promoting art as a major tool for community development. While adding the value of coordination, comprehensiveness, and institutional and political support, program success continues to be a function of pre-existing organizational capacity and neighborhood dynamics (Betancur, Mossberger, and Zhang 2014). For the most part, the traditional challenges of community development still exist and affect outcomes. There are still contradictions between development of place and development of people (Shiffman and Motley 1989), with no real attention paid to the larger forces of unemployment and uneven development, and an emphasis on quick, short-term fixes that focus on the end product over empowerment (Betancur, Bennett, and Wright 1991). Also, NCP has for the most part gotten along with gentrification. An NCP director explained that rather than opposing it, they chose to welcome gentrifiers and redirect their work toward the goal of building a mixed-income community. In the end, assuming that low-income neighborhoods undergoing gentrification can be turned into real mixed-income communities (the jury is still out and so far results are modest), there appears to be a willingness to take the risk and allow the displacement of low-income residents. While to some this can seem a contradiction to the foundation of community development, this strategy is logical for those who believe that the design of the social and physical space can reduce poverty by reducing the number of poor people. As seen in the previous chapter, many agree with this logic. But this hypothetical world would require a mass relocation of the poor (for the most part minorities) into middle-class (for the most part white) communities or vice versa, both highly improbable given the long-standing division of neighborhoods by income and race.

Community Development in the Space of Flexible Accumulation

Operating in an environment of contradiction, practically any community development action has its critics: if you provide social services, you are creating dependency; if you fight displacement, you are antidevelopment and antiprogress; if you develop real estate, you are playing into the hands of gentrification; if you are too conservative, you may hurt the most vulnerable; and if you are too radical, you are likely to run into a wall of resistance. In a context driven by limited resources and constrained by local politics, institutionalized neighborhood-based community development operates at the intersection of the civic and the electoral arenas (Ferman 1996). Although the Democratic machine was traditionally the site of neighborhood-based interventions in Chicago, Mayor Richard M. Daley created a wide-reaching collective by joining foundations and nonprofits, which over time fused donors, neighborhood organizations, intermediaries, and corporations with City Hall.[3] This blurring of the boundaries between electoral politics and civic agendas, between City Hall and civic powerhouses, and between community development and corporate agendas, complicates how we understand and interpret the flow of power and decision making. Who is taking orders from whom? Is this actual neoliberalism? Answering these questions requires looking at the situation from a perspective that neither an ecological nor a political economic framework can reveal, the former because it naturalizes the political arena and therefore excludes it from the analysis, while the latter because it is prone to oversimplify the power dynamics shaping community development.

Whether strategic or progressive, government and elites have adopted the language of community development while incorporating it into the governance apparatus itself, thus bringing community development leaders into its structure and into its fold. This convergence has effectively located community development practice in a contradictory space between its general aims (social justice) and the agenda of its partners (growth). A clear example is the redevelopment of public housing occurring in many cities. Although most community development practitioners agree with the goal of reducing poverty and improving living conditions for poor people, they find themselves up against a wall when their goals are appropriated to reduce the supply of affordable rental housing and to displace poor people from their neighborhoods. The same conflict is evident in other reforms in low-income and minority neighborhoods. Educational interventions that close neighborhood-based public schools only to reopen them as limited enrollment, "at-large" charter schools (Pew Charitable Trusts 2013) not only restrict the choices of poor families, but they also destroy critical neighborhood institutions and in some cases help to gentrify them out (Smith and Stovall 2008). The same can be said of reforms in policing that, as discussed in chapter 4, criminalize residents in some neighborhoods, especially youth and men of color, resulting in large portions of them in prison or with a record that effectively constrains their opportunities. At the same time, efforts are being made to assure that the middle class can defend their neighborhoods, including so-called "castle laws," which allow use of deadly force against anyone assumed to enter a home with the intent to cause harm.[4]

Gentrification, as the previous chapters illustrate, presents a particularly thorny dilemma. On the one hand, nearly everyone wants improvement and some even welcome gentrification outright if it means higher home values and lower crime. On the other hand, these outcomes can also displace lower-income families as housing values and rents rise. To offset this, some CDCs have become developers of affordable housing. As housing values rise, however, so does the cost of development. This is especially challenging when using the low-income housing tax credit, since the rents are fixed and do not adjust with the ebb and flow of income. But even when they are able to creatively finance affordable housing to serve extremely low-income families, CDCs are quite often challenged by higher-income newcomers who assume such development will devalue their homes. Moreover, the number of units they can develop is a drop in the bucket compared to the need and to the depletion of low-income housing associated with gentrification and disinvestment. As we saw in Pilsen, one response to this tension is to produce mixed-income housing that can satisfy low- and middle-income consumers. There was pushback, however, when the CDC advocating this route also supported a for-profit developer's effort to convert a manufacturing facility into housing that, relatively speaking, was not affordable to most of the workers in the neighborhood, thereby pitting one nonprofit against another. Along the way, the antigentrification struggle was neutralized from within the neighborhood because it was considered anti-community-development. This raises the question: can community development have it both ways in the space of accumulation?

Reconceptualizing Community Development: A Third Way

Clearly, all community development efforts have to navigate these murky waters. So does our ability to understand the possibilities and the many roles it plays in neighborhood change. As we have argued throughout this book, both mainstream and critical theoretical approaches limit our interpretation of postindustrial conditions. We propose that a "third way" is needed to conceptualize community development, a theoretical and real space that, as Nicolas Rose (1999) argues, must "become the object and target for the exercise of political power whilst remaining, somehow, external to politics and a counterweight to it" (168). Similarly, Fisher (1996) claims that "oppositional grass-roots efforts must build both democratic, empowered communities and recognize the state as, if not a site of support, then at least a central arena and critical target for oppositional demands." In reality, many community development initiatives actually do closely combine political action with normative positions.

Just as settlement houses called for social reform to address abusive labor practices and the neglect and disinvestment in residential space where immigrants lived, some CDCs today are doing the same. For example, in Humboldt Park a CDC has managed to survive on the strength of both its accumulated assets, particularly land and affordable housing, and community standing that give it some control over the real estate development agenda. And while seemingly shut down, Pilsen Alliance's bare-bones oppositional force promoting people-based alternatives and developing neighborhood leadership has inspired people to organize and push back against outside developers and speculators. Similarly, we have seen unions partnering with neighborhoods to vote out prodevelopment and gentrification representatives and elect their own candidates.[5]

These examples suggest that in this regime of accumulation we should think of neighborhood change in relation to community development as a system that evolves but not naturally, rather as a result of organized efforts and conjuncture. From this perspective, the relationship between community development and accumulation is an ongoing process in which the interaction of different individuals and groups produce different forms of neighborhood change. Every community development actor, each in its own way, is trying to retain or improve its standing vis-à-vis accumulation and commodification of space. While this logic seems to align with a political economic framework, it is certainly not a determined outcome or even one-directional in terms of who has power. In simple terms, it is possible in this regime to have community developers behave like capital investors but also vice versa.

Again, applying insights from Lefebvre and Foucault, we find a far more nuanced and multipolar world in which all kinds of forces pull and push in different directions, competing daily for space and control in this current regime of accumulation. Mainstream perspectives about neighborhood change have played a prominent role shaping community development through two practices: normalization and social control. Normalization aims to produce the right mix of people by race and class in an environment apropos for middle-class values, while social control requires lower-income people to behave like they are middle-class in order to have a right to live in these neighborhoods. As the previous chapters describe, however, people in some neighborhoods have mobilized to resist this approach, including residents of public housing fighting transformation and low-income renters and owners pushing back against gentrification.

Driving these representations and actions are institutional forces striving to retain the conditions necessary to reproduce the existing social order. In contrast, forces of resistance often calling for a new social order push back, giving community development a redefined sense of social justice and redistribution. Still, both sides generally assume the state and its institutions have the power to shape and control the production of space; those that support social control strategies consider this power legitimate and fair while those resisting find it illegitimate and unfair. As a result, both camps tend to set as their goal gaining control of the state, since it is assumed to be the source of the power and stability or the change they seek. From this perspective, community development appears highly unambiguous, corresponding to a modernist, linear, and temporal discourse of change and a clear "us versus them" in the fight for control.

In the space of creative destruction and within this particular framework of normalization and social control, community development actions will always take place around a struggle for control between the so-called "left" and "right." Such stark one-dimensional views, however, actually stand in the way of community development. Applying Lefebvre to our analysis, we should think "about the city as a place where different groups can meet, where people may conflict but also form alliances, and where all can participate in a collective *oeuvre.*" (1992, 207). In this sense, community is produced through encounters and relationships and not through rules and regulations, allowing it to be a diverse, interconnected mosaic. While Lefebvre still blames "the private ownership of land which remains by far the dominant power and which will continue to grow more powerful" (210), he also invites us "to steer urban studies towards possibilities, eventualities, the future" (211). For him and for us, the city is a place of encounter in which we can engage in the task of creating a new form of dwelling together.

As Lefebvre does, we suggest constructing social relations around use values, democracy, and cooperation in order to allow individuals to grow together by engaging in creative endeavors and unmediated interactions. In theory but also in practice, as relations of domination and exploitation are replaced by cooperation, the tensions of competition and hierarchy in human-to-human interactions should diminish and in turn facilitate environments of trust, celebration, and solidarity. In Chicago's Englewood neighborhood, for example, various community development efforts have helped and continue to help people to stay afloat while seeking better options and large-scale change. The same can be said of the many CDCs working around the city and in the United States that have not abandoned their search for justice nor their pursuit of making their neighborhoods better for the people living in them. Much of this work, however, has gotten stuck in the trappings of institutional survival because change is sought through "established channels" that not only support but often require community development practices to be grounded in normalization and social control. This framework presents a significant challenge: follow the rules or lose the resources! In public housing redevelopment, a low-income family's access to housing requires being employed, being in school, or being a volunteer (unless otherwise unable to due to disability or age), and in education reform the new charter and select enrollment schools are not open to all or even to the residents in the neighborhood. Under these circumstances, residents and activists feel like they have lost on both fronts: their options are limited and even eliminated, and what is offered in exchange is not necessarily what they want or is attainable.

Framing community development differently, we promote proposals for new norms of justice and human rights on which to build the city and society that we want and that we can negotiate (e.g., Amin 2009; Fainstein 2011; Thrift 2005). As an alternative to the priorities of commodification, we propose people's welfare as the organizing societal principle of community development and, within it, a deeper commitment to the people and communities deprived of the resources and opportunities to grow to their full potential. This requires moving social science and the practices it influences away from representations of space that mask its production toward nonrepresentational forms that allow us to make space a *verb* (Thrift 2005). As discussed in this book, a critical point of departure is reframing power as being productive rather than coercive and as a constant and multidirectional force rather than simply a one-way flow. Foucault helps us think about how this can be possible by approaching power as something that is present, an everyday phenomenon we are socialized to adhere to and accept but also that we believe can be challenged. In the realm of community development, this means that as a human activity power can and often does embrace approaches that are contrary to the status quo but also that specifically challenge the way space is produced in this current regime of accumulation. Community development as a practice and as a discipline will benefit from taking a more critical position from which to construct options and new futures, and in particular reframing its relationship with and struggle to control the state. Obviously, this is a subject for another book!

In Chicago and elsewhere, significant, perhaps even paradigmatic, change in neighborhoods occurred when capitalism evolved from one form of accumulation to another during the shift from industrial to postindustrial. Civil rights organizing and CDCs were the third way in the 1960s and 1970s, pushing to change structural racism and discrimination while concurrently responding to the daily needs of residents living in disinvested neighborhoods. While still active and needed, these groups are challenged by the production of space in the current regime. If it is antidevelopment to fight City Hall, the banks, and the real estate agents seeking to upscale a neighborhood, then what can a CDC do given a real need for housing that low-income families can afford? Changing this game, structuralists claim, requires changing the power relations.

We see new forms of community development today that suggest that people are not sitting around waiting for the game to change. Take for example the Chicago Anti-Eviction Campaign (CAEC). Formed in response to what was initially happening with public housing and other tenants in subsidized housing, the campaign's mission to prevent eviction also includes homeowners, in part because of the foreclosure crisis but also in an effort to connect people across the housing spectrum and show how all are part of the same problem.[6] While the CAEC does not frame it as accumulation, it recognizes the uneven development pushing resources into Chicago's downtown and predominantly white higher-income communities to the north while extracting from—or at least not investing in—the predominantly nonwhite South and West Sides of the city (Austen 2013). In CAEC's words, the campaign is connecting people with homes and vice versa using legal and extra-legal methods. This includes negotiating with banks to get them to donate foreclosed homes to a nonprofit, which can then lease back to the family, and "liberating" abandoned buildings to move homeless people into "people-less homes" (Austen 2013). While the former works within the existing system, the latter clearly does not. To the CAEC, this is justified because it is a moral problem and we have a moral crisis.

The CEAC is part of a larger nationwide movement based on "positive action campaigns" to "break the immoral laws which allow banks to gain billions while human beings are made homeless."[7] Besides helping families, the larger goal is to accumulate properties that can be put into a land trust in order to secure community control. Of course, land trusts have been around for more than a century, and squatting is not a new strategy. What is compelling about the use of them together in this current regime of accumulation is that it aims to take homes and neighborhoods out of the speculative market and decommodify both. Grounded in the belief that housing is a human right and people have a right to the city, campaigns to liberate housing are operating in Philadelphia; Rochester, New York; Madison, Wisconsin; and Miami. While premature to assess their impact and the likelihood of success, we can see the transformative effect of these efforts at the individual level and to some degree in the space of neighborhoods given the relatively favorable attention in the media, such as the *New York Times Magazine* (Austen 2013). But it's not the press coverage that matters; it's the message that is reframing the problem and the solution. Assuming that community is an obligation that emerges from human kindness, generosity, collective responsibility for taking care of each other, support, and imagination, and the self-fulfillment of doing so, then we conclude there is at least the potential for a *new* third way of doing community development.

The community development trajectory in Chicago and elsewhere is responding to the challenges and conditions each regime brings about and at the same time tries to shape. As traced in this chapter, community development has always been inspired both by demands for rights, opportunities, equal standing in the eyes of the law, and fairness and by particular group interests struggling with racism, classism, and calls for assimilation. Altogether, community development has been as much about normalizing as it has been about establishment of new relations and ending the sources of inequality. Institutionalization may be the main challenge today. This approach certainly limits the options and ways of social change (e.g., Piven and Cloward 1978). Still, community developers have found ways to challenge the status quo, to engage in movements, and advance change, especially on the civil rights front, most recently on gay and human rights. These efforts provide evidence that those marginalized by society can appropriate and turn around the power relations that marginalize them. Along these lines, community development does provide a means to intervene. Still, their absorption into the accumulation approach to community development, whether co-opted or by choice, narrows their possibilities. The critical issue is the extent to which their attachment to the status quo prevents them from engaging in the power struggles that have made the most difference for the poor in the past. Coalitions and movements have often bypassed this limitation, yet at the end of the day, only an independent community development sector can fully challenge the powers that be.

We recognize that community development has been many things for so many people and appropriated for such a wide range of undertakings. In the case of the neighborhood and neighborhood change, the preoccupation has been with the weakest and how to bring them to the fore in the construction of their life and society. While it is a valid starting point, experience has shown how tremendously limited this approach is in actually changing the conditions that create poverty and disinvestment. At the end of the day, we cannot make a panacea of community development but we cannot—nor would we—discard it. Instead, we offer strategies to change how neighborhood change is represented.

Conclusion

There is no other meaning than the one we create in and through history. (Castoriadis 1997, 341)

How should we study neighborhood change today? We began this book by problematizing the assumptions underpinning prominent theories of neighborhood change. We specifically questioned traditional models (mainstream) but also alternatives (critical) developed in response to the lack of attention to the political nature of urban dynamics. Our aim was to reveal the shortcomings of existing approaches and to propose a different way of looking at neighborhoods that could account for how they function as sites of consumption and places for flexible accumulation. We focused our attention on Chicago, in part because we are familiar with its neighborhoods but more importantly because of its role in shaping more than a century of research about neighborhood change that we hope this book will enrich and inform.

In this concluding chapter we weave together what we have learned from our analysis and propose guidance for further investigation. The evidence presented in this book confirms that neighborhoods are important yet limited spaces for study, policy making, and activism. Our intent here is not to provide conclusions but rather to advance an approach for examining neighborhoods and how they change in relation to this current regime of accumulation and creative destruction. We start with the clear forces at work shaping neighborhood space and change over time in our current regime, both conceptually and practically, that fall into three broad categories: Flexible Accumulation, Accumulation by Expropriation, and the Production of New Space (see Figure 7).

First, flexible accumulation has transformed neighborhoods into sites in crisis that are becoming a potential threat to social reproduction, a position

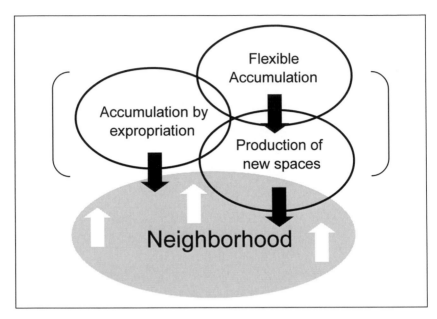

Figure 7. Forces Producing Neighborhood Space
Source: Janet Smith 2015

we know is contrary to how neighborhoods are portrayed, at least in their ideal form. Second, in this regime the state has employed mainstream explanations of neighborhood change to expropriate space through policy and actions that justify restrictive practices and discipline, allegedly to help those most disadvantaged. Third, these expropriated spaces are more likely to be sites of struggle, generating new forms of neighborhood space that are shaped by the spatial practices of people actually living in them. Building on our investigations in Chicago, each of these claims is reviewed below.

Flexible Accumulation: Neighborhoods as Sites of Ongoing Crisis

Capitalism has successfully found a new spatial fix in the real and imagined space of neighborhoods, which has allowed a new period of steady accumulation to take hold over the past few decades. But it is anything but a stabilizing force, as capital producers rely on financial instruments that guarantee a quick return on investment and achieve high levels of liquidity and turnover rates all in a deregulated environment of utmost mobility. The result is inflating property prices, out of control and independent of demand or need; it's now about money making money. Soja defined today's urban dynamics as a "restructuring-generated crisis" (2000, 144). In other words, the *solution* (volatility) has made this regime of accumulation a regime of crisis. And according to Lefebvre it is constant: "The mobilization of space becomes frenetic, and produces an impetus towards the self-destruction of spaces old and new. Investment and speculation cannot be stopped, however, not even slowed, and a vicious circle is thus set up" (2004, 336). As principal nodes, as command-and-control centers, and as core engines of accumulation, cities are the major expression of this societal regime. In the 1970s, in response to these changing conditions, there was an explosion of divergent critical urban theories to help explain the tremendous instability in postmodern capitalist cities. They also revealed the inadequacy of theory developed under previous regimes and, more importantly, called into question whether any fixed explanation of urban dynamics was possible.

We are in a period of crisis in both the actually existing and the conceptual spaces of our cities and neighborhoods. The dominant form of accumulation is by dispossession (Harvey 2005), and as we describe in this book, we see it clearly in the extremes of hyper-ghettoization and hyper-gentrification. Further, data suggests the current restructuring-generated crisis is deepening inequality and fragmentation to the point of producing *urban archipelagos* like we see in Chicago that house both extreme decline and luxurious development with few spaces in between and that are likely to soon go one way or the other. While not nearly as divergent as cities such as Mumbai and Sao Paulo, the stagnation and actual decline of income among a growing number of lower-income residents across the United States is alarming for some (e.g., Stiglitz 2012; Kornbluth 2013). In contrast, neoliberalism maintains the current regime with flexible fast policy (e.g., see Peck, Theodore, and Brenner 2012) that will likely speed up the cycles of creative destruction. Decades of flexible accumulation suggest that as long as cities continue to rely on the frenzy of real estate development as *the* salvation of neighborhoods, we can anticipate continued uneven development that will lift some boats while sinking many others. As the cases in this book illustrate, such an approach has a tendency to accelerate disinvestment in some areas and speculative investment in others, and to uproot people in both.

Efforts to pursue a spatial fix for capital are actually unfixing space in order to prepare it for accumulation. As such, neighborhood change and the extreme forms it takes is symbiotic in the sense that uneven development is necessary to produce more space for accumulation and to sustain the cycles of creative destruction. Given the repeated crises and steep fluctuations in property prices in the last four decades, however, this order may be difficult to sustain as consumers' access to space and capital becomes more restricted. This is perhaps a more pressing concern in the twenty-first century given the wide-scale credit restrictions shaping the housing market recovery after the Great Recession. In this sense, the cure may be more poisonous than the disease and may make some neighborhoods permanently unstable and potentially expendable from a policy perspective. This is suggested in the case of Englewood, with its consistent low housing values and high number of vacant properties over the past forty years. It is also a danger in several other communities on Chicago's South and West Sides, where nearly 200,000 people moved out between 2000 and 2010, as well as shrinking cities like Detroit and Cleveland, to name a few. In the current regime, the scale of investment needed to recover just may be too big.

Another source of risk is the fact that the flow of capital into many neighborhoods continues to be based on fictitious demand generated by speculators promoting fictitious valorization. Despite growing demand for lower-cost affordable housing, the market continues to develop units that are out of reach for most Americans (Joint Center 2014). Neighborhoods are places in which to invest now through mechanisms such as mortgage-backed securities and other instruments for exchanging real estate, but also speculative flipping that pushes up prices and predatory lending that generates space for fast-track profit production and destruction of value. This is quite different from the relatively stable neighborhoods and homes that social reproduction calls for and that theory and practice imagine. Instead, urban dynamics are definitely redefining social reproduction and, we argue, overwhelming and even threatening it.

In Chicago, most of the population loss since 2000 consisted of children under the age of eighteen. While the overall number of white children has remained relatively the same since 1990, the number of African American children has decreased while the number of Latino children has increased. When the trends are mapped out, we find that many of the gentrified communities on the North Side, but also many of the poorer communities, now have fewer children (Voorhees Center 2014). This suggests that it does not matter if families are wealthy or poor since, as documented in this book, both gentrification and ghettoization produce volatile spaces for families. Still, the hardest hit are consistently low-income and nonwhite.

Watching commodification take over some neighborhoods, we see people being pushed against the wall by speculative *rentierism*, investment from outside that is primarily benefiting developers and the state. Even neighborhoods like Englewood can be targeted for predatory value extraction, with its reservoir of available land and property that with the right branding eventually can be repackaged and sold. Those that can afford to invest are likely to do so at a cost, because their livelihoods—often in command-and-control functions, finance, and real estate—also rely in some way on an accumulation-based marketplace. Those who cannot invest have to create alternative spaces of survival, often by breaking the established rules. And the fast-paced commodification that currently embraces neighborhoods as sites to live-work-play generates frenzy at both ends of the spectrum: the frenzy of consumerism among those who can afford to live there and the frenzy of survival among those working in service jobs that do not pay enough to live or play there (Lloyd 2006). This is accumulation for the sake of accumulation at its best.

All neighborhoods are now geographies of risk. In response, occupants do what they can to protect their properties and themselves. This includes making sure others do not pose a risk or a threat to whatever they may have. Soja (2000, 250) refers to this as turning the inside out and the outside in respectively. In both, fear rules! Gated communities are designed to protect home values through rules for behavior among those living there and secured entrances to keep out people who do not belong (MacKenzie 1994, 2011; Blakely and Snyder 1997; Liggett and Perry 1995). One cannot exist without the other. Helping to keep the order outside these gated communities are rules to promote peaceful coexistence that reinforce rather than reframe views about homogeneity and segregation. As a result, all neighborhoods in some way exclude and contain people. In this current regime, however, the focus has been on controlling the spaces that lower-income people can occupy, whether in the ghetto or in new mixed-income neighborhoods.

Accumulation by Expropriation: Neighborhoods as Sites of Domination, Exclusion, and Containment

Producing and then bursting speculative bubbles (financial, technology, and housing), a chronic affordable housing problem, and a mounting artificial debt-based demand help to sustain the propensity for crisis in this regime. Public management is expected to counter extreme threats to social reproduction. In this regime, higher property taxes and more consumers are needed to keep the economy going and greater subsidies are needed to entice the corporate sector to stay or move in. We have argued that a critical component in the production of neighborhood order is the naturalization of change and the acceptance of, but more importantly the application of, mainstream theories by the state to explain it. The result, we propose, is a subsequent appropriation of space that in many cities has helped to sustain racial and economic segregation, which then facilitates the accumulation behavior described above. Even recent efforts to integrate across race and class lines sustains homogeneity as the norm by restricting the proportion of poor people in the mix and by reproducing a long-standing acceptance that racial and economic integration is unnatural.

The homogeneous neighborhood is a powerful and influential represen-tation of space because it is taken for granted and accepted as a given, while heterogeneous space is suspicious, even though many scholars and others have called this logic into question. Created by researchers and policy makers, such rationalizations (Flyvbjerg 2001) produce effects that then sustain misunder-standings but, more importantly, that operate as constitutive forces that define what neighborhoods should be and how they do or do not change. As Bourdieu explains:

> But it is in this constitution of groups that the effectiveness of representations is most apparent, and particularly in the words, slogans and theories which help create the social order by imposing principles of division and, more generally, the symbolic power of the whole theater which actualizes and officializes visions of the world and political divisions (1991, 129–30).

The Chicago School conceived of the order of neighborhoods and why they change by dividing space and reducing its contents in such a way as to poten-tially damage the real people and places they represent. People have been socialized to accept these descriptions as truth and to accept the subsequent justification of heavy-handed—and, we contend, antidemocratic—interven-tions to pre-empt or suppress expected dissidence. Furthermore, accepting the mainstream explanation that naturalizes neighborhood change has helped the power relationships become even more effective and powerful in spatializing inequality. The same is true for explanations that attribute neighborhood change to residents' racial/ethnic/cultural values, behaviors, and choices, as well as the belief that the spatial order of any city is natural and intentionally produced to reflect and reproduce social relations, which are anything but natural.

Rereading what happened in Chicago as whites moved out of different neighborhoods and blacks moved in, we find a continuum between a highly spatialized set of relations of domination, exclusion, and inclusion that pro-duces neighborhood change. In broad terms, Chicago is a familiar story about the expropriation of space in racially changing industrial cities. After World War II, as the immigration of blacks and Latinos increased, racialized prac-tices were introduced to defend the central business district from encroaching slums. First through trial and error and then through aggressive plans, the goal of slum clearance was to halt deterioration and blight supposedly caused by the encroachment of blacks. When the public housing that replaced slums became all-black and the intervention failed to retain or attract whites, a different tack was taken: developing middle-class housing and high-end institutions to buffer the downtown from the neighborhoods. Planning became the official strategy. It allowed space to be cleared and room made for gentrification in the city by progressively pushing minorities and *noncompatible* uses from the areas surrounding the Loop as well as from other locations developers wanted, especially the areas along the lakefront. Veiled by terms such as renewal, removal of blight, revitalization, and redevelopment, these class- and race-based interventions determined where and how investment and disinvestment would take place.[1] The results more often than not concentrated the poorest of the poor in badly maintained and managed buildings in isolated and neglected environments, which made survival at any cost a necessity.

The same principle appears to underpin Chicago's *Plan for Transformation* and the broader renewal of public housing nationwide that began in the 1990s and prioritized strategic locations in cities. In Chicago, it was the sites surrounding the Loop that developers wanted to gentrify. Forgetting that the city along with developers and investors had actually ghettoized public housing, an intense campaign was launched to support the plan. Characterized as welfare queens, murderers, gangbangers, and drug dealers, residents of public housing were portrayed as needing redemption, and subsequently their homes were deemed unsalvageable and unfit for poor families. Creative destruction was also used to expropriate land in low-income minority neighborhoods such as Englewood, which turned the so-called war on drugs into a war on the poor who were mostly black and Latino. These strategies were never applied to middle-income or predominantly white neighborhoods in the city.

Such interventions and their supporting discourses, as Foucault (1992) would argue—and we agree—constitute race and class power relations that sustain the political, economic, and cultural institutions and that reproduce the status quo through the (racialized and classed) production of space. These constitutive forces continue to operate in cities and urban neighborhoods today, though in different ways. Urban space continues to be divided between us and them, often making minorities the enemy within *our social space* to keep away or to keep away from. This fabricated reality produces a human being of convenience, one to pin blame on or target for redemption, that is perpetuated through the spatial practices of real estate professionals, lending institutions, developers, planners, and others that sustain uneven development and segregation. Validated in everyday life, these constitutive forces are camouflaged and effective:

> How do institutions prevail or ensure their effective validity? . . . by and through the formation (fabrication) of the human raw material into a social individual

in which these institutions themselves as well as the "mechanisms" of their perpetuation are embedded. . . . We are all, in the first place, walking and complementary elements of the institution of our society. (Castoriadis 1997, 6–7)

But these institutional constitutive forces are only one part of the story. In order to succeed, the realities of residents' daily practices, resistances, and organized counteractions must be in some way altered, accommodated, or stopped. As this book illustrates, these forces on the ground are also producing the space of neighborhoods and cities.[2] No matter how oppressed, suppressed, overpowered, disenfranchised, or socialized, people partake in the construction, deconstruction, and appropriation of space generated by the forces that establish the official maps and borders around neighborhoods. Yet people actively divert the intended outcomes, limit their efficacy, and actually force change into the process. They carve out their own spaces and practices, which, depending on who is classifying them, may be derelict and perhaps even extralegal or illegal.

Social relations have two or more mutually constitutive and dependent sides, each playing to win (Bourdieu and Wacquant 1992). They are agents of change that "do with what they have" (de Certeau 1988, 18). Thus neighborhoods can never totally mirror the designs imposed from above because they are contested arenas shaped through all sorts of interactions. Of course, just as researchers homogenized space around factors such as income or race, the occupants can do the same to defend, advance, or assert their right to belong, as the Bronzeville initiative in chapter 3 illustrates or as the struggles of gays and Puerto Ricans discussed in chapter 6 suggest. All reveal the uneven spaces created by crisscrossing paths of individual interests, multidirectional networks, and resistance. These actions call into question the assumption that neighborhoods are in any way homogeneous, but more importantly, underscore why we need to differentiate between what is imposed and how life is lived in order to see how neighborhoods are sites of constant struggle.

Production of New Spaces: Neighborhoods as Sites of Struggle for Identity

We assume that the more constitutive power—or social capital in Bourdieu's terms—that residents have, the greater their command of their lives and thus what happens in the places they live. Further, what counts as power or is valued as social capital is largely determined by the current dominant powers or at least marked by their value classifications. The challenge then is how do we classify and interpret the power of people who are in dominated spaces and positions in society, surviving somewhere near the margins?

As a starting point, we revisit the "neighborhood equals community" characterization that underpins the way in which the dynamics shaping urban space is studied. Although it is common to define community as a group of people living in the same place, we think of it as an imagined social space that presumes that bonds and common interests exist. While people do make connections, have face-to-face contact, pursue collective interests, and share the same conditions, these characteristics alone do not constitute community. When we take for granted that a neighborhood *is* a community, then it becomes a site for expectations and judgment based on an imagined, homogenized, and monolithic space. By the same token, community-based organizations and the space they represent are often conflated, and the opinions of the members are assumed to align. This is not to deny that people working with an organization can assemble against powers that alienate them; this book is full of examples of people doing just that. Likewise, we found evidence of people collectively and opportunistically exploiting their common identity in order to keep others out. In any of these circumstances, the struggle for identity engages those that have the power to tie it to space.

As argued throughout this book, some people and institutions have the constitutive power to produce fixed spaces, both physical and representational, and have predisposed people to accept the world as it has been interpreted for them.[3] But people with limited power can also obstruct or in some way mess up what is coming from those with power. In de Certeau's words, "Many everyday practices . . . are tactical in character. And so are, more generally, many 'ways of operating': victories of the 'weak' over the strong . . . clever tricks, knowing how to get away with things, 'hunter's cunning,' maneuvers, polymorphic simulations, joyful discoveries" (1988, xix). Looking at the production of space from a different angle, one that can witness how these constitutive forces interact, is critical if we are to understand how the space of neighborhoods and interpretations of change get fixed and, more importantly, unfixed.

Lefebvre (2004) argues that in any society social relations have to spatialize and materialize in order to exist. It is in the shaping of space that those relations become real and acquire currency and power. For example, the spatialization of dominant-dominated relations is what makes inequality real; this is a condition for inequality to exist. From this perspective, while neighborhoods materialize the relations of inequality, such relations only last because that order is being *fixed* in both physical and mental spaces. In concrete terms, racial segregation continues because people believe that racial integration is unnatural and subsequently they ratify it in their practices. Further, because human beings require signification (Castoriadis 1998), inequality needs some level of legitimacy if it is to be maintained. This can be in the form of evidence, such as lower housing values in mixed-race or racially changing neighborhoods. While force can produce these kinds of results (i.e., lower housing values), a societal regime cannot be maintained for long by sheer force. Instead, reciprocal signification is needed. We see this in the support and reification of the Chicago School's rationalization for why neighborhoods change, and more recently in the sustained belief that there is a culture of poverty that justifies a highly controlled form of mixing in public housing transformation. Both have taken on a life of their own as legitimized representations of space.

Our analysis calls for the continued qualification and deconstruction of any neighborhood characterization. In their daily lives people occupy many spaces inside and outside the neighborhood in which they reside. They participate in multiple social relations in which they do not necessarily occupy the same position; they can be employers or employees, employed or unemployed, parents or children, homeowners or renters, members of this or that party or this or that religious group, old or young, etc. And they can be part of both dominant groups (e.g., as males) and of dominated groups (e.g., as racial minorities) at the same time. Similarly, there are levels and layers in all relations of domination: people can be the dominant within a dominated category or the dominated within a dominant one (Bourdieu and Wacquant 1992).

Because the constraints and possibilities shaping those spaces are always changing, we conclude that neighborhoods must be examined as a collection of spatially connected genealogies if we are to understand how they are constructed and what specific and intersecting structures are producing and reproducing them. Our a priori assumption is that neighborhoods are socially produced, relatively bounded arenas of ongoing struggle and that the struggle takes different forms depending on the societal regime. In this current regime, the dominant forces are pushing neighborhoods toward gentrification and ghettoization, and the struggle is for space that can support social reproduction. These spatial polarities have produced privileged enclaves offering some residents top services and institutions while denying others the basics for social reproduction, such as quality schools, services, and affordable housing. Rather than socializing residents into citizenship, the latter deny people access to basic rights. And in both, the occupants are now consumers and their neighborhood is a submarket of goods and services; while some are oases, many more are deserts lacking access to basic necessities such as food and affordable shelter.

Working-class neighborhoods from the previous regime are in a particular type of struggle as families deal with today's marketplace of contingent jobs, decreasing compensation, and the ultracommodification of everything. Such conditions limit social reproduction and reduce opportunity for an increasing number of households. But it is the speculative fluctuation of home values and rental property generated by the cycles of creative destruction that have made uncertainty a major factor in household decisions including the decision to have children. As a result, we conclude that family life in urban areas has become increasingly constrained, which may explain the overall drop in families with young children. According to the US Census, "the share of households with children dropped from 36% in 2000 to 33.5% [in 2010]. There are now more households with dogs (43 million) than children" (El Nasser and Overberg 2011).

On the assumption that this is the future, perhaps even an optimal new expression of freedom, we are witnessing the intentional transformation of neighborhoods driven by a type of consumerism aimed at a productive and festive lifestyle rather than a reproductive space of opportunity for all. These new spaces of flexible accumulation are based on variety and freedom—live, work, play!—yet they are not necessarily for families with children unless they can afford to purchase services such as education from the private market. Some are willing to pay the price to get the symbolic power and cultural capital unleashed by spatial commodification and accumulation, hence the growth in doggy day care and private child care centers, both of which are expensive.

Today's capitalism makes money by selling distinction (Baudrillard 1983; Debord 1995). In Bourdieu's (1984, 37) words,

[D]istinction is the specific form of profit that symbolic power procures. Lifestyle, as the symbolic manifestation of symbolic capital, exists only by the gaze of the other and as diacritical deviation from the modal, ordinary, common, banal, "average" style, a deviation that can be unwitting or obtained by the stylization of life.

Desire is being manipulated in extreme ways to sell neighborhoods, which turns urban life into a race for distinction. While mass marketing sells this good life to everyone via advertising, the Internet, television, and movies, the reality is that only relatively few can afford it and that most use credit to purchase their lifestyle. Even then, the majority of people are excluded either because they cannot keep up or because they do not have access to the space and means to produce it. As a result, we have at one end of the spectrum people who are purchasing distinction through fetishized consumerism and at the other end acquiring it through criminalization and exclusion. Both ends are more favorable for annihilation than reproduction.

Under Fordism, neighborhood identities were based on ethnicity, class, and race. Today, they are based on prestige, sexuality, lifestyle, and other positive identities found in the place-making rubric used by marketing agencies and planners. The real estate industry relies heavily on naming a space, on branding to sell distinction. But it also counts on stereotyping that can either destroy or increase value. Accordingly, gentrification has helped to replace prior images of slum and blight with diversity, a bohemian lifestyle, and the promise of exclusivity when the replacement process is complete. Selling gentrification requires creating newer and newer enclaves by making the neighborhood space seemingly separate and distinct. This is the case of "East Pilsen," "East Pilsen Artist Colony" and "La 18" all being enclaves of Mexican Pilsen. Rebranding is also established via historical designation. Along these lines, Bronzeville is the aggregation of several community areas under a single brand. Either way, labeling transforms the imagined into a place from which to create value and to speed up the circulation of capital, but it can also be used by residents in places that have been devalued to appropriate power in acts of defiant self-assertion. By no means trivial, these acts of violence, protest, celebration, self-help, and resilience can actually constitute and change the identity of a place.

In Chicago, rebranding is evident in every new map produced by the real estate agents' association. Creating new subdivisions that are either within existing community areas or a combination of pieces from different ones, these new configured markets are based on common consumer interests. Examples include Wicker Park in West Town, Bucktown in Logan Square, Buena Park and Sheridan Park in Uptown, West Gate in the Near West Side, and the South Loop in the Near South Side. Along with these, the city has designated tourist and shopping destinations that reproduce cultural distinction (e.g., Chinatown carved out of Armour Square and Greektown in the Near West Side). Regardless of the label or contents, these new subdivisions, which refine "the patchwork quilt of specialized residential communities" (Soja 2000, 341), are all a new form of segregation for profit. While they are not unlike segregation based on race and class, the identity of these spaces is driven by consumer preferences, or perhaps more precisely by *socialized consumership*. Assuming preferences change over time, the question is this: when and how will the neighborhood change next?

Claiming Neighborhood

We end by highlighting key claims and propositions we make with our analysis both to summarize and, we hope, to inspire and guide new investigations of urban space and change.

Mainstream explanations of neighborhood change are socially produced; rather than taking any of them at face value, we need to focus on understanding their actual effects on the range of social relations in which they emerge. Neither objective nor neutral, such representations can and often do operate as instruments of discipline socializing residents and researchers to perceive and accept extant social relations as natural or inevitable. We ground this claim in a particular way of seeing and interpreting space that assumes that neighborhoods themselves are socially produced and contingent; while real physical places, they also are symbolic and conceptual, contested and highly differentiated.

Incorporating critical theories into the analysis allows us to shift the conversation away from tests of objectivity and toward exposing the power dimensions that neighborhoods represent and the dominant, constitutive, and systemic forces shaping them, along with their mechanisms of domination and social control, as well as to expose the powers resisting them. By exposing the power dynamics involved, we can no longer accept explanations that frame neighborhoods as natural formations and sites for community and change as the repetition of immanent natural law. Furthermore, by tying it to societal regime shifts, neighborhood change becomes conceptually and practically malleable. In today's societal regime of fast-paced creative destruction, neighborhoods are now flexible spaces of uncertainty and instability, which is evident by the way people in them live. We propose that the current societal regime has the potential to seriously compromise social reproduction as creative destruction and, being in a state of permanent crisis, continues to transform the relatively stable neighborhood space of Fordism.

We suggest viewing every neighborhood as constituted and specifically as a product for consumption or confinement. As such, neighborhoods function as end points and their explanation is found in the composition, functions, representations, and boundaries of the site, which are fluid over time even if they appear fixed. Genealogies that document their production can help us analyze power relations and deconstruct the forces that sustain particular notions while dismantling others. In this way, the functions globalizing the production and reproduction of neighborhoods as a type of space, including various classification schemes and a priori definitions, can be revealed and analyzed.

We argue that the presumed neighborhood order is a means to spatialize unequal social relations in which some are dominant and others are dominated. But we also warn against uncritically using polarities such as dominant-dominated to describe these spaces because they construct artificial, mutually exclusive, and monolithic categories that restrict how we interpret neighborhood space. Instead, neighborhoods should be viewed as dynamic spaces shaped and reshaped through ongoing interactions in which people have varying degrees of power and control, all of which are technically, if not practically, in flux. All explanations of neighborhood change must be flexible, and concepts such as domination must be qualified to account for variations and different levels of domination, as well as for efforts to mitigate and mediate them. In short, we need to identify different forms of domination when mapping the trajectories of neighborhood change and think of these explanations themselves as generative rather than reductive.

Any analysis of neighborhoods must include a relatively nuanced investigation of the constitutive power that comes from people challenging their spatialized domination, creating openings for dissent and at times forcing neighborhood space to be reshaped. In their everyday life, people shape spaces through their own strategies, including activities that are considered extra-legal, obstructionist, or evasive. We are not advocating or romanticizing these sorts of activities a priori, and we cannot necessarily consider them liberating since these practices can be highly opportunistic and predatory. Still, we recognize that every occupant of a neighborhood has constitutive power that can dominate or be a source of positive power relations. That means our analysis must look at "the good, the bad, and the ugly" within groups of people and not simply classify them as characteristically monolithic and one-sided. To this end, neighborhoods and the people in them should be examined as arenas of interaction, producing stories and forms that cannot be reduced to predetermined relationships such as developer versus housing advocates, nonprofit versus for-profit, etc.

We must look for evidence of efforts to produce differential spaces in order to understand how and why some neighborhoods change and others do not. The cases of Halsted North and Paseo Boricua illustrate alternative spaces produced by different acts of self-determination, suggesting that a different spatial order is possible, that difference can be creative, and that people always in some way struggle to belong and to be different (i.e., themselves). Further, we assume that acts of differentiation are occurring in every neighborhood. We cannot easily see them, however, when the world is viewed through a lens that homogenizes space.

Neighborhoods and explanations for why they change must be historicized. That means tying these spaces to the conditions that made them possible—different constitutive forces, conjunctures, and power relations—over time. This approach aims to bring out those critical relations veiled by mainstream representations and then challenge explanations that, in their claim to be objective truth, simply reflect and reinforce the status quo.

Rather than using universalizing rhetoric to a priori define the actions of neighborhood-based organizations, we need to establish their actual trajectories, affiliations, activities, constraints, and possibilities. A community development group or elected official can claim to represent the neighborhood, but either one also can be a vehicle for outside forces while at the same time have its own set of interests and factions. In addition, those who claim to represent neighborhoods need to be examined in light of how they view power. In the words of Foucault, "Reform is either carried out by people who consider themselves representatives and whose profession is to speak for others, in their name, and thus is a reshuffling of power, a dis-tribution of power . . . or it is a reform demanded, required by those it concerns and then is not a reform, but a revolutionary action that is meant to question the totality of power and its hierarchy" (1992, 80).

Our work and intention in producing this book was not to propose a new school or to develop *the* theory to guide all investigations of neighborhood change. We do think our approach can help open up and deconstruct previous explanations, and we hope it will entice others to conduct their own investiga-tions that challenge reigning rationalizations. Awareness and reflexivity, how-ever, should not be mistakenly viewed as the only theories to guide practice. With Foucault, we believe that:

> The main political challenge for the intellectual . . . is to explore the possibil-ity of constituting a new politics of truth. The issue is not to "change the con-sciousness" of people or what they have in their minds (assuming that it will mechanically lead them to struggle for change) but the political, economic and institutional regime of the production of truth. (1992, 189)

To the extent that our work is part of a new politics of truth, so is our practice.

Notes

Introduction

1. The Census began this process in New York City in 1900, where it consulted with a community panel to draw tract boundaries that aligned with neighborhoods.

2. This is similar to Bourdieu's (Bourdieu and Wacquant 1992) view of class formation.

Chapter 1. Prevailing Approaches to the Study of Neighborhoods and Change

1. Building on the work of Nietzsche, *genealogy* looks beyond actually existing, taken-for-granted representations to establish how they came about, what powers they represent, and their historical conditions of possibility. Foucault (1972) provides guidance for tracing knowledge production over time through different "generations" of ideas.

2. In Chicago, seventy-five community areas were identified in the 1930s. Today these boundaries remain relatively unchanged with the exception of splitting one community into two (Uptown became Edgewater and Uptown) and adding O'Hare Airport for a total of seventy-seven.

3. Contemporary researchers offer alternative ways to partition the market so that it is not overly simplified. For example, Galster and Rothenberg (1991) assume that demand generated by factors within a submarket is critical to understanding filtering dynamics since it is these factors that determine the degree to which different submarkets come to function as substitutes. But even though their model considers

the complexity of the urban housing market, taking into account individual as well as aggregate demand and variation in the product attributed to the type of housing supplier, it only tells part of the story because it limits the explanation to being a function of supply and demand.

4. Later evidence (e.g., Clark 1993) found similar results with other minority groups.

Chapter 2. Understanding Change in Today's Changing Urban Mosaic

1. We assume that knowledge produced about the experiences of people living in a space can come from different forms of "data," including individuals reporting their direct experience, observations we and others make in that space, and building models using existing data to describe change over time and make comparisons in conditions between spaces. We assume that all data have limitations.

2. According to Cohen and Taylor (2001), Mayor Richard J. Daley (1955–1977) used public housing concentrations to "save" his white ethnic constituency from further black expansion into their neighborhoods.

3. The equity assurance program required owners to pay a one-time fee and wait a minimum of five years before selling their home. To date, only a few claims have been filed.

4. Similarly, following gentrification of Wicker Park in the late 1980s, residents organized as the Old Wicker Park Committee to influence government and real estate agents to prevent construction and retention of affordable housing.

5. For example, people we spoke to in subareas such as Wicker Park (in West Town), Buena Park and Sheridan Park (Uptown), Bucktown (Logan Square), and West Gate (Near West Side) did not know the name of the larger community they lived in.

6. In de Certeau's (1988, xviii) words, "statistical inquiry, in breaking down these 'efficacious meanderings' into units that it defines itself, in reorganizing the results of its analyses according to its own codes, 'finds' only the homogeneous. The power of its calculations lies in its ability to divide, but it is precisely through this analytic fragmentation that it loses sight of what it claims to seek and to represent."

7. Both studies were completed by the Nathalie P. Voorhees Center for Neighborhood and Community Improvement at University of Illinois at Chicago. Janet Smith directed both projects.

8. Evidence of investment and disinvestment was based on property values under the assumption that property values are determined through a combination of conditions and decisions made by investors.

9. The index presented, which is for the period from 1970 to 2000, has been updated to include 2010 data. We chose to use the earlier study to keep the end date parallel with that of the rental housing study.

10. For a complete description of the methodology, see Hudspeth 2003.

11. The observed changes do not apply to individual households or buildings but constitute aggregated conditions based on available statistics.

12. The updated Gentrification Index shows that these trends continued with an increased score in many of the communities identified as "changing, gentrification" and a decreased score in those identified as "changing, decline" (Voorhees Center 2014).

13. Any quote that is identified as "Interview with . . ." was taken from interviews completed by the authors solely for the purpose of this research using research protocol approved by the University of Illinois at Chicago Institutional Review Board (Protocol # 2009–1085). Names of people interviewed by the authors are not included in order to protect their identity.

Chapter 3. Recasting Race/Ethnicity: The Gentrification of Bronzeville and Pilsen

1. Pilsen is the contemporary name for the Lower West Side community area.

2. Bronzeville roughly corresponds to the original Black Belt, which includes the communities of Kenwood and Oakland and sections of Douglas and Grand Boulevard.

3. "Legitimation of the social order is not . . . the product of a deliberate and purposeful action of propaganda or symbolic imposition; it results, rather, from the fact that agents apply to the objective structures of the social world structures of perception and appreciation which are used out of these very structures and which tend to picture the world as evident" (Bourdieu 1989, 21).

4. These multiclass combinations were not unusual, as ethnic groups clustered together and as households serving the wealthy lived nearby.

5. These generalizations help illustrate the overall trajectories of neighborhoods (considered as local or bounded real estate markets of differentiated social reproduction), yet they are layered over highly differentiated processes and social relations on the ground, pushing and pulling in all directions as they "play to win" within predetermined but ever-changing fields (Bourdieu and Wacquant 1992).

6. In *Shelley v. Kraemer*, the Supreme Court ruled that racially restrictive covenants were unconstitutional. Yet covenants did not disappear and continued to be honored by whites.

7. In Bronzeville, higher-class blacks clustered at the edges, mainly to the north and to the southeast, bordering middle- to upper-class Hyde Park. Housing Bronzeville reports that by 1959 high-income families were 17 percent of the population, middle-income 33 percent, and low-income 49 percent (J. Briggs 2006). Then a large proportion of middle- and upper-income blacks left while new immigrants and overcrowded households moved in.

8. Real estate, particularly but not exclusively multifamily buildings, and most businesses in the Black Belt had remained in the hands of whites, who engaged in well-known practices of abuse, foreclosure, abandonment, tax delinquency, and arson to extract value from their buildings. Meanwhile, a self-contained black market allowed many blacks to open their own businesses and accumulate wealth.

9. Construction has been completed and the building is operating as the police headquarters for the city.

10. Cost-burdened homeowners in Chicago went from 25.7 to 49.5 percent, Douglas went from 35 to 52.6 percent, Oakland from 36 to 53 percent, Grand Boulevard from 38 to 48.9 percent, and Kenwood from 39 to 47.5 percent. Cost-burdened renters in Chicago went from 42.3 to 49.8 percent, Douglas went from 35 to 38.2 percent, Oakland went from 36 to 52 percent, Grand Boulevard went from 38 to 59.5 percent, and Kenwood went from 39 to 56 percent (*Chicago Reporter* 2011).

11. Solis was a former head of a Latino group involved with Daley's Democratic machine who, when appointed, moved to Tri-Taylor, a white middle-class corner of the ward, rather than settling in Pilsen.

12. By the time the developer started his work in Pilsen, Lincoln Park was no longer a market for purchasing properties at rock-bottom prices, which was his strategy. But he also did not think Pilsen was going to flip: "Pilsen was always a working class neighborhood. It'll take generations for this to disappear" (Jeffers and Osterman 2003).

13. The city sided with his opponents at many critical times or in critical projects, and it did not help him much in his work (Cunningham 1988). The image he conveys is that of a "lone ranger."

14. According to Wilson, Wooters, and Grammenos (2004), the Protect Pilsen Coalition included a variety of local groups led by an organization that focused on education through development, policy advocacy, leadership training, and action.

15. Betancur experienced this firsthand when he became director of a Pilsen nonprofit, and interviewees confirmed it: "I am finding that many Pilsen organizations do function much like an island; there is not much communication among us." And "In Pilsen, there's been this tradition that organizations do not talk to each other or collaborate." (Interviews with director of an NGO and staff person from a second one)

16. Actually, some of these leaders would change their position vis-à-vis displacing development later on but still wavered on upfront opposition to accommodations.

17. Pilsen had been chosen by LISC/MacArthur as one of sixteen demonstration communities in Chicago, and four local organizations led the implementation of the plan. The plan included goals, projects, and responsible parties within the overall (and ambiguous) purpose of improving the quality of life while settling for output-oriented services and a mixed-income community.

18. Including the alderman, the Chicago Office of Tourism, and the Pilsen Together Chamber of Commerce.

19. Many aldermen receive campaign contributions from the real estate industry and from other businesses in the area that need their (and the city's) support. Referring to the local alderman, Cunningham explained, "It's been hard for [the alderman] to hide his preference for a wealthier class; he rubs elbows with developers and defends development that UIC's Voorhees Center predicts will displace the poor" (1988, 30).

20. He actually supported the proposal.

Chapter 4. Constructing Carceral Space: How Englewood Became the Ghetto

1. The process was documented by Hirsch (1989) and Drake and Cayton (1993).

2. Jackson and McCormick (2005).

3. In 1979, The Citizens Council of Southwest Englewood, addressing the apparent lack of concern of Fifteenth Ward Alderman Frank Brady (1979–1986), filed a missing persons report for him (police eventually found him in City Hall) (Polk and Dumke 1999). Alderman Virgil Jones (1991–99) from the same ward was convicted in 1999 for taking bribes from an FBI mole (Meyer 2012). Alderman Theodore Thomas's reticence in City Council earned him the nickname "Silent Ted." In the arrest complaint and indictment of Twentieth Ward alderman Arenda Troutman, Gary Shapiro, first assistant U.S. attorney, explained "how things get done in the 20th Ward of Chicago. You wanna build something, you wanna improve your property, you need permits from the city, you need zoning, you need the alderman's support . . . you want the alderman's support, you pay the alderman. You pay Arenda Troutman, and best of all in the 20th Ward, and best of all, everything is negotiable" (Bradley 2007).

4. The *Chicago Reporter* staff (2007) reported that an average of seventeen persons attended beat meetings in the Englewood Police District in 1999, which was less than Chicago's average of twenty-six.

5. The tradition of block clubs continues today. They hold an annual meeting under the umbrella Southwest Federation of Block Clubs of Greater Englewood.

6. This includes programs to feed the hungry, clothe the needy, extend a hand to ex-prisoners, provide day care, and accompany residents in their multiple struggles.

7. Fragmentation needs to be carefully assessed. When residents pointed to fragmentation, they were referring to the fact that decision making was split in many ways, which often prevented the development of appropriate infrastructure and services while pulling residents away from collective into individual gains (e.g., patronage).

8. Teamwork Englewood was created by St. Bernard Hospital, Greater Englewood Parish United Methodist Church, and Pullman Bank Initiatives (a subsidiary of the former Park National Bank).

9. The plan lists by name every participant.

10. We recognize that the term "white flight" can be a bit misleading. Certainly, whites flew out of Englewood in response to the racist tactics of the real estate industry. To some extent, this was a rational response on their part as well as a form of forceful relocation, but also there was an element of collaboration as these movers shared the racism by refusing to live with blacks. Ultimately, white flight is deeply embedded in the real estate industry's assigning a negative value to property and neighborhood desirability.

11. Redevelopment began with a false start in 1980 when Mayor Jane Byrne announced a five-year, $11 million renewal plan for "rehabilitating structurally sound buildings and demolishing others, replacing them with single-family dwelling, town houses and small apartments" (Chicago Sun-Times 1980), a plan that never

materialized. In 1988, the city announced the Englewood Plan: Renaissance of Neighborhood Commerce, which sat on the Department of Planning and Development's shelves.

12. This included including Antioch Church, Rebirth of Englewood Development Corporation, Saint Bernard Hospital's Development Corporation, New Birth Community Care Center, the Greater Englewood Parish Housing Association, and ACORN.

13. According to Teamwork Englewood's website, "On January 25, 2016 Teamwork Englewood kicked off the second phase of the Englewood Quality of Life. Over the next several months the task forces will meet to create a new plan for each task force." http://www.teamworkenglewood.org.

Chapter 5. Constructing Flexible Spaces of Accumulation and Social Reproduction

1. Veiling the power relations involved in gentrification and ghettoization, terms like "gentrifiers" and "ghetto dwellers" make individuals agents of gentrification and ghettoization and their activities the result of either creativity (the creative class) or destruction (the irresponsible lumpen proletariat).

2. We do recognize that white ethnics were able to sell or rent their properties in these spaces to the new minorities moving in.

3. Here we are referring to the role played by the headquarters of the Democratic machine in the remaining white neighborhoods that continued many of the practices of vigilantism, racial exclusion, and segregation.

4. Miller (2011) argues that suburban gentrification is occurring in the Chicago metropolitan area.

Chapter 6. Selling the Neighborhood: Commodification versus Differential Space

1. Our gay interviewees expressed distaste for the term "Boystown," which is often used to name the area roughly bounded by Belmont and Grace Streets, and Broadway and Clark. Therefore, we opted for Halsted North, a term they found more acceptable.

2. In contrast, legislation enacted in 2014 allowing gay marriage in Illinois turned the next parade into a celebration.

3. *Community* is used here to refer to identities resulting from ascribed conditions that place all individuals classified as PRs in a relationship based on race/nationality and gays based on sexual orientation. We recognize that such conditions do not affect everybody equally, as other factors and identities (e.g., class or gender) can mediate, mitigate, or intensify the effects of oppression vis-à-vis colonial United States for PRs and heterosexual privilege for gays.

4. The Red Squad was an antisubversive unit of the Chicago police that used both overt and covert tactics to carry out targeted actions against groups such as anarchists and communists and against minority and reform organizations. In reaction

to a lawsuit filed in 1974, the squad destroyed files on 105,000 individuals and 1,300 organizations, and in 1985 the court ordered the unit to dissolve.

5. The terminology "old" and "new" guard was used by opponents of the PRA, who called themselves the vanguard and characterized the PRA as obsolete. This "us versus them" mentality reflects different visions and class interests within the PR community.

6. Initially organized to seek federal empowerment zone designation, the Empowerment Partnership included local institutions, businesses, nonprofits, and others around a comprehensive strategy of business, job, and housing development for actual residents. Although designation was not obtained, many of the collaborations moved forward. The Community of Wellness is a broad coalition of organizations and individuals pursuing comprehensive community health. The Community as Campus was proposed by PRA leaders to address the lack of continuity and collaboration between the different local schools. Their proposal to correct the broken school pipeline was approved by the Board of Education.

7. "Gay" is used here as a generic term for the range of identities reflected in acronyms such as GLBTT or GLBTTQ. Though a class cannot be properly represented by a generic male, it is a commonly understood term; reflecting gay male dominance, the movement has been known as "gay movement." Many of our sources prefer "queer" but acknowledge that many do not relate to it or find it offensive.

8. "The biggest thing that could happen to you was to get home at the end of the day and not having been fired or beaten up, because that was a daily event . . . if you were in a bar, there was a good chance of going to jail because that was a sport for the police, to raid bars" (interview with bar owner).

9. Given the difficulty of obtaining liquor licenses in Chicago up to recently and the risks that gay bars represented, they were owned by well-connected nongay individuals, especially from the underworld, who had to tip the hand of elected politicians or public-sector employees to operate and stay in business.

10. "In the period leading to an election, there were raids of gay bars: they would come and arrest people; their names would be in the newspaper the next day; people would lose their jobs, there were suicides because that was the end of your life" (interview with bar owner).

11. Examining several case studies, Alvarez and Harris (1998, 11) argued that "concentrations of gay and lesbian residential populations are a forerunner to rather than the result of the development of the commercial precincts (i.e. gay or lesbian businesses choose their clientele and not the other way)."

12. The Matachine Society was founded in Los Angeles in 1950 and was one of the oldest organizations in the country.

13. One of the authors lived in the vicinity of HN in the late 1970s when the area was neglected, and Halsted Street was inhabited by PRs with a concentration of antique stores to the south of the street, a grocery store in the middle selling PR food, a few

fringe businesses, and a couple of gay bars. Gays were moving into nearby rentals in droves and some of them were acquiring and fixing property and operating as gentrification pioneers.

14. Safety is still relative, as "gay haters" visit the area to harass and even attack gays.

Chapter 7. Reinventing Neighborhood?
Transforming Chicago's Public Housing

1. In 1929 Harvey Zorbaugh, a University of Chicago sociologist, published *The Gold Coast and the Slum*, which distinguished the Lower North Side (the western section of the Near North Side community area) in order to emphasize the two poles that characterized that neighborhood at the time.

2. While both of these developments are included in the Chicago Housing Authority's Plan for Transformation, most of their redevelopment trajectory happened before the plan was approved in 2000.

3. The Chicago Housing Authority was reluctant to allow this because it was contrary to the intent of dispersing poverty. Eventually, after a couple of years, many of the families moved into a building together.

4. The feasibility of redevelopment was formally determined for each development by determining which would cost more, vouchering out or rehabbing, and nearly eighteen thousand units initially failed this test. After taking into consideration the cost of demolition, this number was recalculated and reduced to eleven thousand units. Compared to New York City and Los Angeles, the two PHAs with larger portfolios than the CHA, this was still a large number to be demolished.

5. HUD sponsored a multimillion-dollar research study called Moving to Opportunity (MTO) that used an experimental approach to investigate what happens when families that are given vouchers to move out of public housing are required to move into low-poverty areas. In total, about 4,200 families across five cities, including Chicago, were involved in the study. While the findings varied across the five cities involved, the general conclusion reached was that after ten to fifteen years out, families that moved into low-poverty neighborhoods had improved "neighborhood outcomes" based on better quality housing and feeling safer, and they had improved mental and physical health. There was no significant impact, however, on employment outcomes for adults or school outcomes for youths (Ludwig et al. 2013). These findings have several caveats, including the concern that "MTO generates too small of a 'treatment dose' on neighborhood environments to provide a meaningful test of 'neighborhood effects' theories" (Ludwig et al. 2013, 7).

6. This comment came from a current Cabrini Green resident, who watched them build the development that she then moved into with her family.

7. Today, the rentals have all been converted to condominiums and Sandburg Village is a well-established neighborhood that bridges the Gold Coast and Old Town.

8. The court required the developer to reduce the income levels to less than 40 percent of area median (about $30,000) in "affordable housing" units subsidized with low income housing tax credits.

9. South Kenwood is the part of Kenwood that is south of Forty-Seventh Street. It has been home to several famous African American Chicagoans including Barack Obama, Muhammad Ali, Louis Farrakhan, and Muddy Waters.

10. As with fuzzy logic, fuzzy space cannot be described with traditional binary sets (where variables may take on true or false values) but instead have a range between 0 and 1.

11. The CHA claims to have lost the list and lost track of the families it had relocated in 1985.

Chapter 8. Building the Organization or Building the Community? Community Development in a Time of Flexible Accumulation

1. See http://www.united-power.org/content/legislative-category.

2. Their approach aimed to send a clear and open message to Chicago's fifty aldermen and the mayor that they are being watched and their action or inaction will be remembered at election time by their growing membership. In spring 2015, the city had its first runoff between the incumbent mayor Rahm Emanuel and Jesus "Chuy" Garcia, along with nineteen aldermen. While Emanuel was re-elected, most agreed that the movement was strong and had won big, especially with the unseating of several old guard aldermen.

3. For example, the union of the MacArthur Foundation, Metropolitan Planning Commission, LISC, city of Chicago, and the Chicago Housing Authority among many others to move forward the Plan for Transformation.

4. While these laws apply to all homeowners, several cases have involved white middle-class owners firing upon nonwhite individuals who have not entered the home (e.g., Trayvon Martin).

5. In 2006–2007, Unite Here, which represents hotel workers, launched a campaign against several aldermen seen to be against their cause. In 2015, the Chicago Teachers Union, as part of Take Back Chicago, helped to successfully run a few candidates for alderman.

6. The Chicago Anti-Eviction Campaign grew out of and is modeled after the Anti-Eviction Campaign in South Africa.

7. This quote was on the Take Back the Land website, which is no longer active since the organization is no longer active. It is also quoted in Smiley and West 2012 (97).

Conclusion

1. While not identified formally as either class- or race-based, the definition of blight meant that low-income neighborhoods were targeted, and in Chicago, as well as other cities, most were nonwhite. See Martin Anderson (1964).

2. This should not be read as an assertion that the oppressed and downtrodden are the agents of change (as in Marx's proletariat). Although elements within the dominant forces take the side of social change, the dominant work to maintain the relations that benefit them at the expense of the rest. Meanwhile, as in Hegel's master-servant relationship, socialized in the game of domination, the dominated also aspire to become dominant; still, by contesting domination, they open cracks in the relationship that can be the basis for other social relations.

3. As Bourdieu (1990, 133) notes, "The most successful ideological effects are the ones that have no need for words, but only of laissez-faire and complicitous silence."

References

Abrams, Charles. 1955. *Forbidden Neighbors*. New York: Harper and Brothers.

Aby-Lughod, Janet. 2000. *New York, Chicago, Los Angeles: America's Global Cities*. Minneapolis: University of Minnesota Press.

———. 2007. *Race, Space, and Riots in Chicago*. New York: Oxford University Press.

Adams, John Kay, and Jerry Cohen. 1959. "Where Englewood Strength Lies." *Chicago Sun-Times*, June 24.

Adler, Jane. 1997. "Polishing Bronzeville: History Comes Alive Again—and So Does the Neighborhood." *Chicago Tribune*, October 12.

Aguirre, Benigno E., Kent P. Schwirian, and Anthony J. LaGreca. 1980. "The Residential Patterning of Latin American and Other Ethnic Populations in Metropolitan Miami." *Latin American Research Review* 15: 35–63.

Ahlbrandt, Roger, and Paul Brophy. 1975. *Neighborhood Revitalization: Theory and Practice*. Lexington, Mass.: Lexington Books.

Aldrich, Howard. 1975. "Ecological Succession in Racially Changing Neighborhoods: A Review of the Literature." *Urban Affairs Quarterly* 10(3): 327–48.

Alihan, Milla A. 1938. *Social Ecology: A Critical Analysis*. New York: Columbia University Press.

Allen, Theodore W. 1994. *The Invention of the White Race*. Vol. 1, *Racial Oppression and Social Control*. New York: Verso.

———. 1997. *The Invention of the White Race*. Vol. 2, *The Origin of Racial Oppression in Anglo-America*. New York: Verso.

Alvarez, Jorge, and Stephen Harris. 1998. "Towards a Model of Gay and Lesbian Neighborhoods." Unpublished paper presented to the ACSP 40th Annual Conference, Pasadena, California.

Amin, Ash, ed. 1995. *Post-Fordism: A Reader*. Oxford: Blackwell.

———, ed. 2009. *The Social Economy*. London: Zed Books

Anderson, Martin. 1964. *The Federal Bulldozer: A Critical Analysis of Urban Renewal, 1942–1962*. Cambridge, Mass.: MIT Press.

Anderson, Matthew, and Carolina Sternberg. 2012. "'Non-White' Gentrification in Chicago's Bronzeville and Pilsen: Racial Economy and the Intraurban Contingency of Urban Redevelopment." *Urban Affairs Review* 49(3): 435–67.

Anderson, Monroe. 2006. "Black Business Owners, Here Is Your Chance." *Chicago Sun-Times*, March 12.

Arnold, Joseph. 1979. "The Neighborhood and City Hall: The Origins of Neighborhood Association in Baltimore, 1880–1911." *Journal of Urban History* 6(1): 3–30.

Atkinson, Rowland, and Gary Bridge, eds. 2005. *Gentrification in a Global Context: The New Urban Colonialism*. London: Routledge.

Austen, Ben. 2013. "The Death and Life of Chicago." *The New York Times Magazine*, May 29. http://www.nytimes.com/2013/06/02/magazine/how-chicagos-housing-crisis-ignited-a-new-form-of-activism.html?_r=0. Accessed on March 3, 2016.

Baer, William C., and Christopher B. Williamson. 1988. "The Filtering of Households and Housing Units." *Journal of Planning Literature* 3: 127–52.

Baily, Jeff. 2008. "Finding the Beat of Chicago's Latino Quarter." *New York Times*, June 29.

Baim, Tracy, ed. 2008. *Out and Proud in Chicago: An Overview of the City's Community*. Chicago: Surrey Books.

Barnes, Jenna. 2012a. "Englewood Residents RAGE against Violence by Developing Own Safety Plan." *Medill Reports Chicago*, Jan 18. http://news.medill.northwestern.edu/chicago/news.aspx?id=198644. Accessed March 24, 2012.

———. 2012b. "In Englewood, Skepticism Surrounds Police Increase." *Medill Reports Chicago*, February 16. http://news.medill.northwestern.edu/chicago/news.aspx?id=200578. Accessed March 24, 2012.

Barrera, Mario. 1979. *Race and Class in the Southwest: A Theory of Racial Inequality*. South Bend, Ind.: Notre Dame University Press.

Baudrillard, Jean. 1983. *Simulations*. New York: Semiotext(e).

———. 2005. *The Conspiracy of Art: Manifestos, Interviews, Essays*. New York: Columbia University Press.

Bauer, Catherine. 1934. *Modern Housing*. New York: Houghton Mifflin Company.

———. 1951. "Social Questions in Housing and Community Planning." *Journal of Social Issues* 7(1–2): 1–34.

Beaty, Paul. 2012. "Violence Weighs Heavily in Englewood." *Chicago News Cooperative*, May 11.

Behrens, Web. 2009. "Pilsen Gentrification: Can Pilsen Pull off Responsible Development?" *Timeout Chicago*, February 16.

Bell, David, and Gill Valentine. 1995. "Queer Country: Rural Lesbian and Gay Lives." *Journal of Rural Studies* 11(2): 113–22.

Bennett, Larry, Nancy Hudspeth, and Patricia Wright. 2006. "A Critical Analysis of the ABLA Redevelopment Plan." In *Where Are Poor People to Live? Transforming Public Housing Communities*, edited by Larry Bennett, Janet Smith, and Patricia Wright, 185–215. Armonk, N.Y.: M. E. Sharpe.

Bennett, Larry, Janet Smith, and Patricia Wright. 2006. "Epilogue." In *Where Are Poor People to Live? Transforming Public Housing Communities*, edited by Larry Bennett, Janet Smith, and Patricia Wright, 301–14. Armonk, N.Y.: M. E. Sharpe.

Berry, Brian J. 1979. *The Open Housing Question: Race and Housing in Chicago: 1966–1976.* Cambridge, Mass: Ballinger Publications.

Betancur, John J. 2002. "The Politics of Gentrification: The Case of West Town in Chicago." *Urban Affairs Review* 37(6): 780–814.

———. 2011. "Gentrification and Community Fabric in Chicago." *Urban Studies* 48(2): 383–406.

Betancur, John J., Deborah Bennett, and Patricia A. Wright. 1991. "Effective Strategies for Community Economic Development." In *Challenging Uneven Development: An Urban Agenda for the 1990s*, edited by Phillip W. Nyden and Wim Wiewel, 198–224. New Brunswick, N.J.: Rutgers University Press.

Betancur, John J., Lee Deuben, and Helen Edwards. 2006. "Gentrification before Gentrification? The Plight of Pilsen in Chicago." Chicago: Nathalie P. Voorhees Center for Neighborhood and Community Improvement, University of Illinois at Chicago.

Betancur, John J., Isabel Domeyko, and Patricia W. Wright. 2001. "Gentrification in West Town: Contested Ground." Chicago: Nathalie P. Voorhees Center for Neighborhood and Community Improvement, University of Illinois at Chicago.

Betancur, John J., and Maricela Garcia. 2011. "The 2006–2007 Immigration Mobilizations and Community Capacity: The Experience of Chicago." *Latino Studies* 9(1): 10–37.

Betancur, John J., Karen Mossberger, and Yue Zhang. 2015. "Standing in Two Worlds: Neighborhood Policy, the Civic Arena, and Ward-Based Politics in Chicago." In *Urban Neighborhoods in a New Era, Revitalization Politics in the Postindustrial City*, edited by Clarence N. Stone and Robert P. Stoker, 81–107. Chicago: University of Chicago Press.

Betancur, John, and Patricia C. Wright. 1988. "The Pilsen Triangle." Chicago: University of Illinois at Chicago Center for Urban Economic Development.

Bezalel, Ronit. 1997. "Voices of Cabrini, Remaking Chicago's Public Housing." Video, https://vimeo.com/8207992. Accessed on March 3, 2016.

Blackie, Robert. 2013. "A Longitudinal Assessment of Gay Space in Chicago: 1970–2010." MA thesis, University of Illinois at Chicago.

Blakely, Edward J., and Mary Gail Snyder. 1997. *Fortress America: Gated Communities in the United States*. Washington, D.C.: Brookings Institution Press; Cambridge, Mass.: Lincoln Institute of Land Policy.

Bluestone, Barry, and Bennett Harrison. 1982. *The Deindustrialization of America: Plant Closings, Community Abandonment and the Dismantling of Basic Industry.* New York: Basic Books.

Bourdieu, Pierre. 1984. *Distinction: A Social Critique of the Judgment of Taste.* Translated by Richard Nice. Cambridge, Mass: Harvard University Press.

———. 1988. *Homo Academicus.* Stanford, Calif.: Stanford Academic Press.

———. 1989. "Reproduction Interdite. La Dimension Symbolique de la Domination Economique." *Etudes Rurales* 113/114: 15–36.

———. 1990. *The Logic of Practice.* Translated by Richard Nice. Stanford, Calif.: Stanford University Press.

———. 1991. *Language & Symbolic Power.* Edited and introduced by John B. Thompson. Cambridge, Mass.: Harvard University Press.

Bourdieu, Pierre, and Loïc Wacquant. 1992. *An Invitation to Reflexive Sociology.* Chicago: University of Chicago Press.

Bowean, Lolly. 2009. "Englewood Violence Limits Summer for Children: For One Family, Kids Spend Time in Safe Havens or Under Watchful Eyes of Parents." *Chicago Tribune*, July 12.

———. 2010. "Bronzeville Still Reaching for Potential." *Chicago Tribune*, February 26.

Bowly, Devereux, Jr. 1978. *The Poorhouse: Subsidized Housing in Chicago, 1895–1976.* Carbondale: Southern Illinois University Press.

Boyd, Michelle. 2000. "Reconstructing Bronzeville: Racial Nostalgia and Neighborhood Redevelopment." *Journal of Urban Affairs* 22(2): 107–22.

———. 2008. *Jim Crow Nostalgia: Reconstructing Race in Bronzeville.* Minneapolis: University of Minnesota Press.

Bradford, Calvin. 2008. "Statements of Calvin Bradford before the National Commission on Fair Housing and Equal Opportunity." Atlanta, Georgia. October 17.

Bradley, Ben. 2007. "Feds Arrest Chicago Alderman." *ABC7News*, January 8.

Bratt, Rachel, Michael Stone, and Chester Hartman. 2006. *A Right to Housing: Foundation for a New Social Agenda.* Philadelphia, Pa.: Temple University Press.

Braudel, Ferdinand. 1982. *The Structures of Everyday Life: Civilization and Capitalism, 15th–18th Century, vol. 1.* New York: Harper and Row.

Brennan, Eamonn. 2013. "Chicago Reveals DePaul Arena Plans." *ESPN.com*, May 16.

Brenner, Neil, and Theodore, Nick, eds. 2002. *Spaces of Neoliberalism: Urban Restructuring in North America and Western Europe.* Oxford: Blackwell.

Briggs, Jonathan E. 2006. "Bronzeville Wants City's Empty Lots. Affordable-Housing Advocates Also Seek Tax for a Trust Fund." *Chicago Tribune*, November 23.

Briggs, Xavier de Souza. 1998. "Brown Kids in White Suburbs: Housing Mobility and the Multiple Faces of Social Capital." *Housing Policy Debate* 9(1): 177–221.

Brownell, Blaine A. 1980. "Urban Planning and the Motor Vehicle." In *Shaping an Urban World*, edited by G. Cherry. London: Mansell.

Bruce-Roberts, Inc. 2004. "Map of Chicago's Gangland, 1931." In *Encyclopedia of Chicago*, edited by James R. Grossman, Ann Durkin Keating, and Janice L. Reiff. Chicago: University of Chicago Press. http://www.encyclopedia.chicagohistory.org/pages/11538.html. Accessed May 31, 2015.

Burgess, Ernest. 1925. "The Growth of the City: An Introduction to the Research Project." In *The City,* edited by Robert Park, Ernest Burgess, and Roderick D. McKenzie, 47–62. Chicago: University of Chicago Press.

Burgess, Ernest, and Donald Bogue, eds. 1967. *Urban Sociology.* Chicago: University of Chicago Press.

Caputo, Angela. 2011. "Loopholes." *Chicago Reporter,* January 1. http://chicagoreporter .com/loopholes/. Accessed May 31, 2015.

Cardona, Adriana. 2011. "The Call to Act Awakens: Residents Unite to Improve Their Community." *The Gate News,* February 22. http://www.thegatenewspaper .com/2011/02/the-call-to-act-awakens-residents-unite-to-improve-their -community/. Accessed May 31, 2015.

Castoriadis, Cornelius. 1997. *World in Fragments: Writings on Politics, Society, Psychoanalysis and the Imagination.* Edited and translated by David Ames Curtis. Stanford, Calif.: Stanford University Press.

———. 1998. *The Imaginary Institution of Society.* Cambridge, Mass.: MIT Press.

Charles, Suzanne L. 2011. "Suburban Gentrification: Understanding the Determinants of Single-Family Residential Redevelopment, A Case Study of the Inner-Ring Suburbs of Chicago, 2000–2010." Working Paper W11-1. Cambridge, Mass.: Joint Center for Housing Studies, Harvard University.

Chaskin, Robert J., and Mark L. Joseph. 2010. "Building 'Community' in Mixed-Income Developments: Assumptions, Approaches and Early Experiences." *Urban Affairs Review* 45(3): 299–335.

Chicago Fact Book Consortium. 1983. *Local Community Fact Book Chicago Metropolitan Area 1980.* Chicago: Department of Sociology, University of Illinois at Chicago.

———. 1984. *Local Community Fact Book Chicago Metropolitan Area Based on the 1970 and 1980 Censuses.* Chicago: Chicago Review Press.

Chicago Housing Authority. 2011. "Jazz on the Boulevard." http://www.thecha.org/ residents/public-housing/jazz-on-the-boulevard/. Accessed April 20, 2011.

———. 2012. *Amended FY2012 Moving to Work Annual Plan.* Chicago: Chicago Housing Authority.

Chicago Rehab Network. 2003. "Affordable Chicago: The Next Five Year Housing Plan 2004–2008, Chicago: Chicago Rehab Network." Chicago: Chicago Rehab Network. http://www.chicagorehab.org/resources/docs/aboutcrn/affordable_chicago.pdf.

Chicago Reporter. 1999. "Englewood Gentrification." *Chicago Reporter.* http://whgbetc .com/englewood/englewood-why-chirep.html. Accessed December 21, 2012.

———. 2001. "Englewood Community Policing." *The Chicago Reporter,* October 1.

———. 2007. "A Brief History of Englewood." *The Chicago Reporter.* http://www.chicago reporter.com/news/2007/10/brief-history-englewood. Accessed January 25, 2013.

———. 2011. "The Devastated Housing Market on Chicago's South and West Sides During the Daley Era." *The Chicago Reporter/Chicago Muckrakers,* June. http://www .chicagonow.com/chicago-muckrakers/2011/06/the-devastated-housing-market

-on-chicagos-south-and-west-sides-during-the-daley-era/. Accessed July 2, 2012.

Chicago Sun-Times. 1980. "Five Year $11 Million Renewal Plan Revealed in Englewood." *Chicago Sun-Times,* August 21.

Chicago Tribune. 1998. "4 Chicago High-Rises Are Demolished." *Chicago Tribune,* December 13.

———. 2002. "Ferd Kramer's Chicago legacy (obituary)." *Chicago Tribune,* July 20.

———. 2011. "Census Shows Changing Neighborhoods: In Some Areas, Gentrification Drove Racial Shifts." *Chicago Tribune,* February 25.

Cintrón, R., M. Toro-Morn, I. García Zambrana, and E. Scott. 2012. *60 Years of Migration: Puerto Ricans in Chicagoland.* Chicago: Puerto Rican Agenda.

Clark, William A. V. 1993. "Neighborhood Transitions in Multiethnic/Racial Contexts." *Journal of Urban Affairs* 15(2): 161–72.

———. 1994. "Residential Preferences and Neighborhood Racial Segregation: A Test of the Schelling Segregation Model." *Demography* 28: 1–19.

Clay, Philip. 1979. *Neighborhood Renewal.* Cambridge, Mass.: MIT Press.

Cochran, William L. 2011. *Englewood: Growing Pains in Chicago.* DVD. Directed by William L. Cochran. Chicago: Maverick Entertainment Group.

Cohen, Adam, and Elizabeth Taylor. 2001. *American Pharaoh: Richard J. Daley—His Battle for Chicago and the Nation.* New York: Little, Brown and Company.

Coleman, Mathew, and John A. Agnew. 2007. "The Problem with Empire." In *Space, Knowledge and Power: Foucault and Geography,* edited by Jeremy W. Crampton and Stuart Elden, 317–39. Hampshire, UK: Ashgate.

Congress for the New Urbanism. 1996. *Principles for Inner City Neighborhood Design.* Washington D.C.: U.S. Department of Housing and Urban Development.

Corfman, T. 2009. "Daley's CHA Dream Deferred." *Crain's Chicago Business,* February 7.

———. 2010. "Cabrini-Green Redevelopment Project Gets Bailout Money from City of Chicago. *Crain's Chicago Business,* January 9.

Cox, Kevin. 1981. "Capitalism and Conflict around the Communal Living Space." In *Urbanization & Urban Planning in Capitalist Society,* edited by Michael Dear and Allen J. Scott, 431–56. London: Methuen.

Craig, Gary. 2007. "Community Capacity Building: Something Old, Something New . . . ?" *Critical Social Policy* 27(3): 335–59.

Cromidas, Rachel. 2010a. "Failed Olympics Bid Leaves Neighborhood in Flux." *The New York Times/Chicago News Cooperative,* January 9.

———. 2010b. "Bronzeville, A Neighborhood Whose Promise Has Been Stalled." *The New York Times/Chicago News Cooperative,* September 2.

Cronon, William. 1991. *Nature's Metropolis,* New York: W. W. Norton.

Cruz, Wilfredo. 2007. *City of Dreams: Latino Immigration to Chicago.* Lanham, Md.: University Press of America.

Cunningham, Peter. 1988. "Podmajersky: Savior or Villain in Pilsen?" *Crain's Chicago Business,* November 14.

Cuomo, A. 1997. "Testimony Before the Government Oversight and Reform Housing Subcommittee." U.S. Department of Housing and Urban Development. http://www .hud.gov/govorhs.html. Accessed February 27, 1997.

Curran, Win. 2004. "Gentrification and the Nature of Work: Exploring the Links in Williamsburg, Brooklyn." *Environment and Planning A* 36(7): 1243–58.

Davila, Arlene. 2004. *Barrio Dreams: Puerto Ricans, Latinos and the Neoliberal City*. Berkeley: University of California Press.

Davis, Stephania H. 1996. "Bronzeville's Golden Past Relies on City for Rebirth." *Chicago Tribune*, May 29.

Dear, Michael J., ed. 2002. *From Chicago to L.A.: Making Sense of Urban Theory*. Thousand Oaks, Calif.: Sage.

Debord, Guy. 1995. *The Society of the Spectacle*. Translated by Donald Nicholson-Smith. New York: Zone Books.

de Certeau, Michel. 1988. *The Practice of Everyday Life*. Translated by Steven Rendall. Berkeley: University of California Press.

DeClue, Denise. 1978. "The Siege of Sandburg Village." *The Reader*, January 20.

Denton, Nancy, and Donald Massey. 1991. "Patterns of Neighborhood Transition in a Multi-Ethnic World: U.S. Metropolitan Areas, 1970–1980." *Demography* 26(1): 41–63.

Didion, Joan. 1979. *The White Album Essays*. New York: Simon & Schuster.

Dill, Thornton, and Ruth E. Zambrana. 2009. *Emerging Intersections: Race, Class and Gender in Theory, Policy and Practice*. New Brunswick, N.J.: Rutgers University Press.

Downs, Anthony. 1981. *Neighborhoods and Urban Development*. Washington D.C.: Brookings Institution Press.

Drachsler, Julius. 1920. *Democracy and Assimilation: The Blending of Immigrant Heritages in America*. New York: McMillan.

Drake, St. Clair, and R. Horace Cayton. 1993. *Black Metropolis: A Study of Negro Life in a Northern City*. Chicago: University of Chicago Press.

Dream Town. 2012. "Englewood Home Sales Statistics." http://www.dreamtown.com/ neighborhoods/englewood.html. Accessed September 17, 2012.

Drover. 2009. "Is Englewood Getting Better? City Data Forum, http://www.city-data .com/forum/chicago/696386-englewood.html. Accessed September 2014.

Duany, Andres, Elizabeth Plater-Zyberk, and Jeff Speck. 2000. *Suburban Nation*. New York: Northpoint Press.

Dumke, Mike. 2012. "The Shot That Brought the Projects Down." *The Reader*, October 14.

Dunlap, Aaron. 2014. "Is the Massive Lake Meadows Redevelopment Back On?" http://chicago.curbed.com/archives/2014/10/29/is-this-epic-lake-meadows -redevelopment-back-on.php. Accessed October 29, 2014.

Dye, Richard F., and David F. Merriman. 2000. "The Effects of Tax Increment Financing on Economic Development." *Journal of Urban Economics* 47: 306–28.

Easterly, William. 2004. *Empirics of Strategic Interdependence: The Case of the Racial Tipping Point*. New York: New York University Press.

Edman, Catherine. 2006. "Being Black in 1958: Director Shares Her Life Story with District 41 Students." *Chicago Daily Herald*, March 3.

Eick, Volcker. 2007. "Space Patrols—the New Peacekeeping Functions of Nonprofits: Contesting Neoliberalism or the Urban Poor?" In *Contesting Neoliberalism, Urban Frontiers*, edited by Helga Leitner, Jamie Peck, and Eric S. Sheppard, 266–90. New York: Guilford Press.

Eigs, Jonathan. 2002. "Eyes on the Street: Community Policing in Chicago." *The American Prospect*, May 17.

El Nasser, Haya, and Paul Overberg. 2001. "A Comprehensive Look at Sprawl in America." *USA Today*, Feb 21. http://usatoday30.usatoday.com/news/sprawl/main.htm. Accessed on March 7, 2016.

Ellen, Ingrid Gould. 1998. "Stable, Racial Integration in the Contemporary United States: An Empirical Overview." *Journal of Urban Affairs* 20(1): 27–42.

———. 2000. *Sharing America's Neighborhoods: The Prospects for Stable Racial Integration*. Cambridge, Mass.: Harvard University Press.

Emmart, William W. 1911. "City Plan." In *Proceedings of City-Wide Congress of Baltimore*. Baltimore: Emmart.

Emms, Stephen. 2008. "Streets Ahead: Pilsen." *The Guardian*, September 19.

Engels, Frederick. 1995 [1872]. *The Housing Question*. London: Pathfinder Books.

Fainstein, Susan. 2011. *The Just City*. Ithaca, N.Y.: Cornell University Press.

Farley, John E. 1995. "Race Still Matters: The Minimal Role of Income and Housing Cost as Causes of Housing Segregation in St. Louis, 1990." *Urban Affairs Review* 31: 244–54.

Farley, Reynolds, and William Frey. 1994. "Changes in Segregation of Whites from Blacks During the 1980s: Small Steps Toward a More Integrated Society." *American Sociological Review* 59(1): 23–45.

Farley, Reynolds, Charlotte Steeh, Maria Krysan, Keith Reeves, and Tara Jackson. 1994. "Segregation and Stereotypes: Housing in the Detroit Metropolitan Area." *American Journal of Sociology* 100: 750–80.

Feagin, Joe R. 1998. *The New Urban Paradigm, Critical Perspectives on the City*. Lanham, Md.: Rowman and Littlefield.

Feagin, Joe R., and Hernan Vera. 1995. *White Racism*. New York: Routledge.

Featherstone, Mike. 1994. "City Cultures and Post-Modern Lifestyles." In *Post-Fordism: A Reader*, edited by Ash Amin, 387–408. Oxford: Blackwell.

Ferguson, Ronald F., and William T. Dickens, eds. 1999. *Urban Problems and Community Development*. Washington D.C.: Brookings Institution Press.

Ferman, Barbara. 1996. *Challenging the Growth Machine: Neighborhood Politics in Chicago and Pittsburgh*. Lawrence: University Press of Kansas.

Firey, William. 1945. "Sentiment and Symbolism as Ecological Variables." *American Sociological Review* 10: 140–48.

Fisher, Robert. 1996. "Neighborhood Organizing: The Importance of Historical Context." In *Revitalizing Urban Neighborhoods*, edited by Dennis Keating, Norman Krumholz, and Philip Star, 39–49. Lawrence: University Press of Kansas.

Flint, Barbara J. 1977. "Zoning and Residential Segregation: A Social and Physical History." PhD dissertation, University of Chicago.

Flyvbjerg, Bent. 1998. *Rationality and Power, Democracy in Practice*. Chicago: University of Chicago Press.

Foote, Christopher L., Kristopher F. Gerardi, and Paul S. Willen. 2012. "Why Did So Many People Make So Many Ex Post Bad Decisions? The Causes of the Foreclosure Crisis." Public Policy Discussion Papers, Federal Reserve Bank of Boston 12-2: 1–62.

Foucault, Michel. 1972. *The Archaeology of Knowledge*. New York: Pantheon Books.

———. 1980. *Power/Knowledge: Selected Interviews and Other Writings, 1972–1977*. New York: Vintage.

———. 1982. "An Interview: Sex, Power and the Politics of Identity." With B. Gallagher and A. Wilson. *The Advocate* 400.

———. 1992. *Microfisica del Poder*. 3rd ed. Madrid: Ediciones la Piqueta.

———. 1995. *Discipline and Punish: The Birth of the Prison*. Translated by Alan Sheridan. New York: Vintage Books.

———. 1998. *The History of Sexuality: The Will to Knowledge*. London: Penguin.

Frankenberg, Ruth. 1993. *White Women, Race Matters: The Social Construction of Whiteness*. Minneapolis: University of Minnesota Press.

Freeman, Lance. 2006. *There Goes the 'Hood: Views of Gentrification from the Ground Up*. Philadelphia: Temple University Press.

Fulilove, Mindy. 2005. *Root Shock: How Tearing Up Urban Neighborhoods Hurts America, and What Can We Do About It*. New York: One World Ballantine Books.

Galster, George. 1990. "Neighborhood Racial Change, Segregationist Sentiments, and Affirmative Marketing Policies," *Journal of Urban Economics* 27(3): 344–61.

———. 1998. "A Stock/Flow Model of Defining Racially Integrated Neighborhoods." *Journal of Urban Affairs* 20(1): 413–52.

———. 2010. The Mechanism(s) of Neighborhood Effects: Theory, Evidence, and Policy Implications. Paper for presentation at the Economic and Social Research Council Seminar: Neighbourhood Effects: Theory & Evidence. St. Andrews University, Scotland, UK. February 4.

Galster, George, Roberto Quercia, and Alvaro Cortes. 2000. "Identifying Neighborhood Thresholds: An Empirical Exploration." *Housing Policy Debate* 11(3): 701–32.

Galster, George, and Jerome Rothenberg. 1991. "Filtering in Urban Housing: A Graphical Analysis of a Quality-Segmented Market." *Journal of Planning Education and Research* 11: 37–50.

Gelman, Erik. 2005. "Boys Town." In *Encyclopedia of Chicago*, edited by James R. Grossman, Ann Durkin Keating, and Janice L. Reiff. Chicago: University of Chicago Press. http//www.encyclopedia.chicagohistory.org/pages/160.html. Accessed September 12, 2013.

Geltmaker, T. 1992. "The Queer Nation Acts UP: Health Care, Politics and Sexual Diversity in the County of Los Angeles." *Environment and Planning D: Society and Space* 10(6): 609–50.

Gills, Douglas C., and Wanda White. 1998. "Community Involvement in Chicago's Empowerment Zone." In *Empowerment in Chicago: Grassroots Participation in Economic Development and Poverty Alleviation*, edited by Cedric Herring, Michael Bennett, Douglas C. Gills, and Noah Temaner, 14–70. Champaign: University of Illinois Press.

Gilman, Sander L. 1985. *Difference and Pathology: Stereotypes of Sexuality, Race, and Madness*. Ithaca, N.Y.: Cornell University Press.

Glanton, Dahleen, Antonio Olivo, and William Mullen. 2011. "Abandoned Homes Multiply in Englewood, and Crime Follows. Foreclosure Crisis 'Is Our Tsunami,' Expert Says." *Chicago Tribune*, June 23.

Glass, Ruth. 1964. *London: Aspects of Change*. London: University College London Centre for Urban Studies.

Glazer, Nathan, and Daniel P. Moynihan. 1970. *Beyond the Melting Pot*, 2nd ed.: *The Negroes, Puerto Ricans, Jews, Italians, and Irish of New York City*. Cambridge Mass.: MIT Press.

Goetze, Rolf. 1979. *Understanding Neighborhood Change: The Role of Expectations in Urban Revitalization*. Cambridge, Mass.: Ballinger Publishing.

Goetze, Rolf, and Kenneth Colton. 1980. "The Dynamics of Neighborhoods: A Fresh Approach to Understanding Housing and Neighborhood Change." *American Institute of Planners Journal* 46: 184–94.

Goldsmith, William, and Lewis Randolph. 1993. "Ghetto Economic Development." In *Theories of Local Economic Development*, edited by Richard D. Bingham and Robert Mier, 100–117. Newbury Park, Calif.: Sage Publications.

Goodwin, Carole. 1979. *The Oak Park Strategy: Community Control of Racial Change*. Chicago: University of Chicago Press.

Gordon, Milton M. 1964. *Assimilation in American Life: The Role of Race, Religion and National Origins*. New York: Oxford University Press.

Gotham, Kevin Fox. 2002a. *Race, Real Estate and Uneven Development: The Kansas City Experience, 1900–2000*. Albany: State University of New York Press.

———. 2002b. "Beyond Invasion and Succession: School Segregation, Real Estate Blockbusting, and the Political Economy of Neighborhood Racial Transition." *City and Community* 1(1): 83–111.

Grimshaw, William G. 1992. *Bitter Fruit: Black Politics and the Chicago Machine 1931–1991*. Chicago: University of Chicago Press.

Grodzins, Morton. 1958. *The Metropolitan Area as a Racial Problem*. Pittsburgh, Pa: University of Pittsburgh Press.

Hackworth, Jason. 2007. *The Neoliberal City: Governance, Ideology, and Development in American Urbanism*. Ithaca, N.Y.: Cornell University Press.

Haines, Kathryn S. 2000. *Improving Community Development in Englewood: Using Collaborative Planning to Enhance Social Capital*. Master's thesis, University of Illinois at Chicago.

Harris, Chauncy, and Edward Ullman. 1945. "The Nature of Cities." *The Annals of the American Academy of Political and Social Science* 242: 7–17.

Hartman, Chester. 1998. "The Case For the Right to Housing." *Housing Policy Debate* 9(2): 223–66.

Harvey, David. 1973. *Social Justice and the City*. Baltimore: Johns Hopkins University Press.

———. 1985. *The Urbanization of Capital*. Baltimore: Johns Hopkins University Press.

———. 1989. *The Urban Experience.* Baltimore: Johns Hopkins University Press.

———. 1995. "Flexible Accumulation through Urbanization: Reflections on 'Post-Modernism' in the American City." In *Post-Fordism: A Reader*, edited by Ash Amin, 362–86. Oxford: Blackwell.

———. 1996. "Cities or Urbanization?" *City* 1(1–2): 38–61.

———. 1997a. *Justice, Nature & the Geography of Difference*. Oxford: Blackwell.

———. 1997b. *The Condition of Postmodernity*. Oxford: Blackwell.

———. 2001. *Spaces of Capital: Towards a Critical Geography*. New York: Routledge.

———. 2005. *A Brief History of Neoliberalism*. Oxford: Oxford University Press.

———. 2006. *Spaces of Global Capitalism: Towards a Theory of Uneven Geographical Development*. London: Verso.

Hill, James. 1997. "Heartbeat of Bronzeville Grows Stronger: Neighborhood Groups Worry as the City Picks Up Their Idea, Runs With It." *Chicago Tribune*, May 6.

Hill, Robert B. 1988. "Understanding Black Family Functioning: A Holistic Perspective." *Journal of Comparative Family Studies* 29(1): 15–25.

Hirsch, Arnold. 1998. *Making the Second Ghetto: Race and Housing in Chicago 1940–1960*. Chicago: University of Chicago Press.

Holloway, Steven R., Richard Wright, and Mark Ellis. 2012. "The Racially Fragmented City? Neighborhood Racial Segregation and Diversity Jointly Considered." *The Professional Geographer* 64(1): 63–82.

Hoover, Edgar, and Raymond Vernon. 1959. *Anatomy of a Metropolis: The Changing Distribution of People and Jobs within the New York Metropolitan Area*. Cambridge, Mass.: Harvard University Press.

Hoyt, Homer. 1933. *One Hundred Years of Land Values in Chicago*. Chicago: University of Chicago Press.

———. 1939. *The Structure and Growth of Residential Neighborhoods in American Cities*. Washington D.C.: U.S. Government Printing Office.

Hudspeth, Nancy. 2003. *Interpreting Neighborhood Change in Chicago*. Chicago: Nathalie P. Voorhees Center for Community and Neighborhood Improvement, University of Illinois at Chicago.

———. 2011. "Everything Must Go: Local Businesses in the Context of Neighborhood Change." PhD Dissertation, University of Illinois at Chicago.

Huebner, Jeff. 2000. "Whose Blues They Choose?" *Chicago Reader*, November 30.

Huffington Post. 2013. "Third Stabbing in As Many Weeks Caught on Video." *Huffington Post Chicago*, July 5.

Hwang, Jackelyn, and Robert J Sampson. 2014. "Divergent Pathways of Gentrification: Racial Inequality and the Social Order of Renewal in Chicago Neighborhoods." *American Sociological Review* 79(4): 807–16.

Hyra, Derek S. 2008. *The New Urban Renewal, The Economic Transformation of Harlem and Bronzeville*. Chicago: University of Chicago Press.

Ihejirika, Maudlyne. 2005. "High School with 'Culture of Failure' to Be Shot." *Chicago Sun-Times*, February 2.

Isaacs, Deanna. 2009. "Pilsen's Ailing Arts District: As 4Art Leaves for Bridgeport, Yet Another Storefront in 'Podville' Goes Dark." *The Chicago Reader*, August 13.

Jackson, Cheryl V. 2008. "South, West Sides Hit by Home Foreclosures; Citywide Numbers up 46%, 108% in Logan Square." *Chicago Sun-Times*, March 27.

Jackson, David, and John McCormick. 2005. "How Fraud Became the Nightmare on May Street: A Block Troubled by Poverty, Drug Abuse and Crime also Falls Prey to Mortgage Scams." *Chicago Tribune*, November 9.

Jacobs, Jane. 1961. *Death and Life of Great American Cities*. New York: Random House.

Jargowsky, Paul. 1997. *Poverty and Place: Ghettoes, Barrios and the American City*. New York: Russell Sage Foundation.

———. 2003. "Stunning Progress, Hidden Problems: the Dramatic Decline of Concentrated Poverty in the 1990s." Washington, D.C.: Brookings Institution Press.

Jeffers, Glenn, and Rachel Osterman. 2003. "Pilsen Uneasy with Development: Some Residents Fear Gentrification." *Chicago Tribune*, December 31.

Jensen, Robert. 2005. *The Heart of Whiteness: Confronting Race, Racism and White Privilege*. San Francisco: City Light Publishers.

Johnson, Steve. 1991. "Lake Parc Place: New Look, New Tenants, New Face For CHA." *Chicago Tribune*, August 15.

Joint Center for Housing Studies of Harvard University. 2014. *The State of the Nation's Housing 2014*. Cambridge, Mass.: Harvard University Press.

Joravsky, Ben. 1998. "Local Options: In Kenwood-Oakland, Community Planning Is a Long, Slow Process." *Chicago Reader*, October 20.

———. 2010. "The Poor Pay Again: The Englewood TIF Coughs up $3 Million to Help Bridge Chicago's Budget Gap." *The Reader*, November 18.

Katznelson, Ira. 1981. *City Trenches: Urban Politics and the Patterning of Class in the United States*. Chicago: University of Chicago Press.

Keating, W. Dennis. 1994. *The Suburban Racial Dilemma: Housing and Neighborhoods*. Philadelphia: Temple University Press.

Keating, W. Dennis, and Janet Smith. 1996. "Neighborhoods in Transition." In *Revitalizing Urban Neighborhoods*, edited by W. Dennis Keating, Norman Krumholz, and Phil Star, 24–38. Lawrence: University Press of Kansas.

Keels, Micere, Greg Duncan, Stefanie Deluca, Ruby Mendenhall, and James Rosenbaum. 2005. "Fifteen Years Later: Can Residential Mobility Programs Provide a Long-Term Escape From Neighborhood Segregation, Crime and Poverty." *Demography* 42: 51–73.

Keely, Louise, and Kathy Bostjancic. 2014. "A Tale of 2000 Cities: How the Sharp Contrast Between Successful and Struggling Communities Is Reshaping America." *The Demand Institute*, February. www.demandinstitute.org/2000cities/report. Accessed March 13, 2014.

Khadduri, Jill, and Marge Martin. 1997. "Mixed-Income Housing in the HUD Multi-family Stock." *CityScape* 3(2): 33–69.

Kimura, D. 2011. "Public Housing Faces $26 Billion in Capital Repairs." *Housing Finance*. http://www.housingfinance.com/urban-development/public-housing-faces-26 -billion-in-capital-repairs.aspx. Accessed May 31, 2015.

Kinchelow, Joe L., Shirley R. Steinberg, Nelson M. Rodriguez, and Ronald E. Chennault, eds. 1998. *White Reign: Deploying Whiteness in America*. London: Palgrave McMillan.

King, David. 2008. "'Imagine Englewood If.' Life in Chicago: Human Stories from Around the Windy City, April 30." http://www.lifeinchicago.net/2008/04/theres -craggy-stretch-of-south-halsted.html. Accessed June 1, 2012.

Kleppner, Paul. 1985. *Chicago Divided: The Making of a Black Mayor*. DeKalb: Northern Illinois University Press.

Kling, Jeffrey, Jeffrey Lieberman, Lawrence Katz, and Lisa Sanbonmatsu. 2004. *Moving to Opportunity and Tranquility: Neighborhood Effects on Adult Economic Self-Sufficiency and Health From a Randomized Housing Voucher Experiment*. Cambridge, Mass.: Harvard University Press.

Kneebone, Elizabeth. 2014. *The Growth and Spread of Concentrated Poverty, 2000 to 2008– 2012*. Washington D.C.: Brookings Institution Press.

Knopp, Lawrence. 1992. "Sexuality and the Spatial Dynamics of Capitalism." *Environment and Planning D: Society and Space* 10(6): 651–69.

———. 1998. "Sexuality and Urban Space." In *Cities of Difference*, edited by Ruth Fincher and Jane M. Jacobs, 149–76. New York: Guilford Press.

Knox, Paul, and Peter Taylor, eds. 1995. *World Cities in a World-System*. Cambridge: Cambridge University Press.

Kobayashi, Audrey, and Linda Peake. 1994. "Unnatural Discourse: Race and Gender in Geography." *Gender, Place and Culture* 1: 225–43.

Kohn, David. 2002. "Tearing Down Cabrini-Green. Cabrini-Green Is Gone. Will The Replacement Work?" *60 Minutes*, December 11.

Kornbluth, Jacob, dir. 2013. *Inequality for All*. 72 Productions.

Koster, Katherine. 2009. "What's the Matter With Pilsen? The Chicago Arts District Falls on Hard Times as Artists Head South to Bridgeport." *Chicago Weekly Online*, November 24.

Kotlowitz, Alex. 1991. *There Are No Children Here: The Story of Two Boys Growing Up in the Other America*. New York: Doubleday.

Kubish, Anne C., Patricia Auspos, Prudence Bron, Robert Chaskin, Karen Fulbright-Anderson, and Ralph Hamilton. 2008. "Strengthening the Connections between Communities and External Resources." In *The Community Development Reader*, edited by James DeFilippis and Susan Saegert, 319–26. New York: Routledge.

Kunichoff, Yana. 2014. "One Year After Closings, How Are Chicago's Public Schools Now?" *In These Times*, June 5.

Lang, Nico. 2012. "Is It Time to Boycott Boystown? Chicago Around Time." *Huffington Post Chicago*, July 26.

Larson, Erik. 2004. *The Devil in the White City*. New York: Vintage.

Lee, Barrett, and Peter Wood. 1991. "Is Neighborhood Racial Succession Place-Specific?" *Demography* 28(1): 21–40.

Lees, Loretta. 1994. "Rethinking Gentrification: Beyond the Positions of Economics and Culture." *Progress in Human Geography* 18(2): 137–50.

Lees, Loretta, Tom Slater, and Elvin Wyly. 2008. *Gentrification*. New York: Routledge.

Lefebvre, Henri. 1991 and 2004. *The Production of Space*. Translated by Donald Nicholson-Smith. Oxford: Blackwell.

———. 1992. *The Production of Space*. Translated by Donald Nicholson-Smith. Oxford, UK, and Malden, Mass.: Wiley-Blackwell.

———. 1996. *Writings on Cities*. Oxford: Blackwell.

———. 2009. *State, Space, World, Selected Essays*. Edited by Neil Brenner and Stuart Elden. Translated by Gerald Moore, Neil Brenner, and Stuart Elden. Minneapolis: University of Minnesota Press.

Lemann, Nicholas. 1992. *The Promised Land: The Great Black Migration and How It Changed America*. New York: Vintage Books.

Lenz, Tom. 1998. "Building a Force for the Common Good." *NHI Shelterforce On-Line* #101. http://www.nhi.org/online/issues/101/lenz.html. Accessed on January 18, 2014.

Levin, Rebekah, Lisa McKean, and Susan K. Shapiro. 2004. *Community Organizing in Three South Side Chicago Communities: Leadership, Activities and Prospects*. Chicago: Center for Impact Research.

Levy, Diane K., Harris Beider, Susan Popkin, and David Price, with Aurelie Broeckerhoff. 2010. *Atlantic Exchange: Case Studies of Housing and Community Development in the United States and the United Kingdom*. Washington, D.C.: Urban Institute.

Liggett, Helen, and David C. Perry, eds. 1995. *Spatial Practices: Critical Explorations in Social/Spatial Theory*. Thousand Oaks, Calif.: Sage Publications.

Lloyd, Richard. 2006. *Neo-Bohemia: Art and Commerce in the Postindustrial City*. New York: Routledge.

Logan, John R., and Harvey Molotch. 1987. *Urban Fortunes: The Political Economy of Place*. Berkeley: University of California Press.

Lowenthal, Martin D. 1977. "The Social Economy in Urban Working-Class Communities." In *New Perspectives on the American Community: A Book of Readings*, edited by Roland Warren, 305–16. Chicago: Rand McNally College Publishing Company.

Luc, Karie Angell. 2008. "Scenic Lake Park Crescent Offers Special Incentives" *Chicago Sun-Times, Today's New Homes*, September 10–12.

Ludwig, Jens, Greg J. Duncan, Lisa A. Gennetian, Lawrence F. Katz, Ronald C. Kessler, Jeffrey R. Kling, and Lisa Sanbonmatsu. 2013. "Long-Term Neighborhood Effects on Low-Income Families: Evidence from Moving to Opportunity." *American Economic Review* 103(3): 226–31.

Luger, Michael, and Kenneth Temkin. 2000. *Red Tape and Housing Costs: How Regulation Affects New Residential Development*. New Brunswick, N.J.: Rutgers University Center for Urban Policy Research Press.

Lutton, Linda. 1998. "Will Development Bury the Barrio?" *Chicago Reader*, April 24.

Lydersen, Kari. 2011. "The Ward Debate in Englewood: With Six Wards Making Up the Neighborhood, Who Is Taking a Leadership Role?" *TimeOut Chicago*, May 4.

MacKenzie, Evan. 1994. *Privatopia: Homeowner Associations and the Rise of Residential Private Government*. New Haven, Conn.: Yale University Press.

———. 2011. *Beyond Privatopia: Rethinking Residential Private Government*. Washington, D.C.: Urban Institute Press.

Maldonado, Eduardo. 1987. "Contract Labor and the Origins of Puerto Rican Communities in the U.S." In *Forging a Community: The Latino Experience in Northwest Indiana, 1919–1975*, edited by Eduardo J. Escobar and James B. Lane, 201–12. Chicago: Cattails Press.

Maly, Michael T. 2005. *Beyond Segregation: Multiracial and Multiethnic Neighborhoods in the United States*. Philadelphia: Temple University Press.

Manley, Theodoric Jr. N.d. *The Revanchist City: Downtown Chicago and the Rhetoric of Redevelopment in Bronzeville*. Chicago: Hoops Institute.

Mann, Leslie. 2009. "Community Profile, Pilsen: Where Change Is Underfoot. Redevelopment Brings Renewed Life to Old Ethnic Neighborhood." *Chicago Tribune, Chicago Homes*, March 6.

Marcuse, Peter. 1985a. "To Control Gentrification: Anti-Displacement Zoning and Planning for Stable Residential Districts. *Review of Law and Social Change* 13: 931–45.

———. 1985b. "Gentrification, Abandonment and Displacement: Connections, Causes and Policy Responses." In *Gentrification of the City*, edited by Neil Smith and Peter Williams, 153–77. London: Unwin Hyman.

Marshall, Jim. 1988. "A Tough Look at Gentrification." *Chicago Tribune*, September 2.

Martinez, Cipriano Hernandez. 1997. "Pilsen and UIC, Voice of the People (Letter)." *Chicago Tribune*, December 23.

Marx, Charles, and Frederik Engels. 1998 [1948]. *The Communist Manifesto*, a Modern Edition. New York: Verso.

Massey, Douglas. 1987. "Ethnic Residential Segregation: A Theoretical Synthesis and Empirical Review." *Sociology and Social Research* 69: 315–50.

Massey, Douglas, and Nancy Denton. 1987. "Trends in the Residential Segregation of Blacks, Hispanics and Asians: 1970–80." *American Sociological Review* 52: 802–25.

———. 1993. *American Apartheid: Segregation and the Making of the Underclass*. Cambridge, Mass.: Harvard University Press.

McCarron, John. 1988. "Chicago on Hold: The New Politics of Poverty." *Chicago Tribune*, August 28–September 6.

McConnell, E. Hoy, and Alexander Polikoff. 2012. "Letter to U.S. Senators Durbin, Kirk; U.S. Congressmen Davis, Gutierrez, Quigley, Rush, Schakowsky; Chicago Mayor Emanuel; Chicago Aldermen Beale, Burnett, Burns, Moreno, Waguespack; CHA Chair Scott, CEO Woodyard; and Ms. Henriquez, Messrs. Donovan, Meiss, Riley, US Department of Housing and Urban Development." December 20, 2012. In authors' possession.

McGlory, Robert. 1993. "The Plot to Destroy North Kenwood." *Chicago Reader*, October 14.

McKenzie, Roderick D. 1925. "The Ecological Approach to the Study of Human Community," In *The City*, edited by Robert Park, Ernest Burgess, and Roderick McKenzie, 63–79. Chicago: University of Chicago Press.

Mele, Christopher. 2000. *Selling the Lower East Side*. Minneapolis: University of Minnesota Press.

Metzger, John. 2000. "Forum: Planned Abandonment: The Neighborhood Life Cycle Theory and National Urban Policy," with responses by Anthony Downs, Kenneth Temkin, and George C. Galster. *Housing Policy Debate* 11(2): 7–66.

Meyer, Graham. 2012. "The Ex Files." *ChicagoMag.com*, June 20. http://www.chicagomag.com/Chicago-Magazine/June-2006/The-Ex-Files/. Accessed September 18, 2012.

Mid-South Planning Group. 1993. *Mid-South Strategic Development Plan: Restoring Bronzeville*. Chicago: Wendell Campbell Associates, Inc. and Applied Real Estate Analysis.

Miller, Ed. 2011. "CReAting Gentrification." PhD dissertation, the University of Illinois at Chicago.

Mitchell, Don. 2003. *The Right to the City: Social Justice and the Fight for Public Space*. New York: Guilford Publications, Inc.

Mitchell, John. 1974. *The Dynamics of Neighborhood Change*. Washington, D.C.: U.S. Department of Housing and Urban Development, Office of Policy Development and Research.

Mollenkopf, John. 1981. "Community and Accumulation." In *Urbanization and Urban Planning in Capitalist Society*, edited by Michael Dear and Allen J. Scott, 319–38. London: Methuen.

Molotch, Harvey. 1969. "Racial Change in a Stable Community." *American Journal of Sociology* 75(2): 226–38.

———. 1972. *Managed Integration: Dilemmas of Doing Good in the City*. Berkeley: University of California Press.

Moore, Natalie. 2012. "Chicago's Highest Murder Rate in Englewood: Community Considers Why the Neighborhood Has This Distinction." *WBEZ.91.5*, January 5. http://www.wbez.org/story/chicagos-highest-murder-rate-englewood-95301. Accessed May 25, 2012.

Moynihan, Daniel P. 1965. *The Negro Family: The Case for National Action*. Washington, D.C.: Office of Policy Planning and Research, U.S. Department of Labor.

National Housing Law Project, Poverty & Race Research Action Council, Sherwood Research Associates, and Everywhere and Now Public Housing Residents Organizing Nationally Together. 2002. *False HOPE: A Critical Assessment of the HOPE VI Public Housing Redevelopment Program*. Oakland, Calif.: National Housing Law Project.

Newman, Kathe, and Elvin Wyly. 2006. "The Right to Stay Put, Revisited: Gentrification and Resistance to Displacement in New York City." *Urban Studies* 43(1): 23–57.

Niedt, Christopher. 2006. "Gentrification and the Grassroots: Popular Support in the Revanchist Suburb." *Journal of Urban Affairs* 28(2): 99–120.

Nina64. 2009. Why Is There So Much Violence and Crime in Chicago's Englewood Community? *City-Data.com/HubPages.com*. http://nina64.hubpages.com/hub/Crimes-in-ChicagoIs-Englewood-Being-Singled-Out. Accessed May 20, 2012.

Northeastern Illinois Planning Commission. 2002. *Census 2000: Summary Tables of Social, Economic and Housing Data for the 77 Communities in the City of Chicago*. Chicago: Northeastern Illinois Planning Commission.

Nyden, Philip. 1998. "Comments." *Housing Policy Debate* 9(4): 741–48.

Nyden, Philip, John Lukehart, and Mike Maly. 1997. "Emergence of Stable Racially and Ethnically Diverse Urban Communities: A Case Study of Nine US Cities." *Housing Policy Debate* 8(2): 491–534.

Nyden, Phillip W., and Wim Wiewel. 1991. *Challenging Uneven Development: An Urban Agenda for the 1990s*. New Brunswick, N.J.: Rutgers University Press.

Omi, Michael, and Howard Winant. 1986. *Racial Formation in the United States From the 1960s to the 1980s*. New York: Routledge.

Orfield, Myron. 2014. "Charter Schools in Chicago: No Model for Education Reform. Institute on Metropolitan Opportunity." Report by University of Minnesota Law School, October.

Orr, L., J. Feins, R. Jacob, and E. Beecroft. 2003. "Moving to Opportunity: Interim Impacts Evaluation: Final Report." Washington, D.C.: Department of Housing and Urban Development, Office of Policy Development and Research.

Osborne, T., and N. Rose. 2004. "Spatial Phenomenotechnics: Making Space with Charles Booth and Patrick Geddes." *Environment and Planning D: Society and Space* 22: 209–28.

O'Toole, Randall. 2011. "Crony Capitalism and Social Engineering, the Case against Tax-Increment Financing." *Policy Analysis* 676 (May).

Ottensmann, John. 1995. "Requiem for the Tipping-Point Hypothesis." *Journal of Planning Literature* 11(2): 132–41.

P., Laura. 2010. No title. Chicago Arts District Web Site. http://www.yelp.com/biz/chicago-arts-district-chicago. Accessed July 18, 2012.

Padilla, Elena. 1947. "Puerto Rican Immigrants in New York and Chicago: A Study in Comparative Assimilation." PhD dissertation, University of Chicago.

Padilla, Felix. 1987. *Puerto Rican Chicago*. South Bend, Ind.: University of Notre Dame Press.

Palen, John, and B. London, eds. 1984. *Gentrification, Displacement and Neighborhood Revitalization*. Albany: State University of New York Press.

Park, Robert, Ernest Burgess, and Roderick D. McKenzie, eds. 1925. *The City*. Chicago: University of Chicago Press.

Patillo, Mary. 2007. *Black on the Block: The Politics of Race and Class in the City.* Chicago: University of Chicago Press.

Pebley, Anne R., and Narayan Sastry. 2004. "Neighborhoods, Poverty and Children's Well-Being: A Review." In *Social Inequality*, edited by Kathryn Neckerman, 119–45. New York: Russell Sage Foundation.

Peck, Jamie, Nik Theodore, and Neil Brenner. 2012. "Neoliberalism Resurgent? Market Rule after the Great Recession." *South Atlantic Quarterly* 111(2): 265–88.

Perry, Clarence. 1929. "The Neighborhood Unit." In *Regional Plan of New York and Its Environs*. New York: Regional Plan of New York and its Environs.

PEW Charitable Trusts. 2013. "Philadelphia and Other Big Cities Struggle to Find Uses for Closed Schools." The PEW Charitable Trusts. http://www.pewtrusts.org/en/research-and-analysis/reports/2013/02/11/philadelphia-and-other-big-cities-struggle-to-find-uses-for-closed-schools. Accessed on March 3, 2016.

Pierce, Neil R., and Carol Steinbach. 1987. *Corrective Capitalism: The Rise of America's Community Development Corporations.* New York: Ford Foundation.

Pilsen: A Center of Mexican Life. 2006. "The Resurrection Project and LISC's New Communities Initiative." http://www.newcommunities.org/tools/qofl.asp. Accessed April 23, 2012.

Pilsen Quality of Life Plan. 2000. "The Resurrection Project and LISC's New Communities Initiative." http://www.newcommunities.org/tools/qofl.asp. Accessed April 23, 2012.

Pitkin, Hanna Fenichel. 1972. *The Concept of Representation.* Berkeley: University of California Press.

Piven, Frances Fox, and Richard Cloward. 1978. *Poor People's Movements: Why They Succeed, How They Fall.* New York: Vintage Books.

Polikoff, Alexander. 2006. *Waiting For Gautreaux: A Story of Segregation, Housing, and the Black Ghetto.* Evanston, Ill.: Northwestern University Press.

Polk, Chanel, and Mick Dumke. 1999. "A Brief History of Englewood." *Chicago Reporter.* http://whgbetc.com/englewood/englewood-history-chirep.html. Accessed May 31, 2015.

Popkin, Susan J., Brett Theodos, Caterina Gouvis Roman, and Elizabeth Guernsey with Lisa Getsinger. 2008. *The Chicago Family Case Management Demonstration: Developing a New Model for Serving "Hard to House" Public Housing Families.* Washington, D.C.: Urban Institute.

Porter, Michael E. 1995. "The Competitive Advantage of the Inner City." *Harvard Business Review* 73 (May–June): 55–71.

Preston, Michael B., Lenneal H. Henderson, Jr., and Paul Puryear. 1982. *The New Black Politics.* New York: Longman.

Puente, Teresa. 1997. "Pilsen Fears Upscale Push May Shove Many Out." *Chicago Tribune,* November 4.

Putnam, Robert. 2000. *Bowling Alone: The Collapse and Revival of American Community.* New York: Simon & Schuster.

Quercia, Roberto, and George Galster. 1997. "Threshold Effects and the Expected Benefits of Attracting Middle-Income Households to the Central City." *Housing Policy Debate* 8(2): 409–36.

———. 2000. "Threshold Effects and Neighborhood Change." *Journal of Planning Education and Research* 20: 146–62.

Rabinow, P. 1982. "Ordinance, Discipline, Regulation: Some Reflections on Urbanism." *Humanities in Society* 5(3–4): 267–78.

Ranney, David, Pat Wright, and Tingwei Zhang. 1996. "Citizens, Local Government and the Development of Chicago's Near South Side." Paper presented at the United Nations Research Institute for Social Development Conference, Istanbul, May.

Ratcliff, R. 1949. *Urban Land Economics*. New York: McGraw-Hill.

Reardon, Patrick T. 2000. "Can Bronzeville Reclaim its Soul?" *Chicago Tribune Magazine*, May 21: 10–16. http://palmtavern.bizland.com/palmtavern/000521_Can_Bronzeville_Reclaim_Its_Soul_full_article.htm. Accessed on September 15, 2015.

Reed, Cheryl L. 2005. "Upscale Blacks Drive Prices Up Forcing Long-time Residents Out: Few in Gentrifying S. Side Neighborhoods Have Qualms about Displacing the Poor." *Chicago Sun-Times*, November 14.

Rice, Roger L. 1968. "Residential Segregation by Law, 1910–1917." *Journal of Southern History* 64(2): 179–99.

Robinson-English, Tracey. 2007. "Englewood Rising; Northwestern Professor Sees Gold Rush in His Old Neighborhood." *Chicago Sun-Times*, October 5.

Rodkin, Dennis. 2010. "Price Cuts, Incentives at Lake Park Crescent in Kenwood." *Chicago Magazine*, October 9.

Roeder, David, and Fran Spielman. 2005. "Pilsen Development News Business: $125 mil. Pilsen Development." *SkyscraperCity.com*, November 17. http://www.skyscrapercity.com/showthread.php/t-283087.html. Accessed July 14, 2012.

Rogal, Brian. 1998. "CHA Tenant Evictions Jump as Buildings Fall." *Chicago Reporter*, December.

Rose, Gilian. 1993. *Feminism and Geography: The Limits of Geographical Knowledge*. Cambridge, UK: Polity Press.

Rose, Nicolas. 1999. *Powers of Freedom: Reframing Political Thought*. Cambridge: Cambridge University Press.

Rosenbaum, James. 1994. *Housing Mobility Strategies for Changing the Geography of Opportunity*. Evanston, Ill.: Institute for Policy Research, Northwestern University.

Rosenbaum, James, and Susan Popkin. 1991. "Employment and Earnings of Low-Income Blacks Who Move to Middle-Class Suburbs." In *The Urban Underclass*, edited by Christopher Jencks and Paul Peterson, 342–56. Washington, D.C.: The Brookings Institution Press.

Rosenbaum, James E., Linda K. Stroh, and Cathy A. Flinn. 1998. "Lake Parc Place: A Study of Mixed-Income Housing." *Housing Policy Debate* 9(4): 703–40.

Rubinowitz, Leonard, and James Rosenbaum. 2000. *Crossing the Class and Color Lines: From Public Housing to White Suburbia*. Chicago: University of Chicago Press.

Ruiz-Tagle, Javier. 2014. "Bringing Inequality Closer: A Comparative Urban Sociology of Socially Diverse Neighborhoods." PhD dissertation, University of Illinois at Chicago.

Said, Edward. 1995. *Orientalism*. New York: Penguin Books.

Sampson, Robert J. 2012. *Great American City: Chicago and the Enduring Neighborhood Effect*. Chicago: University of Chicago Press.

Schelling, Thomas C. 1971. "Dynamic Models of Segregation." *Journal of Mathematical Sociology* 1: 143–86.

———. 1972. "The Process of Residential Segregation: Neighborhood Tipping." In *Racial Discrimination in Economic Life*, edited by Anthony Pascal, 157–84. Lexington, Mass.: Lexington Books.

Schill, Michael. 1997. "Chicago's Mixed-Income New Communities Strategy: The Future of Public Housing?" In *Affordable Housing and Urban Redevelopment in the United States*, edited by Willem Van Vliet, 135–57. Thousand Oaks, Calif.: Sage Publications.

Schumpeter, Joseph A. 1994 [1942]. *Capitalism, Socialism, and Democracy*. 5th rev. ed. New York: Routledge Classics.

Schwartz, Alex, and Kian Tajbakhsh. 1997. "Mixed Income Housing: Unanswered Questions." *Cityscape* 3(2): 71–92.

Sen, Amartya. 2009. *The Idea of Justice*. Cambridge, Mass.: Harvard University Press.

Shiffman, Ronald, and Susan Motley. 1990. "Comprehensive and Integrative Planning for Community Development." University of Nebraska Partnership/Community Paper 17. http//digitalcommons.unomaha.edu/slcepartnerships/17. Accessed on March 3, 2016.

Silver, Christopher. 1985. "Neighborhood Planning in Historical Perspective." *APA Journal* 51(2): 161–74.

Slater, Thomas. 2012. "Missing Marcuse: On Gentrification and Displacement." In *Cities for People, Not For Profit: Critical Theory and the Right to the City*, edited by Neil Brenner, Peter Marcuse, and Margit Meyer, 171–97. London: Routledge.

Smiley, Tavis, and Cornel West. 2012. *The Rich and the Rest of Us: A Poverty Manifesto*. New York: Smiley Books.

Smith, Janet L. 1998. "Interpreting Neighborhood Change." PhD Dissertation, Cleveland State University.

———. 1999. "Cleaning Up Public Housing By Sweeping Out the Poor." *Habitat International*, 23(1): 49–62.

———. 2006a. "Public Housing Transformation: Evolving National Policy." In *Where Are Poor People to Live? Transforming Public Housing Communities*, edited by Larry Bennett, Janet Smith, and Patricia Wright, 19–40. Armonk, N.Y.: M. E. Sharpe.

———. 2006b. "Mixed-Income Communities: Designing Out Poverty or Pushing Out the Poor?" In *Where Are Poor People to Live? Transforming Public Housing Communities*, edited by Larry Bennett, Janet Smith, and Patricia Wright, 259–81. Armonk, N.Y.: M. E. Sharpe.

———. 2013. "The End of Public Housing as We Knew It." *Urban Research & Practice* 6(3): 276–96.

———. 2015. Neighborhoods Matter . . . Neighborhood Matters. In *The Return of the Neighborhood as an Urban Strategy*, edited by Michael Pagano, 3–34. Champaign: University of Illinois Press.

Smith, Janet, and Thomas Lenz. 1999. *For Rent: Housing Options in the Chicago Region*. Chicago: University of Illinois at Chicago, Great Cities Institute.

Smith, Janet, and David Stovall. 2008. "'Coming' Home to New Homes and New Schools: Critical Race Theory and the New Politics of Containment." *Journal of Education and Policy* 23(2): 135–52.

Smith, Neil. 1996. *The New Urban Frontier: Gentrification and the Revanchist City*. London: Routledge.

———. 1979. "Toward a Theory of Gentrification A Back to the City Movement by Capital, Not People." *Journal of the American Planning Association* 45(4): 538–48.

———. 2002. "New Globalism, New Urbanism: Gentrification as Global Urban Strategy." *Antipode* 34(3): 434–57.

Smith, Neil, and Peter Williams. 1986. *Gentrification of the City*. Boston: Allen & Unwin.

Soja, Edward. 1989. *Postmodern Geographies: The Reassertion of Space in Critical Social Theory*. London: Verso.

———. 2000. *Postmetropolis, Critical Studies of Cities and Regions*. Oxford: Blackwell.

South Side Partnership. 1999. "Rebuilding Bronzeville through Collaborative Action: The Concept, Challenges and Opportunities for Southside Partnership, A Position Paper." http://www.iit.edu/~iitcomdev/south_partners/bronzville1.html. Accessed July 6, 2012.

South Town. 2007. "Bronzeville Summit—A Showcase of Development and Information about Bronzeville Today." *South Town*, September 14. http://www.bronzevilleonline.com/. Accessed on October 10, 2008.

Spielman, Fran. 2005. "Ground Broken for Long-Stalled Englewood Campus: Minority Inclusion Disputes Resolved on New Kennedy-King." *Chicago Sun-Times*, November 10.

———. 2013. "Analysis: DePaul Arena Plan Raises More Questions Than It Answers." *Chicago Sun-Times*, May 13.

Spula, Ian. 2014. "Get Ready For a Ton of New Luxury Apartments Downtown." *Chicago Magazine*, August 29.

Squires, Greg. 1994. *Capital and Communities in Black and White: The Intersections of Race, Class and Economic Development*. Albany: State University of New York Press.

Staeheli, Lynn. 2013. "Whose Responsibility Is It?" *Antipode* 45(3): 521–40.

Stiglitz. Joseph E. 2012. *The Price of Inequality: How Today's Society Endangered Our Future*. New York: W. W. Norton & Company.

Stockwell, Clinton E. 2005. "Englewood." In *Encyclopedia of Chicago*, edited by James R. Grossman, Ann Durkin Keating, and Janice L. Reiff. Chicago: University of Chicago

Press. http://www.encyclopedia.chicagohistory.org/pages/426.html. Accessed May 31, 2015.

Stone, M., 1993. *Shelter Poverty: New Ideas on Housing Affordability*. Philadelphia: Temple University Press.

Studenkov, Igor. 2012. "Still Standing, At Last Remnants of Cabrini-Green, Residents Await Uncertain Future." *Chicago Journal*, September 12. http://www.chicagojournal .com/news/09–12–2012/Still_standing. Accessed September 2014.

Suttles, Gerald D. 1972. *The Social Construction of Communities*. Chicago: University of Chicago Press.

Sweeney, Annie. 2006. "Durbin Hears Englewood Frustrations: Meets Gang Members to Explore Their Side: 'A Lot of Broken Lives.'" *Chicago Sun-Times,* April 13.

Tabak, Faruk. 1996. "The Structure of the World Labor Force, 1945–1990." In *The Age of Transition: Trajectory of the World-System, 1945–2025*, edited by Immanuel Wallerstein, Terence K. Hopkins, et al., 87–116. London: Zed Press.

Tamalechica. 2008. "Pilsen and Gentrification." *Tamale Chica Chronicles*, September 28. http://www.tamalechica.com/2008/09/28/pilsen-and-gentrification/. Accessed April 12, 2012.

Taub, Richard P., D. Garth Taylor, and Jan D. Dunham. 1984. *Paths of Neighborhood Change: Race and Crime in Urban America*. Chicago: University of Chicago Press.

Taylor, Ralph B. 2012. "Defining Neighborhoods in Space and Time." *Cityscape: A Journal of Policy Development and Research* 14(2): 225–30.

Teamwork Englewood. 2005. *Englewood: Making a Difference, Quality of Life Plan*. Chicago: LISC Chicago's New Communities Program.

Temkin, Kenneth, and William Rohe. 1996. "Neighborhood Change and Urban Policy." *Journal of Planning Education and Research* 15: 101–12.

Terry, Don. 1995. "Ex-Chicago Housing Chief Says Bureaucrats Hindered His Efforts." *New York Times*, June 7.

——. 2012. "In South Side Neighborhood, Violence Still Hard to Shake." *New York Times*, February 4.

Thomas, William I., and Florian Znanieki. 1958. *The Polish Peasant in America and Europe*. New York: Dover.

Thorne, Eva T., and Eugene F. Rivers. 2001. "Beyond the Civil Rights Industry: Why Black America Needs a New Politics—and How the Black Church Might Deliver One." *Boston Review*, April–May issue.

Thrift, Nigel. 2005. *Knowing Capitalism (Theory, Culture and Society)*. London: Sage.

Tilly, Charles. 1984. *Big Structures, Large Processes, Huge Comparisons*. New York: Russell Sage Foundation.

Time. 1938. "Business in Bronzeville." *Time*, April 18.

Tönnies, Ferdinand. 2001. *Community and Civil Society*. Cambridge: Cambridge University Press.

United Power. 2013. "What Is an Issue Campaign?" http://www.united-power.org/ content/what-issue-campaign. Accessed August 14, 2014.

United States Census Bureau. N.d. "Geography, Geographic Terms and Concepts: Census Tract, *US Bureau of the Census*." https://www.census.gov/geo/reference/gtc/gtc_ct.html. Accessed February 29, 2016.

USA Today. 2012. "Hudson Trial Showcases Violent Chicago 'Hood of Englewood." *USA Today*, April 22.

US HUD (United States Department of Housing and Urban Development). 1997. "FHA's Mixed-Income Housing Underwriting Guidelines, Directive 97–12, issued March 7, 1997." Washington, D.C.: US Department of Housing and Urban Development.

———. 2010. "Interim Assessment of the Empowerment Zones and Enterprise Communities (EZ/EC) Program." Washington, D.C.: US Department of Housing and Urban Development.

Venkatesh, Sudhir. 1998. *American Project: The Rise and Fall of a Modern Ghetto*. Cambridge, Mass.: Harvard University Press.

———. 2008. *Gang Leader For a Day: Rogue Sociologist Takes to the Streets*. New York: Penguin Press.

Vidal, Avis. 1989. *Community Economic Development Assessment: A National Study of Urban Community Development Corporations*. New York: New School for Social Research, Community Development Research Center.

Voorhees Center. 1996. *The Plan to Voucher Out Public Housing: An Analysis of the Chicago Experience and a Case Study of the Proposal to Redevelop the Cabrini-Green Public Housing Area*. Chicago: Nathalie P. Voorhees Center for Neighborhood and Community Improvement, University of Illinois at Chicago.

———. 2003. "Interpreting Neighborhood Change in Chicago." Chicago: Nathalie P. Voorhees Center for Neighborhood and Community Improvement, University of Illinois at Chicago.

———. 2014a. "The Deepening Divide in Chicagoland." Chicago: Nathalie P. Voorhees Center for Neighborhood and Community Improvement, University of Illinois at Chicago. http://www.voorheescenter.com. Accessed July 1, 2014.

———. 2014b. "The Socioeconomic Change of Chicago's Community Areas (1970–2010), Gentrification Index." Chicago: Nathalie P. Voorhees Center for Neighborhood and Community Improvement, University of Illinois at Chicago.

Wacquant, Loïc J. D. 1998. "Three Pernicious Premises in the Study of the American Ghetto." *International Journal of Urban and Regional Research* 21(2): 507–10.

Webber, Maura. 2003. "Pilsen's New Look." *Chicago Sun-Times*, March 17.

Weber, Adna. 1899. *The Growth of Cities in the Nineteenth Century*. Ithaca, N.Y.: Cornell University Press.

Wille, Lois. 1998. *At Home in the Loop: How Clout and Community Built Chicago's Dearborn Park*. Carbondale: Southern Illinois University Press.

Williams, Ashlei. 2011. "Latino Population Shrinks in Some Chicago Neighborhoods, Grows in Others." *Medill Reports Chicago*. http://newsarchive.medill.northwestern.edu/chicago/news-193791.html. Accessed March 21, 2012.

Williams, Debra. 2005. "Englewood: With Help Residents Shape Own Future." *Catalyst Chicago*, June 1.

Williams-Harris, Deanese. 2008. "Bronzeville Ready For Its Renaissance: Neighborhood Faces Challenges, Opportunities and Revitalization Efforts." *Chicago Tribune*, June 27.

Wilson, David. 2007. *Cities and Race: America's New Black Ghetto*. New York: Routledge.

Wilson, David, Jared Wouters, and Dennis Grammenos. 2004. "Successful Protect-Community Discourse, Spatiality and Politics in Chicago's Pilsen Neighborhood." *Environment and Planning A* 36: 1173–90.

Wilson, William J. 1987. *The Truly Disadvantaged: The Inner City, the Underclass, and Public Policy*. Chicago: University of Chicago Press.

Wilson, William J., and Richard P. Taub. 2006. *There Goes the Neighborhood, Racial, Ethnic, and Class Transitions in Four Chicago Neighborhoods and their Meaning for America*. New York: Alfred A. Knopf.

Wittberg, Patricia. 1992. "Perspectives on Gentrification: A Comparative Review of the Literature." In *Research in Urban Sociology: Gentrification and Urban Change, vol. 2*, edited by Ray Hutchison, 17–46. Greenwich, Conn.: JAI Press Inc.

Wittgenstein, Ludwig. 1958. *Philosophical Investigations*. New York: MacMillan.

Wolfe, Eleanor. 1963. "The Tipping Point in Racially Changing Neighborhoods." *Journal of the American Institute of Planners* 29(3): 217–22.

Wood, Paul, and Barrett Lee. 1991. "Is Neighborhood Racial Succession Inevitable? Forty Years of Evidence." *Urban Affairs Quarterly* 26(4): 610–20.

Woodstock Institute. 2012. *2012 Foreclosures Filings and Options*. Chicago: Woodstock Institute.

Wright, Patricia, Richard Wheelock, and Carol Steele. 2006. "The Case of Cabrini Green." In *Where Are Poor People to Live? Transforming Public Housing Communities*, edited by Larry Bennett, Janet Smith, and Patricia Wright, 168–84. Armonk, N.Y.: M. E. Sharpe.

Wyly, Elvin, and Daniel Hammel. 1996. "Islands of Decay in Seas of Renewal: Housing Policy and the Resurgence of Gentrification." *Housing Policy Debate* 10(4): 711–71.

Young, Iris Marion. 1990. *Justice and the Politics of Difference*. Princeton, N.J.: Princeton University Press.

Zenn, Jacqueline. 2011. "Spring Price Reductions at the Lake Park Crescent." *Urban Turf*, June 16. http://chicago.urbanturf.com/articles/article/spring_price_reductions _at_the_lake_park_crescent/3665. Accessed June 23, 2014.

Ziemba, Stanley. 1987. "CHA Urged To Raze 4 High-Rises," *Chicago Tribune*, November 24.

———. 1988. "There Are No Little Plans: Aging Kramer Pushes Kenwood Rebirth." *Chicago Tribune*, April 25.

Zorbaugh, Harvey Warren. 1929. *The Gold Coast and the Slum: A Sociological Study of Chicago's Near North Side*. Chicago: University of Chicago Press.

Zukin, Sharon. 1982. *Loft Living: Culture and Capital in Urban Change*. Baltimore: Johns Hopkins University Press.

———. 1996. *The Cultures of Cities*. Malden, Mass.: Wiley-Blackwell.

———. 2009. *Landscapes of Power, From Detroit to Disneyworld*. Los Angeles: University of California Press.

———. 2010. *Naked City: Death and Life of Authentic Urban Places*. Oxford: Oxford University Press.

Index

JOHN J. BETANCUR is a professor of urban planning and policy at the University of Illinois at Chicago.

JANET L. SMITH is an associate professor of urban planning and policy at the University of Illinois at Chicago.

The University of Illinois Press
is a founding member of the
Association of American University Presses.

———————————————————————

Cover designed by Dustin Hubbart
Cover illustration: map © 2007 Ork Posters

University of Illinois Press
1325 South Oak Street
Champaign, IL 61820-6903
www.press.uillinois.edu